An Illustrated History of the
Philippines

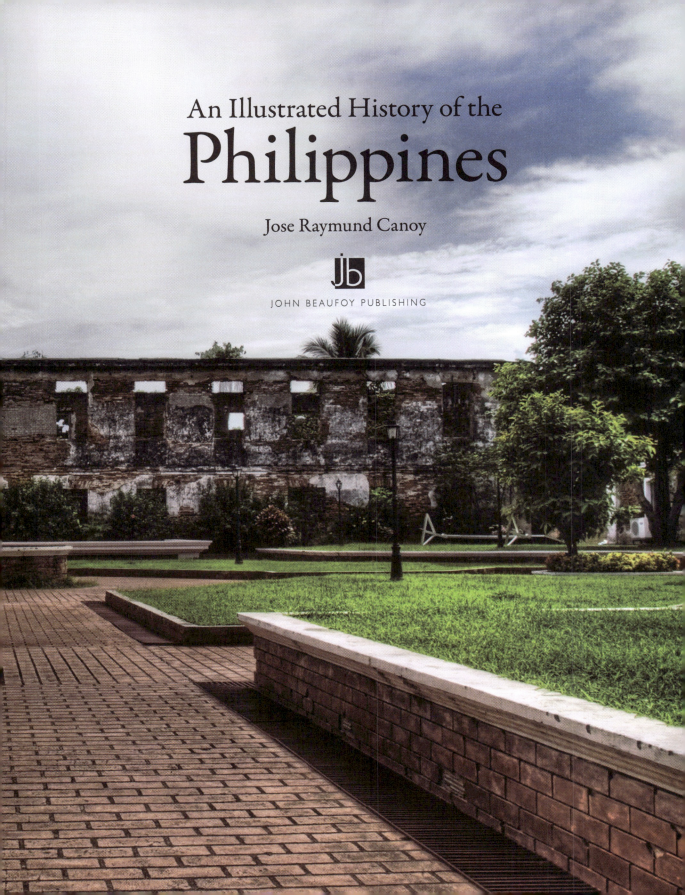

An Illustrated History of the
Philippines

Jose Raymund Canoy

JOHN BEAUFOY PUBLISHING

This book is for my wife, Dorothea, without whom
it would never have been written.
Pochero was the least I could offer in return.

Reprinted in 2024

First published in the United Kingdom in 2018 by John Beaufoy Publishing,
11 Blenheim Court, 316 Woodstock Road, Oxford OX2 7NS, England
www.johnbeaufoy.com

10 9 8 7 6 5

ISBN 978-1-912081-96-7

Design by Nigel Partridge
Index by Marie Lorimer
Cartography by William Smuts
Project management by Rosemary Wilkinson

Printed and bound in Malaysia by Times Offset (M) Sdn. Bhd.

Pages 2–3: Fort Pilar, Zamboanga.

Page 5: A civilian official and a police officer from the nearby city of Olongapo
learn about underwater navigation on their guided goodwill tour of the
Los Angeles-class nuclear attack submarine USS *Pasadena* during the
ship's visit to the former American naval base at Subic Bay, Zambales 2008.

Page 6–7: The façade of Miagao Church, Iloilo.

CONTENTS

1 INTRODUCTION: DEFINING THE PHILIPPINES 8
A Resilient People, A Global Culture, A Weak State

2 THE COMMUNITY AS A BOAT 24
Regional Prehistory and Early Philippine History to AD 1500

3 THE STATE AS A CONVENT 56
The Colonial Experience Under Spain, 1500–1800

4 IMAGINING A NATION 88
Revolution, The First Philippine Republic and its Defeat by the USA, 1800–1910

5 THE TRIALS OF 'BENEVOLENT ASSIMILATION' 120
The Philippines as America's Only Colony, 1901–1950

6 SHOWPLACE OF DEMOCRACY IN ASIA? 152
The Third Philippine Republic and the Post-war World, 1946–1972

7 THE 'NEW SOCIETY' AND ITS AFTERMATH 176
The Marcos Dictatorship, Its Victims, and the Aquinos, 1970–1992

8 NEW FORMS FOR OLD CHALLENGES 204
The Fifth Republic and the Future of the Philippines, 1986 to the Present

Timeline 232
Bibliography 239
Index 240
Acknowledgements 244

1

INTRODUCTION: DEFINING THE PHILIPPINES

A Resilient People, A Global Culture, A Weak State

Like all the other lands of Southeast Asia, the Philippines has a history shaped by the interplay between cultural elements native to the region on the one hand, and important influences from several world civilizations on the other. However, the resulting country presents unique puzzles to the visitor, as well as to the Filipinos themselves. Their own scholars ask: how could such an educated, democratically governed and open people have produced such a deeply unequal society, with such jarring mass poverty? How did such a lively public sphere get caught in a dilemma between a weak government, often unable to provide needed services, security or justice, and the country's aversion to a strong and impartial state? Why has the obvious potential of Filipinos so often been frustrated at home, driving millions abroad to enrich the lives of others? How did this Asian population get to be so Westernized, yet remain essentially itself?

Is this core identity even really 'Asian?' Let us begin here. Filipinos share much of their material culture and patterns of daily life with other nearby peoples. Nevertheless, the particular path that they have travelled to a modern national identity has set this archipelago of more than 7,000 islands apart from the more intertwined collective experiences of its neighbours.

Before Europeans arrived in the region, all the other peoples of Southeast Asia had absorbed centuries of major cultural influences from India and China, and in the cases of the Javanese, Sundanese and Malayic-language speakers of today's Indonesia and Malaysia, also the Islamic world. The Indianized elites of the region ruled complex, state-based societies built on wealth from far-flung tributary hinterlands or

BELOW
The town square of Biñan, Laguna Province, with a typical Spanish colonial layout now struggling with car traffic.

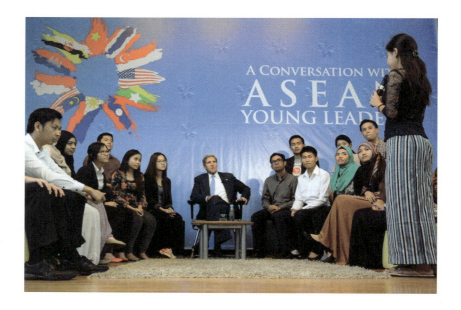

RIGHT

Most Filipinos do not diverge from most other Southeast Asians in outward appearance, belying the considerable gulf between their cultures and historical experiences. In this discussion with US Secretary of State John Kerry, the young woman with the red pattern on her shirt is a Filipina.

BELOW

Despite neither of them being Buddhists, the Indonesian leader Sukarno could share much of a common Indianized culture with the visiting Jawaharlal Nehru as they appreciated a giant Buddha in Borobodur, Java, in the 1950s. The Philippines does not share in this common regional heritage.

trading harbours. Mahayana Buddhism and Hinduism had coexisted as universal faiths before giving way to mainly Theravada Buddhism on the mainland and Islam as the majority faith in present day-Indonesia and Malaysia. Cross-fertilizing cosmologies, writing systems, palace- and temple-building traditions, ideas about universal rulership, literary and artistic styles, iconography and folklore had long shaped both popular and official consciousness in all these cultures. These shared traditions anchor the current identities of many millions of people in the region, providing symbolic and material foundations for the legitimacy of their various modern states.

In contrast, the available record suggests that such affiliations with the great non-Western traditions were a much weaker element in the cultures of the archipelago that was named the Philippine Islands (*Las Islas Filipinas*) by Western explorers arriving in the early 1500s. Outside the far southern territories inhabited by a Muslim minority, little or no clear evidence exists of permanent built structures, multi-civilizational religious syncretism or culture heroes of outside inspiration from the time before Western contact. To be sure, Indianized and/or Islamized rulers and traditions of literacy and metalwork, as well as important Chinese trading links, existed in some communities and regions. However, it was an older set of native cultural patterns – part of an ancient common heritage shared with all Austronesian-speaking people, including the recently Islamized Borneans, Malays and Javanese

– that continued to define community life and personal identity in most of the archipelago.

In the early societies of maritime Southeast Asia, a person's main affiliation was to his or her local settlement, still known in most of the Philippines until today as the *barangay*. Each barangay was originally conceived as an extended kinship group, often believed to descend from one crew of migrant founders navigating the inter-island waters of this region of the world (in most Philippine languages the alternate form '*balangay*' still denotes a widespread sailing boat design). Barangays emerged as centres of exchange between fishermen and the providers of crops, produce, game and minerals from forests and lowlands, as well as the seaborne traders who travelled within the archipelago and linked some of these communities with the wider region, and with the Chinese, Indian and Islamic worlds.

Barangay society eventually stratified under a quasi-hereditary ruler known as a *datu* (still the word for 'the rich one' in many Philippine languages), set over descending grades of warrior aristocrats, animist ritual specialists, craftsmen and other retainers, tribute-paying free commoners and slaves. Although some seaport settlements had joined into loose political confederations under Indianized or Islamized rulers with regional connections, most barangays in the archipelago were autonomous worlds of their own, dealing only with their immediate neighbours. Codes of customary law and justice certainly operated; however, the system functioned through personalistic patronage, not abstract sovereignty. The idea of a permanent, supra-local state, commanding the automatic loyalties of interchangeable subjects, did not really exist. Unlike most feudalisms in the pre-modern world, barangays (and their cognates throughout Southeast Asia) were not primarily territorial concepts. A datu had power over the labour and time of *people* known personally to him, not the barangay's territory or resources per se, which remained understood as commons. This fundamental orientation towards both the local and the personal, at the price of a relatively weak conception and reality of the state, continues to play a major role in Philippine politics and society even today.

At the moment of Western contact, a sense

ABOVE
Monument to Datu Lapulapu in the central Philippines.

BELOW
In the Maranao culture of the southern Philippines, the Sarimanok is a totemic bird that can move between the spirit world and our world. Cognate birds exist in other Austronesian cultures in the region, particularly in Borneo.

ABOVE

Modern-day variations on the datu theme from Sabah, Eastern Malaysia.

of relative cultural distance from the nearby great Asian and Islamic traditions still allows us to group most of the Philippines with certain other parts of the region, such as the upland areas of Borneo and Celebes/Sulawesi and the outlying islands of the Moluccas. However, the course of the next four centuries of Philippine history from about 1550 to 1950 was to be unique in the region, proving to be *the* decisive phase in the formation of the modern nation's identity and orientation. This period witnessed the massive impact on these relatively isolated local cultures of two successive alien imperial powers – Spain and the United States. Of all the competitors in the age of Western colonialism, these two had the most aggressive plans for transforming the identities of their distant Southeast Asian subjects.

A common conclusion among writers of Philippine history is that if European colonialism had not intervened when it did, an expanding Islam would probably have gone on from its already established seaport footholds to provide the archipelago with its unifying faith and high culture. However, we must add that even more crucial for the actual outcome was the fact that it was a specifically *Iberian*, and therefore militantly Catholic, variant of Western imperialism that arrived to shape the Philippine future. Neither the British nor the Dutch had any comparable policy of large-scale social and cultural transformation for their nearby colonial possessions in Southeast Asia. Instead, these Protestant powers often allied with local or regional rulers against their common European Catholic enemies, in the end enabling the survival of various Indianized and Islamized native cultures and elites under European overlordship. If history had taken a different turn, would either of the Protestant powers have been similarly indifferent to Islam's smaller foothold in the Philippines, had they taken the archipelago from the Spanish – as the Dutch came near to doing in the 1640s, and the British in the 1760s?

What actually happened during the Spanish period – among other things – was the creation of an often violent, always tensely militarized, religio-cultural fault line *inside* the archipelago, a divide that in various successive forms has persisted down to this day. It cuts off the Islamized areas of the country (much of the western half of the large island of Mindanao plus the Sulu Archipelago) from the bulk of a largely Christian and Western-oriented population. The emergence of this internal fault line (and its perpetuation during the subsequent American period) was of more than local importance. Together with the hardened borders later drawn by all former European colonies in Southeast Asia, it permanently ended older patterns of exchange between the wider region and most of the archipelago. The Christian Philippines thus shares little sense of cultural affinity with the Muslim parts of Mindanao and the rest of Islamized maritime Southeast Asia lying to the south-west of that island. Even today, for the average Filipino, these geographically adjacent parts of modern Malaysia and Indonesia remain, in psychological terms, far more distant and strange than the faraway but familiar images of hard-to-reach Rome, California, Madrid or New York.

Behind the shield of this southern military frontier, three centuries and more of Spanish rule fundamentally reshaped lowland Philippine society into what is today the third largest Catholic population in the world (after Brazil and Mexico), and the only majority Christian country in Asia of any large size (East Timor at the time of writing being the much smaller other). The violent process by which the essentially animist traditions of the lowland parts of the archipelago were largely replaced with a particularly

BELOW
Festival of moros y cristianos (Moors and Christians) in a modern Spanish town, re-enacting the reconquest of the Iberian Peninsula from Islam. The Spanish exported this festival tradition to the Philippines (where it is known as moro-moro) and Latin America. Only in the Philippines did it actually serve to bolster Christian morale against real local Muslims.

ABOVE
Pope Francis visiting Palo, Leyte, in 2015.

intense form of Baroque counter-Reformation piety – and the accompanying redirection of the Philippine imagination on to the world of Catholic imagery and ritual – is only fragmentarily documented, mostly from the Spanish side. Nevertheless, the resulting faith remains of vital importance for most modern Filipinos' sense of themselves today.

The lightly equipped and staffed official colonial state, understood in the narrow sense, was *not* the agent primarily responsible for laying these Catholic foundations of a future Philippine identity. For the royal, viceregal and colonial governments in Madrid, Mexico City and Manila, the archipelago mostly functioned as a regional base for Spanish efforts to sustain a trade and missionizing network between China and Latin America, and later as a site for large-scale production of agricultural commodities for the world market. Although there was always a modest inflow of bureaucrats, soldiers, entrepreneurial fortune seekers, aspiring absentee landowners and assorted hangers-on into the colony, the archipelago was never the target – unlike the New World – of large numbers of European settlers coming into close contact with the native population outside the Spanish enclaves in the cities.

It was instead the colonial government's reliance on the Spanish missionary clergy for providing primary education, supervising tax collection and labour levies, and many other tasks of civil administration, alongside the spiritual guidance of their parishes, that transformed lowland Philippine society. Largely isolated for three centuries from broader networks while under the bureaucratic control of moralizing religious orders acting on behalf of a distant central government, the pre-colonial barangay hierarchies of personalized local patronage survived to mutate under new labels. Christianized descendants of datus evolved into the *principalia* – prominent local families with significant landholdings and wide circles of dependents. They held quasi-hereditary claims to the minor local government posts open to *Indios*, as the Spanish termed the natives. This defined the upper limits of native engagement with the colonial state. However, the other opportunities for professional advancement and higher education open to the sons of the principalia in Manila, together with a significant amount of intermarriage between Europeans, more privileged Indios and Chinese traders, gradually produced a hybrid identity: *Filipinos*. Ironically, the term had originated in the legal codifications of rigid colonial racial and caste hierarchies, to distinguish locally born Spaniards from the *peninsulares* coming over from Spain.

The loss of Mexico by the 1820s led to the direct administration of the Philippines from Madrid. This, and the subsequent opening of the archipelago to world trade increasingly exposed the Filipino elite to the ideas of the Western Enlightenment, resulting in a generation of reforming modernizers known as the *illustrados*, or 'enlightened ones'. Both the elite illustrados and the Indio masses grew resentful of the casual racism, land grabbing, abuse of local administrative authority and self-serving manipulation of colonial government by unaccountable Catholic religious orders and the oppressive ecclesiastical state-within-a-state they ran with their peninsular allies.

Armed uprisings had constantly broken out in every generation against the dual rule of Spanish church and state, motivated across three centuries by a wide range of personal, religious, cultural, property, racial or group grievances. A final wave of unrest beginning in the 1870s took a clearly political turn, sparked by the frustration of reformist efforts to gain legal equality and representation in the Spanish parliament, and by anger at stepped-up repression by the friars against the native clergy. This culminated in the Philippine Revolution of 1896, the first-ever consciously nationalist anti-colonial uprising in Asia. It attempted to universalize the claim of a Filipino identity to the whole population of the archipelago, although the revolutionary organization itself, the *Katipunan* (usually abbreviated to KKK, see p. 110) overwhelmingly drew its strength from the Tagalog-speaking population of the provinces around Manila, where most of the fighting took place.

While unable to deal the enemy a decisive defeat, one illustrado faction under Emilio Aguinaldo grew strong enough to control the Katipunan and render stable Spanish control

BELOW
A group of acquaintances in the Philippines around the turn of the 20th century, indicating the wide range of intermarriage taking place in the population.

RIGHT
Uniforms of the Philippine Revolutionary Army, 1899–1902.

BELOW
Wives of Filipino politicians work on the American flag to be flown during the ceremonies marking Philippine independence, July 1946.

Panghimagsikang Hukbong Katihan ng Pilipinas
Ejercito en la Republica de la Filipina

of the archipelago impossible. As the US extended the Spanish-American War to Asia and tipped the balance by destroying local Spanish naval forces in the Battle of Manila Bay, Aguinaldo declared an independent Philippine Republic in early 1899. When Spain had surrendered the Philippines a few months previously, however, it had made a point of capitulating not to the Filipinos, but to the superior force of the US as the new imperial Western power. The subsequent Filipino-American War led to the defeat of the Philippine Republic and its replacement in the early years of the 20th century by an American colonial regime that, under various guises, would last until 1946.

Fresh from centuries of Hispanization, the Philippines would spend the next half century and more as a subject of American cultural, political and social re-engineering. This time, administratively empowered Catholic religion would not be the main instrument of further psychological and material transformation. Instead, a new set of political,

economic and ideological techniques would arrive from a young and powerful industrial society that was then rising to a self-appointed global role as uplifter of benighted humanity.

Among these methods were a professional civil service shaped by Progressive-Era cults of technocratic expertise in health care, law enforcement, justice, public works, transportation and many other areas. The traditional economic emphasis on agricultural exports was joined by a new import-based and advertising-driven consumer culture, while mines, agriculture and a local retail market long dominated by overseas Chinese were opened to American business interests. A regime of democratic electoral politics from local to national level on the US constitutional model, accompanied by a relatively free press, would prepare Filipinos for eventual independence on American terms.

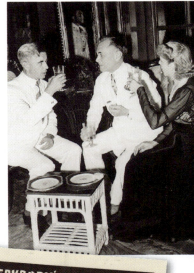

Unlike Spain's reluctance to teach its imperial language, an English-language public education system would produce a generation of Filipinos who thought and felt in American ways, while learning their new roles in public service, culture or the economy. Perhaps even more so than in British India, this eventually created a uniquely globalist and ironic vantage point. Through this highly self-reflective sensibility, the educated Filipino mind of the 20th century could engage deeply with the entire English-speaking cultural tradition.

Filipinos soon joined the colonial administration, and eventually gained control of domestic government as part of the promised transition to independence during the Commonwealth period of the later 1930s. Nevertheless, an authentic investment of popular identification and trust in a strong, impartial and legitimate native state – the major unfinished domestic task at the fall of the first Republic – did not happen. Instead, the debilitating pattern of a relatively weak central authority beholden to special interest networks that had arisen during Spanish times persisted through the end of the American era and beyond.

Despite its commitment to the visible modernization of the state, the economy and the public sphere, the US colonial state had left largely untouched the nation's Catholic religious identity and the Church's enormous material and cultural power in the archipelago. This helped preserve

TOP

Admiral Thomas C. Hart, Commander, US Asiatic Fleet, and Clare Boothe Luce in conversation with Philippine President Manuel L. Quezon, October 1941.

ABOVE

Poster encouraging Filipinos to tune in to English-language Voice of America broadcasts, 1950s.

popular traditions of social deference and elite economic patronage built on conservative Catholic mores. Also largely intact was the public prestige of the Church hierarchy. The European missionary orders, rejuvenated with new cadres of non-Spanish foreign clergy, remained as influential echoes of the religious counter-state of the Spanish period. After the revolutionary Republic had collapsed, even some sections of the anticlerical, nationalist illustrado elite were more committed to the defence of their own properties and regional social positions than to further cooperation with the masses.

These regional illustrado factions and conservative Catholic landowning elites eventually captured most positions in the American-sponsored Commonwealth government, the courts and the increasingly powerful legislature, via an alliance with new urban business and professional groups. Out of the formally democratic constitutional structures imposed by the US, these groups evolved a kind of revolving-door electoral oligarchy based on duelling factions. The parties that were to emerge out of this system in the post-1946 period had no significant ideological differences with each other, but instead were personalistic vote-getting machines that doled out the spoils from electoral victories to maintain the quasi-feudal loyalty of the candidates' followers. Before 1946, these political machines paid lip service to moderate nationalist sentiments while stopping short of demanding immediate independence, and were largely designed to get different elite factions into the game of using the state for the benefit of special interests. It was not rare for a 'traditional politician', or *trapo*, to swing from one such party to the opposing one between election cycles, in a quest for the right coalition to guarantee his career.

As government effectiveness lay permanently vulnerable to the resulting corruption and patronage-based bureaucratic infighting, the original, nationalist-revolutionary militant heritage of the Katipunan became the inspiration for mass organizations based on increasingly hard-pressed farmers, growing numbers of poor city dwellers, students and workers. These groups accused the elite of pseudo-nationalism and the cynical use of the American-designed-and -guaranteed system to advance their narrow class interests, at the expense of the nation as a whole. They sometimes resorted to mass agitation and the threat of armed confrontation, and were frequently suppressed from participation in normal politics by the trapo-controlled courts and militarized constabulary authorities.

BELOW
The first two post-war Philippine presidents, Elpidio Quirino and Manuel Roxas.

Even as the outbreak of the Pacific War in late 1941 ejected the Americans from the archipelago and plunged it into three years of fairly brutal Japanese occupation, the fundamental challenges to the legitimacy and strength of the Philippine state described above still remained unresolved. With the triumphant return of US forces in 1944 and the timely fulfilment of the promise of full independence in 1946, any potential that anti-American nationalism might have carried over from the revolutionary period for mobilizing popular energy to consolidate the newly sovereign state faded away. If anything, the period after 1945 saw the popularity and prestige of the Americans at all-time highs, in the Philippines as in many other parts of the world.

This did much to pave the way for a post-war dependency relationship between the two countries continuing to varying degrees to this day. The increased visibility of the US-allied Philippines in international forums, the provision of relief assistance, decisive CIA guidance in both the defeat of a major rural communist insurgency in the 1950s and the election of at least one president, all encouraged post-war Philippine governments to acquiesce in 'neo-colonial' trade and military agreements. The archipelago became a Cold War platform for some of the largest American military bases in the world. The level of cultural Americanization also continued to rise even after independence, as more and more Filipinos became familiar with the direct,

ABOVE
Premier Hideki Tojo lands in Manila during the Japanese Occupation.

BELOW
A classic image of the American Liberation, a warm and permanent part of Philippine folk memory.

unfiltered images and sounds of original-language American popular culture available from Hollywood, print, radio and television.

The war and its aftermath had irrevocably destroyed much that had been admirable and progressive about the pre-war Philippines; in many material and immaterial ways, the country has never fully recovered from it. Coping with the human and material toll of the Japanese occupation and the American reconquest left little or no remaining capacity to address the long-term structural problems of the weak state as it reappeared in the newly independent country after 1946. Decent if unspectacular fundamental economic performance and the tentative beginnings of industrialization marked the first four post-war presidencies. Nevertheless, struggles among elite factions for control of foreign aid and discretionary funds, mismanagement of relations with ethnic Chinese and others in the Filipino business community, and the increasingly cumbersome growth of state economic bureaucracies encouraged the growth of inequality and the familiar culture of corruption. The resulting erratic economic policy constantly impaired the state's ability to provide services and manage effective programmes of development, worsening the dangers of urban poverty and unrest in a population ironically swelled by advances in public health over the previous decades. The violent legacy of the war years and the anti-Japanese resistance bled over into the normalization of armed private militias, a dangerous new tool in the electoral competition between post-war regional elites and the resurgent political dynasties that had previously captured the 1930s Commonwealth state. This perpetuation (and intensification) of unfavourable pre-war trends suggests why the quest to create an effective, authentically strong and impartial native state in the Philippines has continued to be so elusive, even today.

By the later 1960s, the sense of a debilitating deadlock among increasingly violent elite factions competing for control of the weak state and the stumbling economy had encouraged the resumption of communist and Muslim-separatist armed insurgencies. The charismatic fifth president, Ferdinand Marcos, used these developments to gather a coalition of military leaders, frustrated technocrats and allied elite political machines, and declare a state of martial law in 1972. Initially enjoying significant popular support, the New Society, as Marcos dubbed his dictatorial regime, appeared to many Filipinos to be the first real chance for a strong native state to effectively deal with the many problems the country had inherited from its past. Regime

BELOW
Ferdinand Marcos.

20

propaganda called for the creation of a new, nationalistic mass constituency loyal to the abstract idea of the state itself, and not to any particular special interest group. Invoking Meiji Japan, South Korea, Kuomintang Taiwan and Lee Kwan Yew's Singapore, Marcos promised that the Philippines could be part of a successful Asian model of authoritarian but effective government, pursuing rational technocratic paths to national development.

The closer analogy, however, would be neighboring Indonesia, at the time already under Suharto's New Order dictatorship. But Marcos could not match Suharto's successful juggling of crony favouritism, authoritarian centralism and industrial developmentalism for 30 years – a whole Indonesian generation growing up under a passably effective strong state. Instead, after an initial period of improved public order and economic performance, it became clear to most Filipinos by the end of the 1970s that Marcos was simply the most ruthless and successful elite warlord, or trapo, of all, one who had broken through to a permanent capture of the state for the benefit of his chosen constituencies.

Senior military officers not only took over many lucrative non-combat functions and positions in the bureaucracy, but also expanded the existing counter-insurgency campaigns into extra-legal systems of torture, detention and killing against anyone suspected of opposing the regime. Provision of basic infrastructure and services stagnated, while funds from the government's quasi-monopoly on agricultural export earnings, intensified foreign borrowing and international development aid were all diverted into egoistic showpiece projects, or were simply pocketed by the exclusive network of regime-friendly cronies and the president himself and his wife Imelda – to the tune of an estimated 10 billion US dollars. Flight from the dictatorship boosted further the visibility and already sizeable numbers of dissidents, opposition politicians, professionals, and skilled or service workers in the Philippine diaspora abroad. By the early 21st century, this continuing 'brain drain' of Filipinos out of the country would eventually number around 10 million people – a tenth of the total population, one of the larger diasporas in the world and the largest by far from Southeast Asia.

The assassination of Benigno Aquino, a regime opponent and one of these political exiles, immediately upon his return to the Philippines in 1983 set in motion the events that would lead to Marcos's downfall. This occurred in 1986 in the course of 'People Power', a massive and peaceful popular

ABOVE
Benigno (Ninoy) Aquino, Jr.

BELOW
Bonifacio Global City, a new business district in 21st-century Metro Manila.

uprising in support of a breakaway military coup that brought Aquino's widow, Cory, to the presidency. These events became a model for successful peaceful pro-democratic uprisings around the world in the last decade of the 20th century. However, later repetitions also institutionalized the ritual of 'people power' demonstrations (in occasional conjunction with sympathetic military units), and normalized their function as unpredictable extra-constitutional challenges to any future elected government in the Philippines that creates enough enemies among the various sections of society.

All Philippine presidents since Marcos have had to deal with the myriad consequences of the traumatic failure of his authoritarian strong state to deliver on promises of general betterment and an end to elite factionalism. The massive looting that Marcos's regime undertook set back the national economy even before the impact of the Asian economic crisis of 1997. More generally, the botched opportunities for real development during his tenure in office cast a long-term shadow on the country's economic prospects even through the encouraging signs of recovery – and indeed regionally competitive growth – in the 21st century.

A great intensification of the pre-existing cultural distrust of strong centralized authority is a major legacy of dictatorial rule. But perhaps the most problematic aspect of the restoration of Philippine democracy has been the return of more or less the same pre-Marcos system of elite interests to power. Although now joined by broader representation of interest groups from all sectors of civil society, these elites – including members of Marcos's

ABOVE
*Panoramic view of Biñan,
Laguna Province.*

family itself – have over the last 30 years reclaimed their accustomed posts in the same kind of weak state. Living under a political system deliberately designed to be vulnerable to attempts by special interests to stymie, interfere with or at least slow down the execution of coherent policy, Filipinos watch, whether anxiously or hopefully, for the return of the strong state in some other form.

The histories of countries with strong states fit well in books of orderly chronological chapters, structured via political transitions from one dynasty, regime or government to the next. This book is instead about human resilience in a weak state. It sets the story of the state alongside that of the people in the seven chronological, if somewhat overlapping, chapters that follow: on the pre-Hispanic, Spanish, Revolutionary, American, post-Second World War, Marcos and post-Marcos eras. Stories of the tradition of barangay self-help in the middle of vast urban slums; of maids and nurses abroad or in the homes and hospitals of the rich, sending money home to keep entire villages alive; of fishermen gathering for evening meals on small islands as the familiar hegemony of the US confronts a dangerous future in the South China (or West Philippine, if you prefer) Sea; of the worship of Katipunan heroes as divinities alongside Jesus Christ; of why, if you have ever had a bank card, you might have talked to an invisible Filipino without even realizing it. These and many other stories perhaps contain the answer to a final puzzle, the most compelling of all; if the Philippine state is so weak, why does the country seem so durable and resilient in the shadow of this weakness?

2

THE COMMUNITY AS A BOAT
Regional Prehistory and Early Philippine History to AD 1500

Lying at the far edge of Asia's littoral zone where it meets the Pacific, the Philippines was never on the main maritime trunk routes through which key cultural elements from the great mainland civilizations left decisive imprints on much of the rest of Southeast Asia. To be sure, Islam struck roots after arriving in the 14th century, but today this religion and cultural system is largely limited to the far south. Some Indianized cultural elements – writing and calendar systems, politico-religious concepts and vocabulary – did reach the early Philippines, and the significant commerce with China and regional neighbours from early times also had an impact on the archipelago's cultures. However, the evidence for such contacts is spotty, and experts differ on the nature and significance of exchanges in goods, ideas and people between these islands and the rest of Asia before about AD 1300.

Clearly, such linkages were not robust enough to leave behind the characteristic Hindu-Buddhist monumental architecture, regionally networked aristocratic courts or annalistic memory cultures found today in neighbouring countries. Instead, an older pattern of localized chiefdoms, some superficially Indianized or recently Islamized and linked to China-centric trade systems, but all retaining predominantly Austronesian cultural features, persisted as the dominant form of community organization in the archipelago until the coming of Europeans. It was the culture-world of these settlements, some beginning to consolidate into larger polities, that faced the repeated shocks of massive Western cultural and social re-engineering after 1500 – and again after 1900.

Even the circumstances of the archipelago's

OPPOSITE
Mt Banahaw and its surrounding volcanic complex. A view over the waters of Laguna de Bay, the largest lake in the Philippines. Photo taken from Cardona, a town in Rizal Province.

BELOW
Outrigger watercraft of traditional Austronesian design in use for millennia in the waters of the Visayas, central Philippines.

physical emergence are detached from the geological history of most of the rest of maritime Southeast Asia. However, the Philippines occupies a surprisingly central place in debates about how prehistoric peoples and cultures spread through the region.

Except for narrow Palawan Island in the west, originally a Baja California-like breakaway strip of the South China coast, the Philippines consists of complex ridges uplifted from the sea floor at the juncture of the tectonic plates under Eurasia, Australia/India and the Pacific. The resulting island country lies on the western edge of the volcanic Ring of Fire around the Pacific Rim. Earthquakes are common, with the occasional major ones being very destructive.

Mountainous and with a generally humid tropical climate, the archipelago features narrow coastal lowlands except for two major riverine plains on the largest island of Luzon (the Central and Cagayan Valleys), and two more on the second largest island of Mindanao (the Agusan Valley and the Cotabato Basin). Smaller level areas can be found in Mindoro, and on Panay, Negros and Bohol in the Visayas islands in the middle of the country.

When anatomically modern humans first began entering Southeast Asia in the later phases of the last ice age (60,000–80,000 years ago), most of the region was still part of an expanded Asian mainland exposed by

RIGHT

Outline map of Sundaland with waterline at 120m (394ft) below present level. Courses of ice-age rivers are estimates from bathymetric surveys.

lower planetary sea levels. Back then, today's Borneo, Java, Sumatra, Malay Peninsula and Indochina were the uplands of what paleogeographers call Sundaland – a single, dry-land subcontinent almost three times the size of India. In contrast, Sulawesi/Celebes and the Maluku/Moluccas and Nusa Tenggara sub-archipelagos in eastern Indonesia, as well as most of what became the Philippines, have been separate islands since their formation.

During the final warming phases 8,000–15,000 years ago that ended the last glacial period, the melting ice caps raised global sea level by about 120m (394ft), drowning the broad central plains and river basins of the Sundaland subcontinent. This created today's Gulf of Thailand, the southern reaches of the South China Sea, the Strait of Malacca and the Java Sea, while leaving dry the uplands to where various early human populations must have retreated – the peninsulas, islands and archipelagos of the current regional map.

In contrast, the outlines of the ice-age Philippines were already roughly those of today's archipelago. The sea-level rise did not greatly alter the relatively steep Philippine coastline, apart from submerging some coastal areas north of the Bicol region, around Sulu, and northern Palawan, widening the narrow water gap between Palawan and Sundaland-Borneo, and drowning the narrow ancient plains and valleys between some current islands in the Visayas.

Our understanding of early human migrations into the Philippines and the rest of Southeast Asia before and after the break-up of Sundaland remains very tentative. Preliminary radiocarbon dating of a bone fragment from Callao Cave in the northern Philippines shows it to be around 67,000 years old, although its relationship to true, anatomically modern humans is still debatable. A series of bones from Palawan's Tabon Caves are definitely modern human, and date to 45,000–57,000 before the present (BP). Such Philippine finds are in the same league as the oldest verified modern human remains uncovered elsewhere in Southeast Asia to date – from Laos (c. 60,000 years BP) and from Niah Cave in the east Malaysian state of Sarawak (c. 45,000 years BP).

The earliest settlers' ability to cross both the possible channel between Palawan and Sundaland-Borneo and the broader waters between northern Palawan, Luzon and the central Philippines may therefore already have been well developed.

The earliest Southeast Asians did not closely resemble present-day inhabitants. Although these pioneering people left some traces in the genetics of many modern Filipinos, the first migrants' closest modern relatives are Aboriginal Australians, Papuans and perhaps the Ainu of Japan, probable descendants of further ancient treks southeastwards and northwards. Anthropologists label this earliest wave of humans 'Australoids'. Their descendants persist today in a few isolated populations in upland Southeast Asia; dark-skinned and small in stature, they are known in the Philippines as Negritos, or Aetas.

It was a different group of humans, arriving millennia after the Australoids, who were the probable ancestors of the current majority population in the Philippines and the rest of the region. Scholars disagree about this second group's geographical origins or limiting physical and cultural characteristics, and also about the exact role of the Philippines in their migrations. About the only things we can say with certainty are that the vast majority of Filipinos today speak languages belonging to the Malayo-Polynesian branch of the Austronesian language family; and that most have ancestry, physical features, cultural practices and genetic markers that are associated with other speakers of these languages in the rest of maritime Southeast Asia. Although many other ethnic groups have contributed to the Filipino heritage in recent times, the term Austronesian (derived from the Greek '... of the southern islands') can serve to denote the ethnic identity of the majority of people in today's Philippines.

The break-up of the Sundaland subcontinent 14,000–6,000 years ago accelerated on its way towards the region's current geography. This was a time of lowlands becoming swamps, then new lakes, bays and finally shallow seas, of proliferating coastlines, changing vegetation and new weather patterns based on seasonal monsoons, and ever-broadening expanses of water crossable only with constantly improving boat-building and navigational skills. The emergence of the Austronesian peoples (and perhaps their separation from the nearby mainland Austroasiatic ethnolinguistic groups) probably took place sometime shortly after (or while) this rapidly changing landscape and seascape was stabilizing into the maritime Southeast Asian map of today. Even without the flooding of many possible archaeological sites, correlating the ancient spread of language and culture with the transmission of

ATI-ATIHAN, THE FESTIVAL OF AUSTRALOIDS-TO-AUSTRONESIANS

A distant echo of the supplanting of the Australoids by the Austronesians in the Philippine lowlands has lived on in the Ati-Atihan festival in the Visayas region. This commemorates a late instance of these ethnic replacement events, one that took place well within historical times. *Ati-Atihan* means 'imitate the Atis' – *Ati* being a regional variant of *Aeta*, the general term for Australoid groups in the Philippines. Somewhat like the logic behind the Native American role in the Thanksgiving holiday in North America, the festival dancers dress like Atis supposedly celebrating the events around their own handing over of the lowlands of Panay to Austronesian settlers from Borneo in the 1200s. Amid the festival gaiety, there is a certain melancholy irony – most of the 'Atis' dancing in the festival are actually modern mainstream Austronesian lowland Filipinos.

genetic characteristics is difficult. Demonstrating the physical replacement of one population by another through violence, migration or intermarriage – or the exact relationship between language use and physical markers of ethnicity – is complicated. Much of the evidence that could help us better understand the stages leading up to the emergence of the Austronesians in the Philippines and the rest of Southeast Asia could lie inaccessible in vanished river valleys and submerged ancient coastlands.

In more recent prehistory after the break-up of Sundaland, seaborne Austronesian-speakers fanned out to occupy a larger contiguous area of the globe than any other language family, ranging west to Madagascar, east to Polynesia and the islands off Latin America, north to Taiwan, Hawaii and perhaps southern Japan, and south to New Zealand. The exact role played in these later migrations by the Philippines and Borneo (which lie closest to the centre of this enormous area) is also unclear. There is frequent debate among the experts, because the evidence is not conclusive.

The first attempt to explain the movements of the Austronesians through the Philippines was by the American anthropologist H. Otley Beyer in the 1930s. Beyer held that four waves of settlement had taken place. First came proto-human hominids, or 'Dawn Men' like *Homo erectus* (Java Man and so on), then the Australoid Negritos, both arriving from the south on land bridges. Later, the tool-using 'Indonesian' hunter-gatherers

BELOW
Regional and transregional Austronesian cultural expansion. The large pink area encompasses the current known limits of Austronesian migration and travel by sea; in red are the land areas within the overall expansion zone.

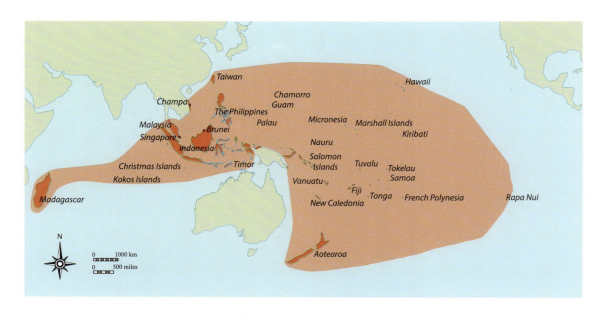

and the more advanced Iron-Age 'Malay' agriculturalists also arrived from the south, but by boat, each successively driving earlier groups before it into the highlands and replacing it in the lowlands. Beyer's model was taught in schools for many decades and remains well known among lay Filipinos, but has lost support among serious researchers and scholars.

The Filipino anthropologist F. Landa Jocano has objected that speaking of 'Malays' or of 'Indonesians' in this context is anachronistic, as these ethnic identities only emerged in fairly recent historical times. Jocano suggests instead that Southeast Asian groups developed their current ethnic identities after having already lived in the region for a very long time. Reacting to changes in their physical environment and the effects of trade and travel, they slowly differentiated away from common origins in an early settler population that cannot be classified into any of the present-day ethnic categories.

Other explanations reverse Beyer's proposed south-to-north direction for the arrival of Austronesians in the Philippines, and emphasize the importance of the archipelago in the emergence of such ethnic characteristics. Probably the most commonly accepted such model comes from Australian archaeologist Peter Bellwood. Building on the work of American linguist Robert Blust, Bellwood's 'Out-of-Taiwan' model notes the distribution of Austronesian languages and analyses their evolutionary relationships. Bellwood then links this to archaeological evidence of a Neolithic culture in southeastern China that practised rice, pig and chicken farming, with expertise in watercraft and navigation. He concludes that the Austronesian ethnic pattern originated in Taiwan and southeastern China, with the Philippines being the first short migration jump southwards. Once in the archipelago, according to Bellwood, Austronesian languages and cultures diversified further, before fairly quickly dispersing southeastwards to Polynesia and southwestwards to Borneo, and to the rest of maritime Southeast Asia and beyond to Madagascar.

Bellwood's model of rapid southwards migration is in turn challenged by the British epidemiologist and science writer Steven Oppenheimer. He

ABOVE
Early 20th-century colonial Japanese anthropological photograph of the Tao (Yami) ethnic group from Orchid Island (Ponso no Tao) near Taiwan. The Tao have many cultural and linguistic affinities with Ivatan and other ethnic groups in the northernmost Philippine island chains, directly south of them. The word 'Tao', or its variants, continues to mean 'human being' in most Philippine languages.

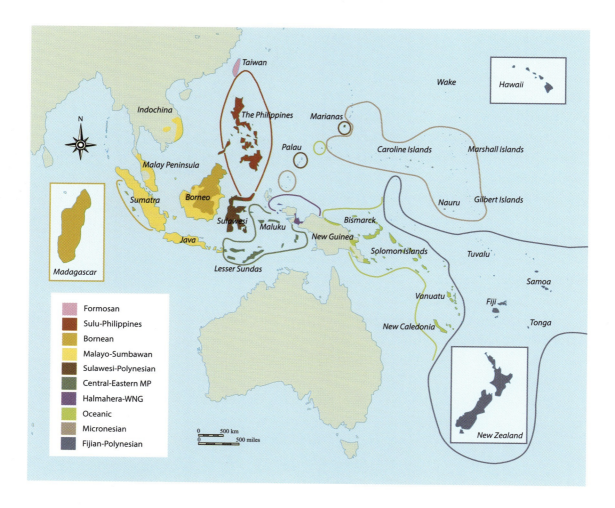

ABOVE

Geographic and typological distribution of the Austronesian language family.

argues that a rapidly flooding Sundaland may have generated environmental refugees who settled more northerly parts of East Asia such as Japan and the south China coast, positing a *northwards* direction for Austronesian cultural and genetic flow through the Philippines. Oppenheimer deploys an occasionally speculative combination of comparative folklore and paleogeology, but he is supported by data from the Human Genome Project, which reports very little genetic diversity in the north-east compared to Southeast Asia. This suggests that much of the current population of East Asia may be the result of a second migration event from the south, after the Australoids. Rising seas and population pressure may have dispersed this second wave of settlers northwards through Indochina and the Philippines, while leaving those who stayed behind in Southeast Asia to develop maritime

'Austronesian' (as well as mainland Southeast Asian 'Austroasiatic') ethnic and cultural identities.

Finally, the American anthropologist Wilhelm Solheim warns against overdependence on specific ethnic designations or one-way culture flows in the Austronesian homeland debate. Instead, he offers the concept of a 'Nusantao Maritime Trading and Communication Network' (NMTCN) during the Southeast Asian Neolithic (starting around 7,000 years ago, as the last major meltwater pulses were completing the break-up of Sundaland). Derived from the words for 'southern island people' in many Austronesian languages, 'Nusantao' is Solheim's term for interlinked chains of seafaring communities operating in a large area with the Philippines close to its centre, some of whom today do not speak Austronesian languages. These networks

EARLY MUSICAL INSTRUMENTS

Spanish sources have noted how rituals, celebrations and storytelling were often accompanied by music. However, it is notoriously difficult to accurately recover ancient musical forms and individual pieces, particularly after so many cultural intrusions since 1500. Some Philippine musical instruments in use since early times are also found in variant form elsewhere in Austronesia.

BELOW: *Also known as the 'crocodile lute', or 'boat lute', the* kudyapi, *or* kutyapi, *is a stringed instrument played to droned scales to accompany traditional vocalists. It is shared by the Muslims of southern Mindanao and the animist Lumad communities of the rest of the island. It also used to be found in various places in the Visayas.*

ABOVE: *The* kulintang *is a gong-chime-based ensemble preserved in the Muslim courts but once found over a wider area of the early Philippines. It is part of a family of such ensembles unique to Southeast Asia (and pre-dating any outside cultural influences) that also includes the* piphat *of Thailand and the better known* gamelan *of Java.*

Some mobile populations of 'sea people' still exist on the very edges of state awareness and control. While the Orang Laut of western Malaysia and Indonesia are more integrated into state structures and identities, the Sama-Bajau of the Philippines, Malaysian Sabah and eastern Indonesia are sometimes undocumented and therefore stateless in practical terms, subject to discrimination, harassment and exploitation by more settled populations or local government authorities.

BELOW

The proto-historic Nusantao trading system included luxury goods such as this nephritic jade earring (one of a pair) from sometime between the 3rd century BC and the 1st century AD. It was found in Vietnam.

nevertheless developed a shared trading and migration culture, out of which emerged the 'Austronesian' ethnicity. Present-day examples of these Nusantao networks include the Sama-Badjao of the Philippines and Nusa Tenggara, the Orang Laut (sea people) of Malaysia, Borneo and the Riau Archipelago, and other groups based off the mainland Asian coast. For millennia, their ancestors have been circulating genes, sailing, fishing and tool technologies, vocabulary, ideas and goods within a common zone of coastal and offshore settlements from Taiwan, the South China and Vietnamese coasts, the Malay Peninsula and the Straits of Malacca, then over to the Philippines, northern Borneo and the islands of eastern Indonesia and Northern Papua.

Within this large area, Solheim argues for a core Nusantao trading zone encompassing the central Vietnamese coast, northern Borneo, the Moluccas and the south-west-central Philippines. Based on findings from archaeological sites at Sa Huynh in Vietnam and Kalanay in the central Philippines, he suggests that between about 2000 BC and AD 100, seaborne trade and travel between these three or four centres was the impetus for cultural and

LEFT
The key sites in the early history of the Philippines.

Callao Cave
CAGAYAN VALLEY

CENTRAL VALLEY
Mali-lu? (Manila/Tondo)
BATANGAS
"San-hsü"?
Laguna Copperplate Inscription
Mt. Banahaw
Ma-I?
BICOL
MINDORO
Madja-as Federation
Kalanay Cave
PANAY
"P'i –she-ya"
CEBU
PALAWAN
Butuan
Tabon Caves
Golden Tara
AGUSAN VALLEY
COTABATO BASIN
Bruneian Empire
Basilan Island
Maguindanao
Sulu Archipelago

ABOVE
The most striking single find recovered in the Philippines from the Sa Huynh-Kalanay culture is the Manunggul Jar, a secondary (bone) burial vessel found in the eponymous cave on Palawan island. The top of the jar lid shows a boat with two figures, the rear one paddling and possibly a shamanic bearer of the dead to the Afterworld across or under the water, the one in front with the crossed hands of a ritually buried corpse. The jar has become an icon of sorts for Philippine prehistory, appearing among other places on the country's official paper money.

linguistic diffusion in the region's early Metal Age. Apart from the Philippines and Vietnam, the characteristic Sa Huynh-Kalanay pottery is found in many other places in mainland and maritime Southeast Asia, as are the signature bronze drums of the near-contemporary, but probably not Austronesian-speaking, Dong Son culture in northern Vietnam.

The Nusantao culture of Sa Huynh is a probable ancestor of Champa, a historically attested, early Austronesian-speaking state that emerged in the same part of central and southern Vietnam around the 2nd century AD. In contrast to Champa, which left extensive monuments and documentation in the records of neighbouring civilizations, much less is known about the the related Metal Age centres in the Philippines like Kalanay in the period AD 200–1000. After the 1st millennium AD, however, glimpses of them re-emerge in the first reports from written sources about the archipelago.

A noble couple from the Tagalog region with gold jewellery as pictured in the Boxer Codex, a late-16th-century illustrated manuscript, possibly by a Chinese artisan, but probably made for Luis Perez Dasmariñas, an early Spanish governor-general of the Philippines.

THE CHINESE VIEW – TRADING ENTITIES

Setting aside ambiguous descriptions of Southeast Asian islands in the works of the classical geographer Ptolemy, the first reliable foreign source to mention the Philippines is a Chinese Sung dynasty edict of 972. This lists locations overseas from which 'southern barbarians' came to trade with China. Along with Borneo, Java, and Srivijaya and Aceh in Sumatra, and the Arabs, it mentions a community known as 'Ma-i', noted as observing the syncretic Hindu-Buddhist religion commonly found in early Southeast Asia. Place-name research and archaeological finds suggest this was a port, either on the Philippine island of Mindoro or on the nearby coast of southern Luzon, today the province of Batangas.

Ma-i sent a direct trade mission to China in 985 AD; however, it was never part of the formal tribute system by which the Chinese legitimized relations with their more important trading partners further south.

That distinction falls to Butuan, another early Philippine trading community in north-east Mindanao near the modern city of the same name. It first appears in a Sung memorial of 1001 AD, as a regular source of official tribute missions to China. In 1007, the 'king' of Butuan unsuccessfully petitioned the Sung ruler for the same tributary status rank as Champa, with whom Butuan also conducted regular trade. This strongly suggests that the prehistoric trading patterns of the Sa Huynh-Kalanay network from

CHINESE INFLUENCES

The hundreds of borrowings into Philippine from Chinese languages tend to address practical, familial, commercial and material concerns; food items, objects of everyday use and relational terms for family members; *suki/su-ki* (regular customer), *ate/a-chi* (elder sister), *bwisit/bu-wi-sit* (bad luck), *pansit/pansit* (noodles), *sangla/sangley* (trader), *lumpiya/lun-pia* (spring rolls) and *kuya/ko-a* (elder brother), to name but a few. Other traces of Chinese influence on material culture include umbrellas to designate royalty or status, porcelain as prestige displays in homes, the manufacture of gunpowder, and (via Chinese in Java) cast metal cannon, mining technology, bronze and steel metallurgy, and (independently of Christianity) the institution of godparents.

Solheim's earlier Nusantao period may have persisted into historical times, nurtured by multilateral trade with China. By 1011, a final petition resulted only in the enrolment of the Butuan envoy as an honorary general of subordinate rank in the Chinese military.

It took until the 1170s for the next mention of a contact from the Philippines to appear in the Chinese records. This time it was no peaceful trade mission, but rather attacks by southern sea pirates that the reports called 'Pí-she-ya' in the monsoon season of 1171 to 1172, plundering ports along the southern coasts of Fujian province. The historian William Henry Scott suggests that these 'Pí-she-ya' raiders may have been Visayans (*mga Bisaya*) from the central Philippines. He points to reports by later Spanish chroniclers of oral epics still being sung in that region as late as the 1660s, commemorating naval raids on China by an Odysseus-like figure known as Datu Summangol, to win the hand of a Princess Humayanun from the Visayan island of Bohol.

After the first Pí-she-ya raids, the Chinese understandably developed a heightened interest in these islands south of Taiwan. By 1206, their surveys

added new locations in the archipelago to the already registered Ma-i and Butuan: Mindoro, Palawan, Basilan Island off western Mindanao, and 'San-hsü' (probably islands between Mindoro and Luzon). By 1225, Lingayen Gulf in western Luzon, and even perhaps Manila (*Mali-lu*), appear in these Chinese lists.

In the 14th century, Sulu and Maguindanao in the southern Philippines were added as Chinese tributaries, with Sulu listed as a vassal under the Bruneian Empire of Borneo. This may reflect a shift in Chinese trading patterns away from Butuan because of disruptions to the trading system stemming from the overthrow of the Sung by the Mongol Yuan dynasty in the 1270s. The return to power a century later of a new native Chinese dynasty, the Ming, saw new restrictions on private Chinese trade overseas replacing individual traders with once- or twice-yearly government-sponsored trading and tribute missions.

Despite the new government restrictions, the Ming period has left us with the bulk of the evidence for Chinese trade with the Philippines. Blue Ming pottery has been found at many sites, often far away from the trading ports recorded in Chinese sources. The American anthropologist Laura Lee

BELOW
A resident Chinese couple in the Philippines, late 1500s.

Junker notes that the Chinese trade affected not only those ports that were directly linked to China. It also enriched communities that were distribution hubs for the dispersal of Chinese goods throughout the archipelago, as well as collection points for Philippine products destined abroad. The large entrepot of Cebu, for example, is not as prominent in the Chinese records as other ports, but clearly functioned as a market and transshipment centre for half the archipelago – a role it has continued to play until today. Through it flowed the tortoise shells, sea cucumbers, hemp, cotton, yellow wax, gold, betel nuts and pearls from surrounding islands and the Moluccas, in exchange for the transshipped Chinese goods from Luzon and Sulu – porcelain, silk, tin, iron tools, bronze gongs, lacquerware, fans, gunpowder and parasols – that assured the prestige and power of many local leaders in the central and southern Philippines.

THE OFFSPRING OF SULU IN CHINA

In 1417, a 'king' of Sulu, Paduka Pahala (or Paduka Bathala in some accounts), sailed with his extended family and court to pay tribute to the Yongle Emperor of the Ming Dynasty. Although successful in establishing diplomatic relations on his arrival in China, he died on his way home from a mysterious ailment at Dezhou in Shandong province. The Chinese built him a tomb complex that still stands today and settled some of his family in the area to maintain his ancestor cult. In an interesting parallel to the religious future of their original home-land in the southern Philippines, their descendants were eventually assimilated as members of the Hui ethnic group after converting to Islam. The descendants of Paduka Pahala's two sons comprise the An and Wen clans in Shandong province today. With their links to an earlier and more amicable era in the two countries' relations, these clans have become a focus of efforts to improve the currently tense relations between China and the Philippines over maritime disputes.

While rebel Chinese military leaders have occasionally sought refuge in the Philippines from internal conflict on the mainland, most Chinese who visited the archipelago were merchants, craftsmen and occasionally settlers looking for arable land. These were people of low status in imperial society and thus unlikely pushers of imperial political or cosmological ideas. This is in contrast to the experience of Vietnam – the only major state in the region to come under direct Chinese suzerainty (in AD 111–939) – which today retains a massive Chinese element in its culture. Unlike in Vietnam, there is no evidence for major encounters between local Philippine elites and Chinese officials, clergy or scholars bearing the mandarin ethos of Confucianism or the doctrines of Buddhism.

The Chinese sources focus instead on commercially relevant information, describing tribute-paying Philippine 'barbarians' in stereotypical terms as imperial subordinates. This type of documentation gives us only occasional insights into the actual cultural and social characteristics of the early Philippine communities catalogued. A bit more information is available from archaeological findings, occasional notes in annals from the rest of Southeast Asia and reports from external Arab sources. We can also extrapolate conclusions from what is known about related Austronesian polities and communities in the rest of maritime Southeast Asia during these centuries. However, the most detailed and useful picture by far of ways of life in the archipelago at the point before they faded under the impact of Christianization can be found in the extensive observations of Spanish

Diorama figures of immigrant Chinese market traders from the Bahay Tsinoy, a museum of Chinese-Filipino culture in the walled city of Intramuros, Manila. 'Tsinoy' is a portmanteau term in Tagalog derived from 'Intsik' – a common if sometimes derogatory term for Chinese – and 'Pinoy', a term for Filipino.

clergy and scholars who recorded details of the Philippine scene in the couple of generations between the later 1500s and mid-1600s.

All these different sources suggest that a number of early Philippine communities had taken on cultural influences from Indian civilization even before the earliest mention of the archipelago in the Chinese accounts. The French historian and archaeologist George Coedes has described the emergence of what he termed 'Indianized kingdoms' in many other places in Southeast Asia in AD 100–1000. In most cases this was not the result of invasion or migration, but of the eager adoption by local elites of selected elements of mixed Hindu-Buddhist religious systems and models of court culture brought to the region by Brahmic priest-scholars who accompanied traders. Creatively grafted by many Southeast Asian rulers on to local social and cultural systems, such elements of Indian civilization enhanced these leaders' authority and power.

The most successful of these Indianized rulers controlled expansionist political entities that wielded influence over many parts of the region from the first centuries AD to about 1500. Apart from Champa, already in a trading relationship with the early Philippines, other early examples of Indianized kingdoms were Funan in Indochina and Tarumanagara in present-day Indonesia. Much larger ones emerged between the 6th and 11th centuries – the Indonesian thalassocracies of Srivijaya and Majapahit, and the Khmer-speaking state of Angkor centred in present-day Cambodia. There is scattered evidence that their rulers considered the Philippines to be within their contemporary spheres of cultural and economic – but not necessarily political – influence throughout this long period.

The common use of the term 'empire' to describe such polities implies a level of centralization and territorial control familiar from the Mediterranean, Near Eastern and Chinese experiences, but misrepresents how these Southeast Asian polities actually functioned. These remained systems of influence over people and labour, rather than power over territory. Also, in contrast to empires in other parts of the world, their geographical borders were often hazy and indeterminate. As a more useful way of describing them, scholars have employed the Sanskrit word *mandala*, originally denoting a ritual circle representing the Hindu-Buddhist idea of a world microcosm.

A mandala polity drew its identity from a ceremonial and commercial/political centre, but included separate communities only partly integrated into the centre's economic and administrative system. Like feudal systems in Europe, Japan and elsewhere, mandalas featured hierarchical relations of suzerain and tributaries. Compared to the average vassal in the classic feudalisms however, subordinate mandala communities had far higher degrees of autonomy. Mandalas emphasized customary and personal, rather than legally codified, feudal relationships, and were often non-exclusive. A vassal might have dealings with more than one overlord. The ruler of a vassal community could play off mandalas against each other and preserve considerable local freedom of action; for the mandala centres themselves, half-integrated vassals on the peripheries were useful as buffers to avoid too much direct conflict with each other.

Because of the geographic logic that funnelled most Philippine trade directly to China rather than to the southern entrepots that controlled Indonesia's

OPPOSITE

Candi Bajang Ratu in Trowulan, site of the capital of the Majapahit mandala, Java. The structure is designated a Hindu-Buddhist temple (candi) in current Indonesian terminology, but is actually a ceremonial gate into the inner precincts of the capital. Although the rulers of Majapahit were aware of the Philippines, their influence reached its extreme outermost limits in some barangays there and left no permanent built structures in the Indianized communities of the archipelago as material evidence.

BELOW

A general view of the major Southeast Asian mandalas of the Classical period (9th through 14th centuries AD).

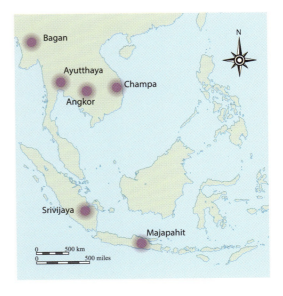

41

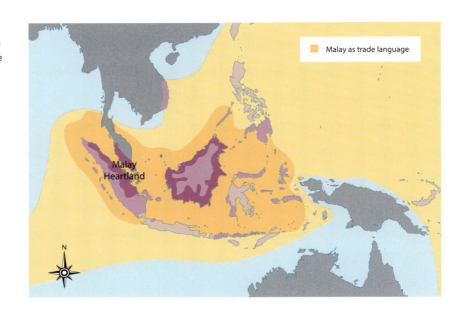

supply chains and transshipped hemispheric cargo, the Philippines always remained at the extreme northern or eastern edges of most mandalas' awareness and influence. Indian chronicles attest to travel by traders and Brahmic priests directly to Indonesia from the early centuries AD. However, there are no records of direct contact between the Philippines and the subcontinent that would explain the traces of modest Indianization that exist in the archipelago's cultures. The conduit was much more likely the low-volume local trade with nearby vassals in Borneo of the great mandalas further south and west. These modest exchanges were sufficient to introduce the basic idea of the Indianized kingdom (*karajaan/kerajaan*) and its monarch, the *raja*, to some Philippine regions to enhance the Austronesian concept of a chiefdom or datuship (*kadatuan*), without necessarily transmitting the Indian original's implications of territoriality or hereditary succession.

The secondhand nature of this transmission ensured the absence in the Philippines of the more elaborate Indianized cults centred around rajas elevated to the status of divine cosmic rulers (*devarajas*, or *chakravartins*) legitimated by resident Indic priests and disposing over mandalas of their own. The neighbouring bringers of Indianization would have had every reason instead to recruit early Filipino communities into the vassal networks of the mandalas that already existed in Indonesia and the Malay Peninsula. A key intermediary in this process was the Malay-speaking sub-regional power

A modern statue of Rajah Humabon, ruler of the port of Cebu at the time of first Western contact. Absent are any of the visual attributes of Indian kingship, and any definite hint of Indianized court life. Instead we have an image of a classic tattooed Visayan pintado chieftain, recognizable all over the Austronesian world.

centre of Brunei in northern Borneo, which underwent Indianization as a vassal of the Srivijaya and Majapahit mandalas before adopting Islam in the 12th century.

Some lowland Philippine languages retain traces of contact with bearers of Indian civilization. Tagalog, spoken in the regions around Manila, is notable for abstract or metaphysical Sanskrit or Pali borrowings such as *agham*

THE LAGUNA COPPERPLATE INSCRIPTION

The blending of Southeast Asian with Indian cultural elements is apparent in the earliest written document known so far from the Philippines, the Laguna Copperplate Inscription (LCI). Written on a rolled-up metal sheet, this text currently represents the beginning of the country's recorded history. It was discovered in 1989 near the town of Lumban, southeast of Manila. The LCI's internal dating uses a Hindu calendar widely known in Southeast Asia during the early first millennium AD, allowing the document to be dated quite precisely to 21 April in the year AD 900. The LCI uses a script closely related to the Old Kawi used in contemporary Javanese courts, and a trade language blending Old Malay, Sanskrit, Old Tagalog and Old Javanese. It attests to the clearing of a debt owed to the ruler of the Indianized realm of Tundun (Tondo, today a district of Manila) by the family of a certain Namwaran, thereby earning their manumission from slavery. Place names mentioned in the LCI indicate the spread of Indianizing influence from Tondo to hinterlands around the Manila Bay area. Other place and personal names suggest that Tondo had strong cultural, trade and administrative links via Brunei with Medang, a Hindu-Buddhist predecessor kingdom to Majapahit in central Java, and perhaps also with Srivijaya, Medang's powerful contemporary rival in neighbouring Sumatra.

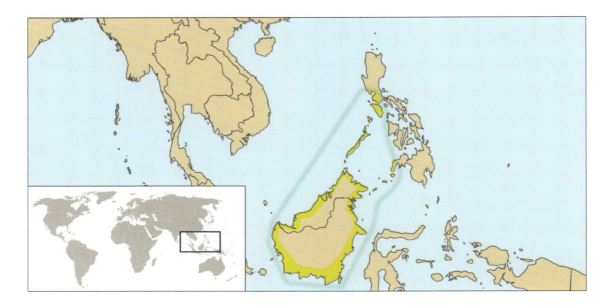

ABOVE

The Bruneian Empire at its greatest extent in the 15th century. Coastal areas in yellow indicate parts of Borneo and the Philippines where the Bruneians exercised significant political, economic and/ or cultural influence or hegemony. The area of water bounded by the darker blue line drawn around Borneo and the western Philippine littoral indicates the zone of Bruneian naval power.

(science, knowledge), *Bathala/Batara* (the Supreme Being), *budhi* (conscience), *diwa/deva* (soul/spirit), *dukha* (suffering) and *guro/guru* (teacher). Philippine academic Juan R. Francisco has identified about 336 other loans from Sanskrit into Tagalog and other Philippine languages.

Yet despite the archaeological and historiographical sensation caused by recent discoveries such as the Laguna Copperplate Inscription (see p. 43), the available evidence for Philippine contact with the Indianized realms further south, taken as a whole, remains relatively sparse. A strong if contested tradition credits the settlement of the Visayan island of Panay (and the designation of the entire Visayas region as a memorial to Srivijaya) to *Madja-as*, a federation of immigrants from Pannai, a Srivijayan vassal state. A golden statue of the Shivaite-Buddhist divinity, Tara, found near the Agusan River in eastern Mindanao, appears to be the work of local craftsmen, replicating an original perhaps associated with Javanese miners working in the area. Assorted items of ritual jewellery and seals with Indic scripts have been unearthed from sites in the nearby Butuan area. Apart from linguistic traces and the enduring presence of itinerant clans of Tamil small traders and moneylenders since early times, this is more or less the entire catalogue of concrete evidence available for Indianization in the early Philippines.

Whatever modest Indianization occurred in the archipelago, the detailed information about Philippine communities from early Spanish suggests that the original Austronesian cultural traditions remained the dominant factor in determining the character of daily life at the moment of Western contact. This included a rotated-field system of swidden farming; domestication of oxen and water buffalo; low to moderate levels of metal usage; highly developed seafaring and navigational skills; a formal system of indigenous social hierarchies; a durable animism with deep Austronesian roots and attached cults of ancestor worship; music and dance performances as expressions of an oral epic tradition, and in some regions, a cultural emphasis on tattooing.

In this phase of Philippine history, the cultural differences between lowland and upland communities remained relatively minor, at least in contrast to the radical separation of Westernized lowland society from the older patterns by the end of the Spanish period. Nevertheless, the largest and most complex early Philippine communities tended to develop on the coasts. The sea was central to everyday life in such places, the means of survival and the generation of wealth, as well as the access to other communities vital for cultural exchange and development. Further inland in some areas were communities more dependent on agriculture. With low population densities, land use was generally unregulated and free of notions of exclusive private property. Millet, bananas, the sago palm (*lumbia*) and taro root (*gabi*) were the most widespread cultivars. Rice and millet fields were optimized for rainfall drainage and irrigation at the foot of mountains or along rivers, and

THE EARLY PHILIPPINES THROUGH SPANISH LENSES

The first century or so of Spanish colonial presence after about 1580 produced an impressive series of travel reports, ethnographic studies and country surveys. These reports were written by Ferdinand Magellan's chronicler, Antonio Pigafetta, after Spanish first contact in 1521, and by Miguel de Loarca (1582) and Juan de Plasencia (1589) in the wake of Miguel de Legazpi's definitive voyage of colonization at the close of the 16th century. At about the same time, the new Spanish government in Manila commissioned the anonymous author of the Boxer Codex to produce this profusely illustrated country study, from which some of the illustrations of early Filipinos and others in this present volume come. Later came reports by Pedro Chirino (1604), Antonio Morga (1609), Francisco Colin (1660) and Ignacio Alcina (1688). All of these documents have to be read with care, in the context of the Spanish colonizers' own cultural assumptions and prejudices. Nevertheless, from all of them we get evidence that well into the first century after initial contact, and earlier phases of engagement with the Chinese and Indianized worlds, most lowland Philippine communities had kept forms of material culture, ideology and community organization more or less unchanged from the Austronesian early Metal Age.

RIGHT

The paraw *(also known as the* proa, perahu *and* prau*) is a narrow-hulled outrigger watercraft design found in various forms throughout the region. It may have a symmetrical layout with a central hull carved out of hardwood and bamboo outriggers on each side, or an asymmetrical layout with a single hull and a single counterweighted outrigger on one side only.*

in some regions in upland rice terraces, whose complex irrigation systems were similar to those developed in Java and parts of Indochina.

Lowland interior communities were also places where things from the sea brought by the coastal settlements could be exchanged with the products offered by people coming down from the mountains. Some upland and lowland groups also responded to over-water and local demand by developing mining and blacksmithing industries for gold, copper, coal, iron and other resources, sometimes aided by Chinese who settled locally. Other industries encountered by early Spanish chroniclers included weaving, pottery, poultry and livestock raising, lumbering, wine-making, and large-scale freshwater and salt-water fishing.

Regionally optimized watercraft and navigation techniques were among the signature Austronesian technologies that continued to shape Philippine life before and after Western contact. The wide, large, people- and cargo-carrying *balanghai* was only one of a range of boat designs. The *caracoa* was a sleek, double-ended warcraft that could advance and reverse without needing to turn around. Double outriggers with fighters at extra rowing stations allowed fast combat manoeuvring. Similar principles also characterized the smaller *paraw* and *banka* used near coasts, in rivers and bays. It was sometimes used to escort *caracoas* from the Visayas or Mindanao during *pangangayaw*, or *mangubat* (sea raids), to other parts of the archipelago and beyond.

As already noted, early Filipinos had repurposed 'balanghai' from a term for a medium-sized passenger boat to denote the archipelago's basic primary unit of political organization, the barangay. With their far-flung Austronesian cognates indicating distant origins in the prehistoric dispersals, barangays were independent communities of 30–100 families, founded originally on mutual kinship support and obligation. Like many pre-modern communities around the world, barangays featured a tripartite class structure of nobles, freemen and bonded labour (for the latter, we may use the approximation 'slave', a roughly comparable status in other societies). The functional elaborations of this basic structure differed from region to region.

Among the Tagalog-speaking groups, a nobleman was a *gat*, or *ginoo* (both meaning 'lord'), with the noble class as a whole termed *maginoo*. The title datu (cognate with Malay *dato* and Javanese/Fijian *ratu*), today meaning 'the rich one' in most Philippine languages, could also be found in some Luzon communities, although the term was more typically applied to ruling nobility in the Visayas and Mindanao. Datu and the collective *kadatuan* are thus perhaps the most useful generic designations for community leaders. In most parts of the archipelago, wives or consorts of nobles went by the title *dayang*, or Lady. Although there is evidence of hereditary restrictions to datuships in some parts of the archipelago, charismatic individuals who showed skill or courage in battle, or who gathered followings of fighting men and the allegiance of slaves, or even began as slaves themselves, often rose to datu status.

Monopoly of power by a permanent ruling family only became an established principle in the Muslim sultanates. The arrival of Islam provided a theological basis for a more stable monarchy in the 14th century – a role that had been played earlier by Hinduism or Buddhism in the rest of the region, but not in the Philippines. Nevertheless, piety, age, wealth, descent and character continued to play a role in the ratification of a successor in Philippine

BELOW

A noble (kadatuan) couple from the Visayas in the distinctive red clothing of their class.

ABOVE
Portrait of the Sultan of Sulu and members of his court, taken at a meeting with representatives of the British North Borneo Company, 1899.

sultanates that, in the same way as Saudi Arabia today, featured very large extended ruling families.

In some regions, Spanish observers noted councils of elders with advisory functions. In Sulu, a council of prominent datus with the Malay-language designation *ruma bichara* continues to provide advice to the sultan in matters pertaining to politics, law and religion to the present day. In most of the archipelago, some laws were customary and transmitted by oral tradition, while others were written down after being promulgated by the chieftain and his council of elders. Disputes were settled by the datu in consultation with the elders.

Among the categories of people who belonged to the ranks of the freemen were warriors, merchants, craftsmen, slaves who won their freedom, and some (but not all) cultural or ritual specialists and healers. The term for this social level in most of the archipelago was *timawa*, or *timaua* – people with land and property, commanding followers and slaves, but also obligated to serve the datu and the community. Tagalog regions additionally recognized among timawa the Indianized subcategory of *maharlika*, hereditary warrior bodyguards of the datu and other nobles who shared in the spoils of war.

People became slaves because of indebtedness, defeat in war, illegitimacy, criminality, or voluntary or involuntary purchase. Slaves were termed *alipin* in Luzon, *oripun*, or *olipun*, in the Visayas. Some (called *aliping namamahay*) had entailed households of their own, kept property and passed it on to their families, and had specific labour and tribute obligations. Other slaves (the *aliping sagigilid*) lived with their masters, had no property rights and no fixed terms of service, and could not marry without their master's consent. In contrast to some other systems of slavery, most alipin/olipun in the early Philippines could redeem their freedom with gold or other payments stipulated by customary law.

Living partly outside the basic tripartite social structure, ritual specialists existed in all early Philippine societies, practising a shamanistic animism rooted in the original Austronesian heritage. In Tagalog-speaking areas, the term for the more prestigious of such figures, who communicated with the higher gods and the spirit world, was *katalonan*. In the Visayas the title was *babaylan* (related to the *bobolian* of nearby Borneo). In the upland regions these shamans had other names: *mambonong*, *mumbaki* and *mansib-ok*. Beneath these respected ritual figures were people of more modest status operating in the broad zone between ritual magic and medicine. In the Visayas until today, such folk healers had names like *mananambal* and *hilot*.

Archaeological evidence from grave sites and contact-era Spanish descriptions of burial practices suggest that, like most human communities, early Filipinos cultivated good relations between dead and living members

WHAT ROLE DID MONEY PLAY?

Although barter was the main method of trade in the archipelago and between it and neighbouring lands, hoards of what the Spanish called *piloncitos* – small, rounded gold cones with characters stamped at the bases – have been found in various parts of the country. They resemble Javanese currency of the 10th and 11th centuries, and also Thai specimens dating to the period of Srivijayan influence. Even without corroborating evidence of a widespread money economy, they suggest at least that regional coinage flowed into the archipelago's economy, perhaps in the way that Spanish coinage later circulated in the colonial Caribbean even among communities that ultimately cut up the coins to access their precious metal.

of the community. Ancestor worship developed from this, as a link to the rest of the non-human inhabitants of the spirit world. Supernatural entities among Tagalogs were called *anito*, a word with cognates in the region such as the Malay *hantu* (ghost), attesting to very old Austronesian roots. Another term for these entities, *diwata*, was more common in the Visayas and fused the concepts of spirit and deity. It also suggests the impact of Indianization on Philippine cosmology, ultimately deriving from *devata*, a Sanskrit term for intermediary divinities between the high gods and the worlds of men and nature.

In their everyday lives, early Filipinos practised divination and relied on magic charms and amulets (*anting-anting*, or *agimat*) against both this-worldly and supernatural threats and curses (*barang*). Alongside the benevolent anitos and diwatas were malevolent or unpredictable supernatural beings. The *manananggal* (separators) detached their own upper bodies to fly off with hanging entrails and snatch babies from sleeping mothers. The *sigbin* was a huge, kangaroo-like being, perhaps a folk memory of marsupials that had survived in the region till the Mesolithic period. The *aswang* was a ghoul or witch that fed on the dead and could enchant and sicken the living. The *kapre* was a bipedal, horse-like creature that loved smoking rolled-up herbal cigars. The banyan tree (*balete/dakit*) was the haunt of spirits or the

GODS OF THE ANCIENT FILIPINOS

Early Filipino communities had varied, overlapping pantheons of higher divinities with cognates in other Austronesian traditions. They occupied the usual functional niches found in such systems around the world: Idiyanale and Apolaki were the Tagalog gods of agriculture and labour, and Siginarugan and Dalikamata the Visayan gods of the underworld and medicine, to name but a few. Presiding over most pantheons was a distant deity in charge of the whole cosmos, known in the Visayas as Laon and in Tagalog areas as Bathala (from Sanskrit *Batara*). Like the metaphysical Alfadur (All-Father) who evolved from the tribal Odin in the final phases of Norse paganism, the figure of Laon/Bathala suggests that a shift from animism to a more abstract deism may have been under way in some Philippine communities during the last few centuries before Christian contact, even in parts of the archipelago not exposed to Islamic monotheism.

gateway to the Otherworld. The *Agta* was a reclusive black giant, etymologically probably a folk memory of the Aetas – the vanished Australoids of the uplands and forests.

Such traditional belief systems survived repression during the Spanish period and persist in the lives of many Filipinos today. Similar to the pre-Christian folk heritages of Ireland and Latin America, Philippine animism has taken on new form in the saints and rituals of folk Catholicism, co-existing fairly comfortably with the canonical structures of the official Roman Catholic faith.

BELOW
A Filipino-Japanese joint project launched a microsatellite called Diwata DS-1 in 2016. Primarily used for weather and natural disaster tracking, and environmental management, it keeps watch over the country like its supernatural namesake, the diwata, but in this case from a low non-geostationary orbit.

WRITING AND LITERATURE

A Filipino syllabary called *baybayin* developed from older scripts common to Indianized Southeast Asia, most likely Javanese Kawi (itself a derivation of the classical Pallava from Tamil regions in India). Baybayin recorded business transactions, folk tales, poetry, songs and other literary compositions, and was written or incised from left to right and top to bottom with a metal stylus on bamboo strips, bark or banana leaves using the coloured sap of trees as ink. Baybayin had three vowels (A, E or I, and O or U) and 14 consonants (B, K, D, G, H, L, M, N, NG, P, S, T, W and Y) with a vowel associated with each and

the other vowels (or vowel suppression) indicated by diacritical marks. It continued in moderate use among Christianized lowland Filipinos alongside the Roman script in both handwriting and print, until the end of the 19th century.

Ancient Filipino literature survives in two forms: in the recorded oral traditions and sung epics of many communities throughout the archipelago encountered by Spanish or latter-day collectors; and in a limited number of manuscripts recording pre-Islamic epics preserved by the Muslim courts of Mindanao. Unlike Finland, Greece, the Celtic lands and many other nations, the Philippines does not have an 'official' native epic cycle expressing a dominant national identity. Neither did the archipelago fully share in the pan-regional dispersal of the *Ramayana*, the Indianizing civilizational epic that – modified by Buddhism or Islam – links separate ethnic traditions in Indochina, Malaysia and Indonesia. In the Philippines, instead a number of regional epics survive that are familiar only to the ethnic groups that produced them in remote areas outside mainstream Christian Philippine society.

The *Darangen* of the Maranao in Mindanao, the *Hinilawod* of the upland Visayans, and the arguably *Ramayana*-influenced *Life of Lam-Ang* among rural Ilocanos of northern Luzon are three of the most prominent among the 27 that have survived. These 'ethno-regional' epics do not generate feelings of personal ownership for the majority of mainstream Filipinos, in the way that narratives from the Catholic tradition do. Nevertheless, the Philippine state and cultural establishment have appropriated some of them in the 20th century as symbols of national identity.

ISLAMIZATION IN THE PHILIPPINES

The processes of political consolidation represented by the great mandalas of Southeast Asia in the early centuries AD were just getting under way in the Philippines of the 1400s and 1500s. Despite the occasional 'paramount' datus who bore the Sanskrit title of raja, Indianization played only a modest role. Islam had been providing the main impetus in the century immediately prior to Western contact, before the Spanish deflected consolidation into a completely unprecedented colonial centralization.

While most of Indochina maintained a Buddhist cultural orientation

ABOVE

A Malaccan soldier armed with flintlock and kampilan (Austronesian sword) encountered by early Spanish observers in the Philippines, late 16th century.

WINNING SULU FOR DAR-UL ISLAM

Although it is difficult to separate legend and embellishment from the actual facts, traditional accounts of the Sulu Sultanate mention missionizing efforts of 'Arab' teachers called *makhdumin* as early as the late 14th century. They parallel the advent of the semi-legendary 'Nine Saints' (*Wali Songo*) who began the Islamization of Java at about the same time. Islam's early footholds in Sulu were deepened by Baguinda Ali, a migrant from Sumatra who became Sulu's raja (indicating that by then the existing Indianized system had still not fully given way to Islamic models of rulership). By the middle of the 15th century, however, Sharif Abu Bakr, another charismatic migrant from Palembang, was able to establish the Muslim Sultanate of Sulu. Later sharifs such as Muhammad Kabungsuan accomplished large-scale conversions in mainland Cotabato and Lanao on Mindanao soon afterwards.

into modern times, the Indianized mandalas of Maritime Southeast Asia were slowly giving way by the 1300s to Islamic successor states. Beginning in Aceh in Sumatra, Islam spread to the heart of the Malay world via the key entrepot of Malacca, and from there to most of coastal Indonesia. It was from the recently converted Malaccan vassal state of Brunei in particular that Islam's representatives eventually came to Sulu in the southern Philippines.

The coming of Islam brought concretely territorialized concepts of state sovereignty. The Sulu Sultanate in particular staked out considerable regional power in the South China Sea and Moluccas area. By the 16th century, Sulu's hegemony straddled the present-day boundaries of the Philippines, Indonesia and East Malaysia, ironically ending Brunei's traditional role as transmitter of successive pre- and post-Islamic cultural influences to the central and southern Philippines. The chronically hostile relations between Muslim states in Mindanao and the lightly Indianized communities of the Visayas that were coming under Spanish rule in this period then ended the further penetration of Islam into the central Philippines.

Further north, however, the dynastic ties between Brunei and the Manila Bay area had already produced a Muslim ruling class in the large trading and fortified settlement of Manila itself, in neighbouring Tondo,

RIGHT

The dynastic and state flag of the Sulu Sultanate in the 19th century was recognized by most of the European maritime powers present in Southeast Asia.

and along the shores of the large lake later named Laguna de Bay by the Spanish. Although these leaders began carrying Islamized proper names such as Soliman (Suleyman) by the 1500s, they retained the Indianized title of Rajah and ruled over communities that remained largely unconverted from their ancestral and only lightly Indianized animism.

On the eve of first contact with the next major cultural force to arrive in the archipelago – Spanish imperial Catholicism – the Philippines thus featured several separate cultural and political milieux that coexisted alongside each other with varying degrees of tension. In the middle of the archipelago were the Visayans, largely unaffected by Islam and displaying varying degrees of secondhand Indianization alongside cultural memories of founding migrants from the great mandalas to the south. There were also the Muslim sultanates of the far south, and the partly Indianized federated communities in the Manila Bay area still in the process of a transition to Islam. Everywhere in the archipelago, however, the vast majority of ordinary people still lived by the ancestral Austronesian traditions. From upland mountain ranges to rice-growing plains, from coastal trading settlements to lives lived permanently on boats, many communities participated in a barter-based economic system whose ultimate logic rested on northwards links to China, not the mandala systems further south.

Of all these varied traditions, only a few animist communities in the remote uplands and coasts, and the established Muslim sultanates in the south, would clearly retain anything like their former identities after the massive changes brought by the coming three centuries.

3

THE STATE AS A CONVENT
The Colonial Experience Under Spain, 1500–1800

On his first voyage to the Caribbean in 1492, the Genoese explorer Christopher Columbus believed he had reached Asia by sailing west from Europe, but most European cartographers quickly realized that the real Asia must still lie an unknown distance further westwards. In the rivalry between Columbus's Castilian employers and neighbouring Portugal for global trade and empire, the Americas were a complete surprise – a vast New World that would take many generations to explore and exploit. Nevertheless, the Crown of Castile, with the larger kingdom of Spain just beginning to coalesce around it, would also persist with the original project to reach the east by sailing west. Three and a half centuries of European rule in the Philippines would be the second surprise result of Spain's circling of the globe.

To avert war between two Catholic powers, the papally approved 1494 Treaty of Tordesillas earmarked most of the newly discovered Americas for westwards Spanish exploration and colonization, while ratifying the ongoing eastwards Portuguese takeover of trade routes via southern Africa and the Indian Ocean all the way to the coveted Spice Islands of Southeast Asia. The treaty tried to define a north–south meridian dividing the two global empire-building projects – but only in the well-charted mid-Atlantic; there was not yet enough information to draw a counterpart longitudinal line in the still-mysterious antipodes on the other side of the globe.

In 1511, the chief Malay entrepot of Malacca fell to Portugal, and along with it control of the final sea approaches to East Asia from the Indian Ocean. From there, the Portuguese almost immediately set up outposts in the Moluccas – the Spice Islands long sought by European traders, lying in the easternmost sub-archipelago of present-day Indonesia. There was a growing realization among Western mapmakers that these Moluccas lay close to the other, antipodal line of longitude that should demarcate Spanish from Portuguese claims in Asia. However, navigational science was still not precise enough to establish on whose side of this line the Moluccas lay.

OPPOSITE
Portuguese memorial to Prince Henry the Navigator, sponsor of the first Iberian voyages of discovery.

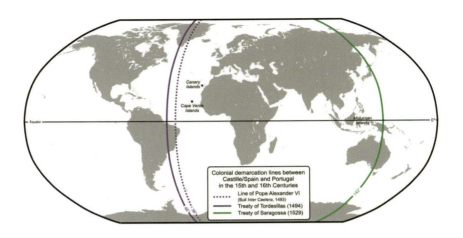

Technical difficulties with the determination of longitude shifted the Tordesillas line westwards several degrees in the years before and after 1500. The corresponding line in the Pacific remained undetermined until the Treaty of Zaragoza in 1529, seven years after the survivors of Magellan's expedition circumnavigated the globe.

THE PACIFIC PROJECT

Reaching the western coast of Mexico in 1513, the conquistador Vasco Nuñez de Balboa saw an unknown ocean stretching far beyond into the sunset. Charles I, King of Spain, authorized an expedition to find a route through this new body of water to Asia, there to establish a Spanish presence pending clarification of the Spice Islands' exact location with regard to the Spanish-Portuguese divide. The leader of the expedition was Ferdinand Magellan, a disgruntled Portuguese veteran of the Malacca campaign. His five ships left Spain in August 1519; only three survived the Atlantic crossing to clear the tip of South America. Making it into the seemingly calm ocean Balboa had sighted, Magellan named it the Pacific. After anchoring off what is today Guam, he made the first known European landfall in the archipelago we call today the Philippines in early March of 1521, at Homonhon islet off the island of Samar.

After celebrating Mass at a nearby island called Limasawa, the Spanish met a local ruler, Kolambu, who directed them onwards to the larger island and port of Cebu. They were received there by a ruler with an Indianized title, Rajah Humabon, who accepted Christian baptism shortly afterwards. Whatever Humabon may have understood to be the significance of his act, he promptly convinced Magellan to intervene in a dispute with Lapulapu, ruler of the smaller, nearby island of Mactan. When Magellan attacked Mactan with a small force on 27 April 1521, eyewitnesses report that he was cut off from his own men, badly wounded by Lapulapu and killed by the latter's warriors. The expedition sustained further losses while zigzagging down to Brunei and loading a valuable spice cargo in the long-sought Moluccas. *Victoria*, the last remaining ship, set sail homewards through the dangers of the Portuguese-patrolled Indian Ocean and African coasts. Under the command of Sebastian Elcano, it limped back into Sanlucar de Barrameda late in 1522, the first known ship to have sailed around the world.

Between the *Victoria*'s return and 1570, Spain sent four more expeditions to clarify the geographic relationships between the Spice Islands and the new archipelago Magellan had discovered, and to deepen the Spanish claim to both. The Loaisa expedition first returned to the Visayas and Mindanao in 1526, but ended disastrously with its members' arrest in the Moluccas, and the transport home under Portuguese guard 10 years later of the last 24 survivors. This was the last effort at an exploratory voyage of global circumnavigation from Spain itself to the Philippines. With the destruction of the Aztec Empire in Mexico in 1521 and its replacement by the Viceroyalty of New Spain, a more convenient base had emerged on the west coast of Central America from which to launch Spanish expeditions to Asia and back, without the dangers of a transatlantic crossing and a return

via Portuguese-controlled Indian waters. An expedition under Alvaro de Saavedra Ceron from New Spain to Mindanao in 1528 failed to chart a return route to Mexico, however, and met a fate similar to Loaisa's – Portuguese captivity in the Moluccas.

In 1529, the Treaty of Zaragoza drew a Pacific counterpart to the Tordesillas line in the Atlantic, to finally divide the entire globe clearly between Spanish and Portuguese interests. The boundary lay about 1,700km (1,055 miles) east of the Moluccas – about where the land border on New Guinea between Indonesia and independent Papua lies today. Zaragoza assigned all of the Spice Islands to the Portuguese, while placing most of the Pacific Ocean in the Spanish zone. The archipelago Magellan had reached had not yet been officially named, and was not mentioned in the

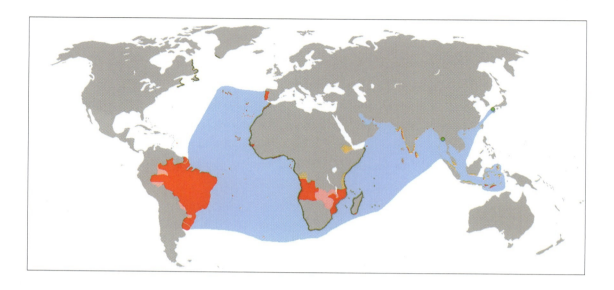

treaty, but by implication it lay fully within the Portuguese zone, technically excluding Spain from any rights to its exploration and control.

Charles I, however, was cultivating dynastic and political connections with Portugal that seemed to promise amalgamation of their overseas acquisitions. In the meantime, doubt about the exact longitudinal boundaries of Portuguese Brazil had led that colony's edges to creep over the Tordesillas line into the Spanish side, setting a precedent for similar encroachments in the opposite direction in Asia. Finally, reports from the earlier expeditions had indicated no spice production in the archipelago, giving the Portuguese no pressing reason to object. The voyages continued.

THE ARCHIPELAGO IS NAMED AND TAKEN

The first post-Zaragoza expedition under Ruy Lopez de Villalobos reached the archipelago from Mexico in 1543. He met the same depressingly familiar end in the Moluccas – imprisonment by the Portuguese – before dying from tropical fever, or as one of his jailers put it, 'from a broken heart'. Villalobos nevertheless left a major mark on posterity, for it was he who named the archipelago the Philippine Islands (Las Islas Filipinas) in honour of Charles' son, the crown prince Philip of Asturias, who was to become King Philip II on his father's abdication in 1556. Philip's reign brought Spain to the apex of its adventure as the first imperial power with truly global reach. Alongside his efforts to establish hegemony in Europe; another expedition was duly

ABOVE
Charles I (on the left) and his son Philip II.

launched from Mexico under Miguel Lopez de Legazpi, arriving in the Philippines in early 1565.

As his pilot and adviser, Legazpi had recruited an elderly Augustinian monk in Mexico named Andres de Urdaneta, a veteran of the failed 1526 Loaisa expedition who had led its survivors home from years in Portuguese captivity. With Urdaneta at the helm, Legazpi's expedition reached Cebu in early 1565 – where they found a settlement burnt to the ground on the orders of its current ruler, Rajah Tupas, who wished to deny it to the Spanish. Legazpi's chronicler, Miguel de Loarca, reports the rediscovery by a Spanish soldier of a statuette of the Child Jesus (the *Santo Niño*), during a search of a burnt house. Magellan himself had supposedly given it to Rajah Humabon's wife after that first Mass and the couple's conversion, 40-odd years earlier. The story (whether true or not) is the foundation of the oldest Catholic devotional cult in the Philippines, and the ideological justification for the

Miguel Lopez de Legazpi on an early-20th-century 500-peso Philippine bill.

later Spanish argument that Legazpi's expedition restored legitimate authority to an already Christianized community.

To avoid renewed harassment by the Portuguese, Legazpi quickly shifted his base of operations from Cebu to a more defensible anchorage near the present-day city of Iloilo on the neighbouring island of Panay. From there, he set about cementing alliances with leaders of other key barangays in the Visayas. The most prominent of these treaties was a sandugo blood compact between Legazpi and two datus on Bohol island, Sikatuna and Sigala. According to Spanish accounts, the two rulers were eager for allies against the Portuguese raids that had repeatedly plundered Bohol. Without attestations from the Boholano side, it is difficult to say more about what other reasons may have motivated the two datus to mingle their body fluids with those of the conquistador.

Having dispatched Urdaneta back to (successfully) chart the first Spanish return route to Mexico, Legazpi directed his attention to accounts of large trading settlements further north, in a large bay with an excellent harbour on the big island of Luzon. These were the partly Islamized communities of Manila and Tondo already encountered in the previous chapter.

RIGHT
The Santo Niño de Cebu. This appears to be a manifestation of the same cult as the Child Jesus of Prague, brought by Habsburg influence to both cities in the 16th century. The Holy Child is indeed dressed as a prince of the Habsburg court.

For Legazpi's generation of conquistadores, the last stages of the reconquest of Iberia itself from Islam were still a powerful cultural memory. Encountering Muslim influence, here on the other side of the world, must have been a further spur for the Spanish to take over the Manila Bay area as soon as possible. Legazpi sent a detachment north in 1570 to investigate, under his grandson, Juan de Salcedo, and an experienced campaigner named Martin de Goiti. Attempts to arrange a treaty with Manila's Rajah Soliman proving unsuccessful, the Spanish laid siege to his settlement and burnt it to the ground.

The two commanders returned north in force in 1571, this time with Legazpi himself, reinforced by now-allied Visayans from the central parts of the archipelago. After trying to rally the leaders of the surrounding Tagalog region, Soliman finally capitulated the following summer, ending the possibility of any further spread of Islam from a northern Philippine centre. With the exception of southern Mindanao, this event cut off much of the archipelago almost completely from its modest cultural, dynastic, economic and religious links with Malacca, Brunei and the rest of the Malay/Javanese cultural worlds. This victory on 3 June 1572 is the founding

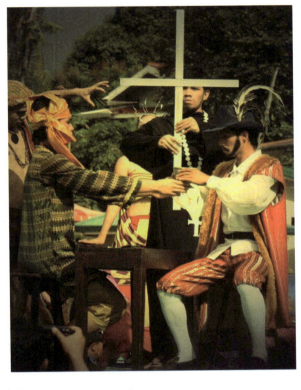

ABOVE
A re-enactment of the Blood Compact for a festival near Tagbilaran, Bohol.

THE NEVER-SECURED SOUTHERN FRONTIER

The Spanish raided Sulu in the far south of the archipelago, and also Brunei (whose rulers were related to Soliman), in 1578 and eliminated the Bornean sultanate's naval presence from Philippine waters. However, Christian forces were overextended, and unable to establish stable control on the large southern island of Mindanao lying between Borneo and the Visayas. The Muslim sultanates in the far south of the archipelago thus survived, never fully integrated into successive Philippine states. Over the next 300 years of Spanish rule to their north, they continued to raid the Visayas and the southwestern coasts of Luzon. Moro raids now combined punitive religious retaliatory intent against the Spaniards and their Christian allies with the more traditional preoccupations of economic plunder and slave raiding that had motivated previous centuries of Philippine piracy, regardless of religion.

date written on Spanish Manila's charter as the 'distinguished and ever loyal city', to which Legazpi promptly moved the seat of European power in the archipelago, leaving smaller garrisons in Panay and Cebu to anchor the Visayas.

Over the 1570s and '80s, further Spanish expeditions ranged widely over lowland Luzon. Across the Tagalog-speaking central plains, volcanic ranges and lakesides around Manila, into the nearby Pampango and Pangasinense-speaking areas and the Ilocano-speaking regions further north, and southeastwards through the coastlands of the Bicol peninsula, they founded fortified towns (of which the UNESCO-listed Vigan in the Ilocos region is the best-preserved example today) as regional bases for Spanish control over diverse populations.

DEFENDING THE PRIZE

From their forward bases in the Moluccas, Formosa and the Pacific island groups to the east of the Philippines, the Spanish could see that they faced serious external threats apart from Portugal, Brunei and the Muslim south. China's political instability in the later 16th century also stirred up pirates and renegade military leaders all along that empire's southern coasts. One of them, the warlord Limahong, attacked newly Spanish Manila in 1574, perhaps with a view to founding an independent Chinese settlement free of imperial control.

With Legazpi having died in 1572 from a stroke after berating an aide too vigourously, and Goiti killed in the initial Chinese assault, the defence

ABOVE
Vigan Old Town.

OPPOSITE TOP
The Spanish takeover of the archipelago.

OPPOSITE BELOW
Bird's-eye view of early Spanish Manila.

INTRAMUROS

Even as Manila developed in the next two centuries into one of Asia's classic colonial port cities, Europeans remained a small proportion of its population. The district of Intramuros ('within the walls') was the city's fortified Western core, with its strongpoint of Fort Santiago at the mouth of the Pasig River. By the 1600s, Intramuros was surrounded by burgeoning non-European districts such as Binondo, Quiapo, Malate and Parian. Here, subjugated Indios (as the Spanish had begun to call the archipelago's natives) and other Asian trading populations lived and worked. This pattern of segregation repeated itself on a smaller scale in Visayan ports like Cebu and Iloilo, where the Spanish maintained settlements housing smaller contingents of European administrators, entrepreneurs, landlords and soldiers.

ABOVE: *Santo Tomas Plaza, Intramuros, Manila, before the Second World War.*

of the fledgling colony fell to Salcedo and the new governor, Guido de Lavezares. Soliman and Lakandula, disgruntled by Spanish failure to follow through on promises to respect their aristocratic rights, threatened a revolt. Promises of reform reconciled the two datus and won the vital commitment of their manpower to the defence of the Spanish city. Limahong was repulsed, and when his fleet sought a new landing point on Luzon's northwest coast, Salcedo pursued and destroyed it with a Spanish-Tagalog force.

The Chinese imperial authorities quickly sent a delegation demanding either Limahong's extradition or his head; they got neither, since the pirate chief had disappeared. Governor Lavezares nevertheless responded with a successful diplomatic exchange that in 1576 culminated in a commercial treaty, the sending of the first Catholic missionaries from the colony to China, and a system of regulating the immigration of Chinese traders and artisans into the colony. Here, prospects were better for many of them than at home, while their commercial and industrial skills would prove very useful to the Spanish – who had little interest in the development of similar capabilities among the archipelago's natives.

The uneasy coexistence with the Chinese did not mean the end of external threats to the colony. The 17th century saw the rise of the hostile naval

and commercial power around the globe of the Protestant Dutch, newly free of Spanish Catholic rule in the Low Countries. The Netherlands took over many Portuguese outposts and naval bases along the southern coastlands of the eastern hemisphere. Seemingly incapable of understanding that God had already apportioned the world at Tordesillas and Zaragoza between Catholics, Dutch flotillas threatened the Philippines three times between 1600 and 1647, before being repulsed by understrength Spanish forces reinforced by native auxiliaries.

The increasingly aggressive presence of the Dutch East India Company in what is today Indonesia led to Spain's withdrawal in the 1660s from its overstretched garrisons in the Spice Islands, to Fort Pilar at Zamboanga on the western tip of Mindanao, a stronghold against nearby Muslim sultanates as well as other European powers operating further south. In 1637, the Spanish temporarily

occupied Muslim Lanao on the Mindanao mainland, and Jolo in the Sulu Archipelago. The northern threat from the Chinese warlord Koxinga in the 1660s led to Spanish withdrawal from Zamboanga, and only intermittent refortification throughout the early 1700s; the problem of Muslim raids on the Christian coasts would not be solved until the very last decades of the Spanish presence in the Philippines.

Such military sacrifices contributed to Spain's decision to keep the colony even if it did not generate compelling levels of profit. Without the realistic possibility of significant numbers of settlers from Spain or Latin America to exploit the islands' resources and land, the colony functioned mainly as a base for asserting a Spanish presence in that part of the world, and for attempts to Christianize the rest of Asia. Subsidies from the metropole or Mexico, taxes and levies from the Indios, and eventually profits from the galleon trade, in which the archipelago served as a staging point between Mexico and China, kept the fledgling colony afloat.

GOVERNING THE INDIOS

The structure of colonial government followed patterns developed in Spanish America. The sovereignty of the King was exercised through the Viceroyalty of Mexico, to which the Philippines was administratively attached. On the spot in Manila was the colonial governor-general, answering ultimately to the Royal and Supreme Council of the Indies in Spain via Mexico. The governor-general also had to coordinate with the local *Real Audiencia* in Manila, a composite legislature and supreme court of appeal composed of high officials and other prominent Spaniards resident in the colony. The governor-general was also the trustee of the Crown's role as source of all private property rights, as well as manager of the royal estates and the Crown's other private interests in the archipelago.

Also following the Latin American pattern, early colonial rule over most local communities outside the port cities operated through the *encomienda* system. Originally reserved for veterans of Legazpi's initial campaigns, an encomienda was a 'trusteeship' over a certain area and its native population. It was not an outright grant of tenure, being in theory heritable for only two or three generations before reverting back to Crown control. Also in theory, it involved a commitment by the *encomendero* to ensure that the natives, who were forbidden to leave the area, could pursue their traditional

LEFT
Puerta de San Lucia, a secondary gateway to the government district inside Intramuros.

livelihoods in their traditional communities in peace and security, while being instructed in the Catholic religion and Castilian language. In return the encomendero had rights to the labour and goods produced by these communities, and a share in the tax revenues extracted from them.

In practice, most encomenderos ignored their responsibilities and squeezed the maximum amount of profit and use out of their charges, using extra-legal violence, legally sanctioned chicanery and intimidation. Although the encomienda system was officially abolished in the 1750s, in places it persisted even afterwards because successive governors-general often ignored the policy limiting heritability to the second generation, and occasionally even created new encomiendas long after the original conquest. Other forms of land tenure eventually emerged: leased Crown estates, private *haciendas*, the remnants of local community smallholdings and the ever-increasing proportion of land owned outright by the Catholic Church.

The encomiendas were eventually supplanted in most areas by the governmental subunits of the central colonial state. With the exception of special military districts, the lowlands were gradually organized into provinces (*alcaldias*), and by the end of the colonial period a few autonomous cities (*ciudades*) on the model of the capital Manila. Each province or major city was administered by a civil governor (*alcalde mayor*), a position reserved for Spaniards. Alcaldes mayores had judicial, police, fiscal, registry,

notarial, permit-issuing and other administrative powers, supervised encomiendas in their jurisdiction, and could greatly augment their relatively low official salaries with officially granted, often monopolistic personal trading franchises (*indultos de comercio*) in essentials like rice and salt. Governors and their officials thus often acted as powerful private entrepreneurs in the economies under their control, with everyone obligated to do business with them for staples and basic services.

Each province consisted of a number of townships, or *pueblos*. Each pueblo in turn contained a main town, the *poblacion*, then a number of village districts, or *barrios* (many of them direct successors of pre-Hispanic barangays) and their outlying satellite hamlets (*sitios*). Installed in the poblacion's *municipio*, or town hall, the pueblo's mayor bore the title *gobernadorcillo*, or 'little governor', a characteristically patronizing Spanish diminutive, indicating the highest level of political authority available to a native Indio under the colonial system. Under the gobernadorcillo were the several district or village heads (*cabezas de barangay*, or *cabezas del barrio*).

The native gobernadorcillo and his council of cabezas formed the core of a district's principalia, the class of elite Indios whose wealth, reputation and/or influence accorded them formal dignities and privileges from the Spanish Crown. Among these were the right to be addressed by the feudal honorific *Don* or *Doña*, recognizing their equal legal standing with other local nobilities in the Spanish-speaking world. Members of the principalia sat in advisory councils at the provincial level and enjoyed access to economic preferences. They were freed from many tax obligations – in return for lucrative but unpopular and personally risky roles as tax farmers or collectors. These dignities and privileges also applied to their immediate families, and in practice often extended even beyond their time in office. Although these offices were, strictly speaking, not hereditary, descendants and relatives of such notables often continued to enjoy heightened prestige, titles, status and long-term political power in the community. This was partly because the colonial government tended to appoint members of prominent local native families with pre-Conquest datu lineages to the principalia, thus perpetuating the Austronesian elite aristocracy under new labels. Even today, the central role of a good number of local political dynasties in the routine democratic functioning of Philippine communities can be traced back to these families' roots in the principalia of colonial times.

RESISTANCE TO SPANISH RULE

Flight was not the only response to the widespread abuse of natives. The early datu-led resistance during the colony's foundational years foreshadowed a constant pattern of native revolt throughout the entire period of Spanish rule. Between 1581 and 1661, at least eight major uprisings are recorded; there were many more minor ones. Almost all of them had the abolition of forced labour and confiscatory taxation as explicit central demands, along with the obvious wish to be rid of arbitrary and often abusive rule by outsiders. Among the earliest was the attempt in the 1580s to remove Tondo from Spanish rule, led by the native auspiciously baptized as Augustin de Legazpi, and his more traditional ally Magat Salamat, both supported by arms smuggled in from Japan. In 1621, separate and long-running revolts broke out in Bohol (under a traditional ritual specialist, Tamblot) and Leyte (under the apostate ex-Christian shaman Bankaw, who had welcomed Legazpi in 1565). The anti-Christian thrust of both uprisings (and the native names their leaders carried) suggests a desire to return to traditional,

LEFT

Principalia of Leganes, Iloilo, at a community event, second half of the 19th century. Notice the white shirts worn untucked underneath formal jackets. There is no evidence of a specific regulation to support the common folk belief that the Spanish required natives to wear their semi-transparent shirts untucked to prevent assassination attempts with knives or belts. Most cultures in Southeast Asia wear shirts untucked because of the heat and humidity, though this way of dressing does seem to have become a signifier of native identity, as opposed to European.

FORCED LABOUR AND ITS DISCONTENTS

In addition to the burdens of often arbitrary taxation and tribute in kind, all natives outside the privileged ranks of the principalia were liable to a system of forced labour, the *polos y servicios*. Such 'donations' of time and effort were required from each male Indio of working age for a specified number of days a year (often exceeded in practice), to be applied to tasks ranging from domestic service, work on Spanish-owned farms or infrastructure such as roads and buildings, or military service. The constant interruptions to one's own effort to earn a living, particularly the long absences required for service in the colony's public works, military forces and shipyards, demoralized much of the population. The Spanish reacted to Indio efforts to evade the *polos y servicios* by accusing the natives of being feckless, lazy and workshy, incapable of sustained effort and long-term planning. Many of these stereotypes have survived till today, sweepingly applied to Filipinos by some foreigners – and even by some Filipinos to their own countrymen – ignorant of the long tradition of passive resistance to forced unpaid labour and confiscatory taxation.

LEFT: *A volume of stories about Juan Tamad (Lazy Juan), a stock figure from colonial-era Tagalog folklore reflecting Spanish attitudes about lazy natives. Perhaps the best-known of these stories is one about how Juan, wishing for some fruits from the guava tree, lies down underneath a branch with his mouth open waiting for one to fall, instead of climbing up to pluck the fruits.*

pre-contact Visayan religious belief systems in addition to more generic material grievances. Between 1641 and 1661, other revolts broke out in Samar, Pangasinan and Pampanga, and among the Ilocanos.

Unlike comparable colonial uprisings in the rest of Southeast Asia, Indio revolts in the Philippines before 1800 for the most part did not invoke surviving pre-colonial loyalties extending beyond the immediate region or province. This isolation was one reason why Spanish military pacification campaigns could defeat them. The actions of the Spanish state alone, however, would not have been enough to produce the enthusiastically Christian, Western-oriented character of the lowland society that developed in the Philippines between the 1570s and 1870s. The emergence of this new culture was due to the remarkable job of social and psychological engineering accomplished by the government's partner, competitor and sometimes adversary, the Catholic Church.

CHURCH AS STATE

As was the case in Latin America, the early decades of the colony had witnessed the efforts of conscientious churchmen to denounce corrupt civil officials. Championing the natives against the more abusive early Spanish colonizers was ultimately a contest for power between church and state, based on the question of the ultimate source of moral authority that legitimized Spanish occupation. The first Bishop of Manila, Domingo de Salazar, advanced in 1582 the remarkable doctrine that sovereignty and ultimate self-determination remained in the hands of the Indios as fellow children of God. For Salazar, the islanders had merely and voluntarily (through their chiefs) entered into (revocable) compacts of alliance and fealty with the Spanish, bringers of the True Faith and good government. It was the duty of all Spaniards, laymen and religious, to ensure that there would never be grounds for such revocation.

ABOVE
Present-day decorative carvings of Sikatuna and Tamblot in a Bohol museum.

Early in the history of the colony, this doctrine gave the Church plenty of opportunities to protest the obvious abuses in the early encomiendas. By the 17th century, Salazar's doctrine also gave the clergy a leading role in transforming the lowland Philippine landscape through the archipelago's

THE DAGOHOY REVOLT

None of the uprisings in the early centuries of Spanish rule were fought in the name of a nationwide 'Filipino' identity; such a concept did not yet exist. Nevertheless, for modern Filipino nationalists, they constitute an honoured roster of predecessors. Perhaps the most spectacular and sustained effort to end Spanish rule anywhere in the Christian parts of the archipelago before the late 19th century was the Dagohoy Revolt. For a remarkable 84 years from 1744 to 1829, Francisco Dagohoy and thousands of his supporters effectively made most of the Visayan island of Bohol an autonomous zone where Spanish rule did not function. Starting as a narrow personal grievance over the Church's refusal to accord Dagohoy's brother a Christian burial, the uprising fed on the accumulated discontent of a broad rural population. These people abandoned the pueblos into which Bohol had been divided, be-

coming *remontados*, literally those who 'remounted', retreating back into the uplands of the island's interior. There they established self-sufficient farming settlements, protected from any effort to reimpose control by the colonial government by fortified defence lines and the early warnings of sympathizers in the remaining Spanish-controlled towns. Despite having thrown off the rule of both colonial church and colonial state, the Dagohoy communities – and Dagohoy himself, as seen in his complaint about the refusal of his brother's Christian burial – seem to have remained resolutely Catholic. In contrast to Tamblot on the same island a century earlier, the Dagohoy Revolt was a testament to how, by the mid-1700s, Christianity had ceased to be experienced by even the most recalcitrant Indios as an external imposition, becoming instead a central component of a new, self-sufficient native identity and culture.

version of the *reduccion* (resettlement) system pioneered in Latin America. Foreshadowing policies of population reconcentration in other Western colonial contexts over the next few centuries, this policy intended to 'reduce' the number of natives living outside Spanish religio-political supervision, thereby making them more taxable, educable and controllable.

Most of the *reducciones* in Latin America had been achieved via the joint effort of the colonial state and the Church. In the Philippines, these

THE PATRONATO REAL

The governor-general of a colony was also the local administrator of the *Patronato Real* (royal patronage). This was an agreement by which the Pope allowed the monarchy to regulate the activities and presence of the Catholic Church throughout the entire Spanish empire. Originally won by the Crown as a concession from the Vatican after the reconquest of Spain itself from Islam, the Patronato Real, at least on the face of it, gave the civil government in the Philippines decisive authority over the Church. This included the power to set the boundaries of mission territories for the different missionary orders, veto papal pronouncements and instructions within a colonial jurisdiction, route any clerical contact with Rome through the Mexican ecclesiastical hierarchy, approve personnel appointments to clerical posts, supervise clerical activities outside the strictly ritual/theological sphere and punish abuses. In return, the colonial state was obligated to protect the interests and property of the Church and provide for the material upkeep and support of the clergy. The state was also responsible for paying regular salaries and stipends to ecclesiastics at all levels for the many non-clerical public responsibilities that churchmen, recreating medieval European patterns, eventually took on in local communities throughout the archipelago.

This last obligation was particularly significant in creating a situation where the Church ended up enjoying massive autonomy from the colonial state, becoming very often the only representative of Spanish authority in many Philippine communi-

ties. This was partly because the civil administration remained relatively small and overstretched throughout the entire period of Spanish presence. Although some conscientious and energetic civil officials did made their way to the Philippines, at the local levels in particular the colony also had more than its share of corrupt timeservers and careerist chancers, who barely attended to the needs of their jurisdictions and mostly looked for opportunities to enrich themselves before returning home.

In many communities, the longer-serving European clergy perforce took on an array of local administrative tasks such as civil residence registry, supervision and teaching in local schools, subjudicial arbitration of community disputes, management and rental of the growing inventories of Church lands, assignment of compulsory labour and even public tax collection. It was often not clear whether the government thereby controlled a powerful tool of pacification and ideological propaganda to ensure a cooperative population, or if the Church had managed to enlist the authority of coercive governmental force in the running of what was essentially an ecclesiastical state-within-a-state. From the beginnings of the colony, missionary religious orders not under the authority of the Bishop of Manila were also prominent in official colonial policy making and public affairs. As a consequence, the actual working relationship between church and state was often contentious, and occasionally even violent. Each side aggressively defended its prerogatives even as both exploited and dominated the local populations.

LEFT
A possibly posed photograph showing Jesuits missionizing native Filipinos in around 1900.

resettlement programmes relied much more on the efforts of the Church, in particular its well-organized and disciplined missionary orders, the Augustinians, Dominicans, Franciscans and Jesuits. Many of them were avid learners of the local Austronesian languages spoken in their particular *doctrinas*, or mission districts, and more than a few were able compilers of anthropological and scientific information about these new peoples and landscapes. These early missionaries encouraged the cooperation of natives with the resettlement effort via inducements such as offers of town housing to heads of families, and recommendations to the civil authorities of traditional elders to elevate to the principalia. The prospect of gaining an education for their children in the new ways of European civilization as a passport to social and economic mobility also attracted many families to these resettlement programmes, as central to the friars' power in the colony was their control of education as well as cultural and intellectual life. Not only were all schools at the village level in the hands of the local clergy, but in 1581 the Jesuits had arrived in the colony with a mission to set up seminaries for the training of priests and the provision of secondary educations for paying secular students. They quickly set up the Colegio de San Jose, the first Western college in the archipelago. Although it did not survive, by 1611 the Dominicans had founded what became the University of Santo Tomas, the

ABOVE
Main facade, University of Santo Tomas.

oldest extant Western university in Asia.

By the second century of Spanish rule, most of the lowland population was successfully re-settled in civil poblacions and their respective doctrinas. For the more reluctant, churchmen could call on the threat of armed force from the colonial state; the truly recalcitrant fled to the uplands outside the orbit of Christian lowland culture. Perhaps the largest percentage of Indios, however, found a compromise, moving with various degrees of dexterity between the worlds of Christianized town and traditional countryside by living in the outlying barrios and sitios dependent on a poblacion. The Church adjusted by establishing a network of subsidiary chapels in major villages, and instituting a rotating circuit of catechism and Masses among them that still operates in the present day.

The interrelated issues of 'visitation' and 'secularization' were to shape

BENEATH THE BELLS

A major emotional draw for country and town alike lay in the aesthetic and emotive appeal of the Catholic religion itself in its most Baroque form, and the feast days, sacraments, music, Masses, religious sodalities and organizations that embodied it. Along with the more practical kinds of inducements, these new expressions of the numinous and divine were all available when one lived 'beneath the bells' (*abajo*

de las campañas), that is, within hearing distance of the church that stood at the centre of the new pueblos emerging in the countryside, the headquarters of the local doctrina. The relative absence of symbols and practices from the other great Asian religions in the majority of the archipelago north of Mindanao meant that Catholicism was alone in providing, in a manner compatible with the indigenous traditions of Austronesian animism, a colourful symbolic narrative around which a community could reorient itself. The Church and its ancillary infrastructure and programmes was simultaneously a de facto civil administrative centre, a ritual site for instruction and immersion in a new faith (and the gradual assimilation of that faith into local traditions), the source of general education and literacy, and the forum for the community's cultural life and general sociability.

LEFT: *A Church festival in present-day Santa Ana, Bulacan province.*

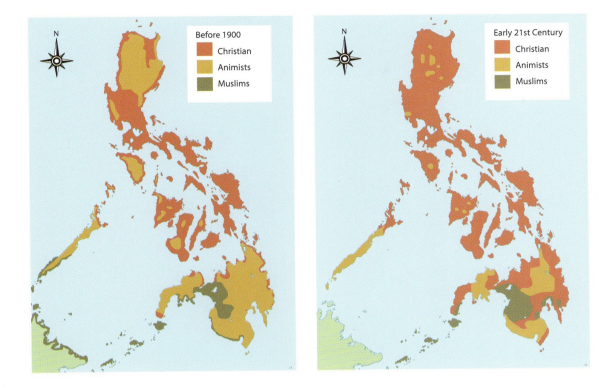

ABOVE
The spread of Catholic Christianity from 1800 (left) to 2000 (right).

the development of the Church in the colony, defining the contest over power between the autonomous missionary orders – the aforementioned Augustinians, Dominicans and Franciscans, and later the Jesuits – on the one hand, and the colonial archdiocese of Manila on the other. Visitation involved the power of the bishops of a regional Church hierarchy to monitor and control the local representatives of missionary orders headquartered in Rome. However, the friar orders successfully avoided the efforts of the Archbishop of Manila to impose visitation on them until the end of the Spanish colony and beyond. Under their own provincials or regional superiors based in the archipelago or in other parts of Asia, they operated in the Philippines without any formal supervision closer than their orders' headquarters in Europe. Secularization was the term for the intended gradual replacement of the friars, who came exclusively from Spain, as soon as trained local clergy could be raised – in this case, Filipino priests ordained by the local bishop. Secularization, too, was successfully resisted, as successive generations of European friars through the history of the colony held to the position, often phrased in the crudest of racial stereotypes, that natives

ABOVE
Present-day Filipino Franciscans. With most of the missionary orders today thoroughly Filipinized, the commanding position the orders had in everyday community life has ironically disappeared.

were unqualified or simply constitutionally unable to serve as parish priests.

As the decades passed, the central and highly autonomous role of the missionary Spanish parish priest in lowland community life made it increasingly difficult to avoid the temptations of power and influence that had dangled before the civil administrators. The colonial regime's reliance on the clergy for routine administrative tasks offered many opportunities for personal enrichment. Other routes to corruption lay in the growing tendency for friars in rarely audited parishes to charge fees for Masses, sacraments and other religious services, and in the use of compulsory polo labour and food or produce tributes (often with a surplus to be sold on) for the upkeep of the local clergy.

Perhaps the most important way that a religious vocation became a lucrative calling for those who sought lives of ease, power and luxury lay in the concessions granted to the various missionary orders, as well as the regular diocesan clergy, to own land. The Patronato Real had originally assigned land parcels or shares in the produce from local encomiendas to the Church, from which the clergy was supposed to derive both maintenance and its operating income. Apart from such government bequests, the Church's role as landowner also grew through pious donations and legacies, direct purchases using the income from fees and tribute, and foreclosing on loans to farmers who had pledged their lands as collateral. Most of this property was then rented out to native tenants who either tilled the land themselves or, as so-called *inquilinos*, sublet them to their own tenants.

If some churchmen in the early decades of the colony had acted as voices of conscience against official abuse, the roles had begun reversing by the mid-17th century, as civil officials started calling out the corruption emerging in the ecclesiastical state-within-a-state. The missionary clergy retaliated, sometimes violently, against any perceived challenge to its autonomy. One such dramatic confrontation occurred in the late 1640s, when the Augustinian friars engineered the imprisonment of former governor-general Sebastian Hurtado de Corcuera over a dispute during his incumbency about the right of sanctuary in a church for a soldier convicted of murder. Behind the immediate issue lay a growing sense that the missionary orders were becoming a law unto themselves. This was also evident in an incident in 1719, when

BELOW
The Assassination of Governor Bustamante and His Son, *by Felix Resurreccion Hidalgo, 1884. Hidalgo was perhaps the finest Filipino painter of his generation. Although his success was an inspiration for Filipino nationalists, he took no active part in their efforts at home or abroad. His career took him mostly away from the archipelago. He died in Spain in 1913 but was buried in Manila.*

a mob led or egged on by missionary friars stormed the governor-general's palace and knifed to death the incumbent, Fernando Bustamante. In this somewhat medieval drama, but with an opposite outcome to the tragedy of Thomas à Becket, the clergy were retaliating against Bustamante's imprisonment of Francisco de la Cuesta, the Archbishop of Manila, for conspiracy over accusations involving the right of church sanctuary for officials involved in misappropriated government funds. The elevation of the good archbishop himself to the post of acting governor-general for the next few years after Bustamante's assassination (until a reversal arrived from Spain) underscored the point the clergy wanted to make.

ECONOMIC DEVELOPMENT OF THE COLONY

Despite the occasionally homicidal levels of tension between them, the Spanish church and state were partners (alongside powerful and wealthy individual Spaniards resident in the colony) not only in the exploitation of the Philippines itself, but also in the highly profitable galleon trade, where the Philippines served as the Western Pacific anchor and transshipment point for trade between Asia (mostly from China) and Acapulco in Mexico. Urdaneta's original return voyage of 1565 had laid the foundations for a trade system that brought to Mexico Chinese spices, ivory, lacquerware, luxury handicrafts and silk destined for European markets, while return voyages brought payment in Mexican silver destined for China, as well as provisions, manufactures and passengers bound for the Philippines.

Very little of the trade was in items from the colony itself, which therefore did not receive incentives to develop manufacturing or agricultural export industries. The profits also remained in the hands of Spanish investors, who jealously guarded their monopoly. This failure to exploit the archipelago's natural resources, and the investment of the overwhelming majority of official, private and Church capital in the galleon trade, went hand in hand. Loss or capture of the galleons or Chinese junks en route to Manila represented a financial disaster for the colony. The shareholders in the galleon trade used the proportion of their wealth not expatriated to Spain to enhance the overall standard of living and cultural activity in Manila and acquire land in the provinces, but otherwise did little to develop the colony's internal economy or infrastructure.

LATERAL IMPERIAL TRAVEL – MEXICO AND THE BASQUE COUNTRY

The galleon trade resulted in the transfer of some Nahuatl or other Mesoamerican vocabulary to the Philippine languages, new crops and livestock like turkeys, maize, tomato, cacao, avocados, yams and potatoes, Catholic religious cults of Mexican, sometimes pre-Christian origin like the Black Nazarene and Our Lady of Guadalupe, and the Mexican ancestry of some Filipinos. Small colonies of Filipinos descended from galleon crews developed not only in Acapulco and other Mexican cities, but even in the bayous of Louisiana, briefly under Spanish administration in the 18th century, where they were known as 'Manilamen'. Among the Mexican soldiers, administrators, businessmen and clergy who came over to the Philippines were many people of Basque origin. Like the Scots, Irish, Cornishmen and Welsh who fanned out into the British empire in search of better lives, many prominent Spanish-Filipino families today trace their descent back to Basque ancestors, via Mexico.

Chinese food and desserts bought from street vendors became part of daily life in the Philippines during the Spanish period. Although chopsticks did not make it in the long run, most Filipinos eating noodle dishes today like bam-i, sotanghon *and* bihon *no longer automatically associate them with Chinese origins.*

Separately from its investments in the galleon trade, the Church accumulated enough capital from its other domestic activities to become a powerful factor in the modest amount of long-term economic development taking place inside the colony itself. By the 18th century, Church-sponsored community benevolent associations known as *obras pias* ('pious works') had started acting as banks, extending credit not only to agricultural tenants and farmers, but also to early commercial enterprises – transport services, construction contractors, artisanal manufacturers, fisheries and the like. Much of this latter entrepreneurial activity outside agriculture, however, was not undertaken by the native population, but by Chinese immigrants.

Absent a large European settler influx, Chinese commercial activity in the Philippines, which had already been going on for a very long time before 1521, somewhat ironically received a significant boost from the coming of Spanish rule. Latent or active anti-native discrimination by most of the Spanish (and some of the Chinese), travel restrictions for Indios, a legal system of contracts enforceable across ethnic groups, increased demand for craftsmen and entrepreneurs, systems of mutual Chinese support, and the monetarization of the colonial economy encouraged growth in the resident Chinese trading population. By the early 17th century, the Chinese already outnumbered the Spanish, and had their own district in Manila, the Parian.

Fanning out from the capital and other ports, the Chinese found roles in the smaller towns and the countryside as travelling retail merchants, wholesalers, storekeepers, artisans, and construction gangs or wage labourers. Between the galleon trade and the rent-labour-tribute focus of the Spanish imperial sector on the one hand, and the barter-and-produce-based native economy on the other, Chinese commercial and artisanal activities comprised the third – and most dynamic – separate track of the Philippine colonial economy. Because of the structural roadblocks to native participation outside purely local networks and the reluctance of the Spanish to involve themselves in domestic trade, middlemen of wholly or partly Chinese background provided the cash-based links between the local

THE CHINESE – A COMMUNITY CAUGHT IN BETWEEN

Despite periodic efforts to restrict their entry and limit their increasingly important role in the colonial economy, conflict occasionally erupted between the Chinese on the one hand, and the native and European communities on the other. In 1603 and 1639, these chronic tensions escalated into Chinese uprisings and native-Spanish pogroms that took tens of thousands of lives, each side of course blaming the other for starting the trouble. In 1662, the warlord Koxinga had not only done the colony an unwitting favour by eliminating the Dutch threat from Formosa; he also threatened a possible repeat of the Limahong invasion. Although the invasion failed to materialize, it triggered further repressive measures against local Chinese populations. By the 1700s, however, the disturbances accompanying the transition from the Ming to the Ching dynasty had receded enough to reduce the threat of external warlord or imperial incursions. Meanwhile, the local Chinese community was undergoing a process of partial assimilation through marriage with native communities that was to continue – with far-reaching political, social, economic and cultural consequences – until today.

RIGHT: *A gigantic statue of Koxinga guards the coast at Gulangyu Island off the coast of Xiamen, Fujian Province, China.*

economy's products and the urban consumer markets of Manila. They sold Chinese and other imported goods in rural markets across the archipelago, and provided credit and supply chains for native micro-enterprises, laying the foundations for the prominent Chinese role in the Philippine economy that has lasted until the present.

THE FADING OF SPANISH PRIMACY

Despite the development of the Chinese-based internal trade sector, the Philippine colonial economy before 1800 can hardly be described as dynamic. This was a reflection of the increasingly outmoded mercantilist economic policies intended to enrich the motherland via extractive exploitation of colonies that characterized Spain's approach to its overseas possessions. Having created the world's first global empire in the 1500s, by 1650 Spain itself was entering a protracted period of decline. Costly imperial conflicts with other European powers bred economic and political instability at home – despite the influx of wealth from the New World – and had already led to the permanent loss of the Netherlands and Portugal. The War of the Spanish Succession in the early 1700s eliminated the Habsburgs' claims and put members of the French Bourbon dynasty on the throne in Madrid. Although Bourbon Spain held on to most of its overseas possessions throughout the following century and slowed imperial decline somewhat via efforts at economic and administrative reform, Spain was no longer fully in control of its own destiny.

Spain's decline became apparent during the British occupation of Manila in 1762–1764, a relatively minor episode in the worldwide Seven Years' War that pitted a victorious British-led coalition against Bourbon France and its allies, including by 1759 the Bourbon relatives ruling in Madrid. This Spanish humiliation left a permanent impression on many inhabitants of the colony. Three years after the formal declaration of hostilities between London and Madrid, the British East India Company launched an expeditionary force from Madras that took Manila in late 1762, burning parts of Intramuros (and incidentally destroying or looting many of the earliest documents of the Spanish colony, including records of the Christianization of early barangays and datus).

Despite the surrender of the colony by Archbishop Manuel Rojo as acting governor-general, a Spanish resistance movement under Simon de

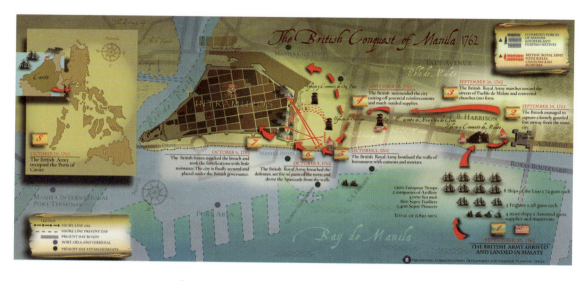

ABOVE

The British Conquest of Manila, 1762.

Anda managed to rally many natives to a provisional government based in the provinces of Pampanga and Bulacan. Yet the British intervention laid bare in many ways the fragility of the Spanish hold on the islands. Fighting for their survival against the British in Luzon, the Spanish were unable to maintain their naval patrols against Muslim Moros, who stepped up their raids on coastal settlements in the Visayas. The slave markets of Sulu received a boost from the Christian captives taken on these raids, and the uptick in Moro activity triggered by the British invasion was to continue into the 19th century and the sultanate's gradual rapprochement with the British Crown. Most of the Chinese in the archipelago, nursing memories of Spanish-inspired pogroms, restrictions and confiscatory taxation, supported the British occupation, supplying volunteer labour and troops who fought de Anda in Pampanga.

In the end, Spanish power could not dislodge the British. The latter only evacuated the Philippines because news of its capture had taken so long to get to Europe that the colony had fallen under provisions of the 1763 treaty, returning to Spain all territories 'not specifically mentioned' in the complicated swaps that left the British in control of Canada, Florida and India at the expense of France and Spain. Spain had lost, then regained the archipelago to suit the needs of other, greater powers. In that sense, despite the vigorous Spanish reprisals against those who had aided the invaders, the British occupation marked the beginning of the end of the old colonial order in the archipelago.

REFORM AND RENEWAL

The end of the 18th century did, however, see some efforts by the Spanish in the Philippines to encourage a more vigorous economy as a basis for a more secure colony, using techniques such as the rationalization of cash-crop agriculture for export and the creation of comprehensive trading and development authorities. Both approaches were decades in advance of comparable

THE BRITISH AS A CATALYST FOR REVOLT

Apart from the actions of the Chinese and Muslims, Spain's authority over the Christian majority population of the colony was permanently compromised by the British occupation, despite de Anda's success in rallying native support in the countryside around Manila and bottling up the British in the capital. In addition to the lease of life granted to the Dagohoy Revolt on Bohol mentioned earlier, the collapse of effective Spanish control in Pangasinan because of the British invasion also emboldened Juan de la Cruz Palaris to lead an uprising demanding reforms in that province in late 1762. This became a significant threat to the de Anda government until it was put down and its leaders executed in March 1764. Further away from the capital, other anti-Spanish rebellions received significant encouragement from the British. The most notable was Diego Silang's uprising in the Ilocos region of northern Luzon. Silang expelled the Spanish from the coastal city of Vigan and set up an independent government at the end of 1762, abolishing the tribute and the polo labour drafts, confiscating Church properties and expelling the local Spanish administration. Although he seems to have been motivated by a reformist agenda and did not wish for a complete break with Spain, he also exchanged friendly communications with the British, who (perhaps semi-seriously) appointed him civil governor of his region for their occupation government, and threw in the resounding title of 'Captain in the War for His British Majesty'. However, Silang also answered to an even higher power; he had already appointed Christ as his Captain General, with himself as Adjutant on Earth. He was nevertheless assassinat-

ABOVE: *British troop movements into Luzon.*

ed by the Spanish mestizo Miguel Vicos in May 1763 with the blessing of the local bishop and the higher ecclesiastical authorities in Manila. Silang's widow, Gabriela, carried on the struggle for several months, finally being captured and hanged with 90 of their followers later that year, and becoming a subsequent icon for nationalist Filipina feminists.

ABOVE

A Manila cigar factory at the end of the 19th century.

19th-century developments in the Asian colonies of other European powers, such as the *cultuurstelsel* export crop system in the Netherlands East Indies, and the tea- and opium-growing experiments of the British East India Company. These innovations were undertaken by one of the ablest and most energetic administrators in the entire history of the colony, Governor-General Jose Basco (1778–1787), who introduced these reforms designed to make the Philippines independent of subsidies from Mexico.

In 1781, Basco established the *Real Sociedad Económica de Amigos del País* (Royal Economic Society of Friends of the Country) in Manila, patterned on similar organizations in Spain and Latin America. Throughout its periods of activity over the next century (constantly interrupted by shifts in government policy), the society encouraged cultivation of new crops for export – tobacco, indigo, tea, silk, opium poppies and abaca (hemp), the growth of local industry through investment funding and a vocational school system, and provided grants for advanced study of economic and business techniques abroad. Basco established a government tobacco monopoly in 1782 that brought in large profits for the colonial administration and made the Philippines a leader in world tobacco production.

Back in the imperial centre, however, despite some effort at internal reform, the relative decline of Bourbon Spain was well advanced by the middle of the 18th century. In the Western European countries that were Spain's imperial rivals, growing numbers of entrepreneurial and educated urban people were driving a process of political, economic and technological modernization known as the Enlightenment. In Spain, however, the power and influence of a conservative aristocracy, the royal bureaucracy, big landowners and like-minded elements within the Catholic Church persisted mostly unchallenged over a largely rural and small-town society. Only the modest beginnings of a commercial, urban and intellectual middle class – the natural constituency for Enlightenment ideas – had emerged in the kingdom by 1800. The practical result for the Spanish state – a loss of resilience and international competitiveness – was becoming irreversible, while Spanish society was entering a period of increasing polarization. This decline in Spain would have far-reaching consequences for its Philippine colony in the coming 19th century.

4

IMAGINING A NATION
Revolution, The First Philippine Republic and its Defeat by the USA, 1800–1910

In the first half of the 19th century, following on the loss of Spain's empire in the Americas and political chaos in Spain itself, diverse groups in the Philippines began to develop a new and separate national consciousness. Aware of the stagnation and exploitation that had come to characterize life in the archipelago, these people at first sought solutions within the framework of liberal reformism, as loyal citizens of the Spanish state. By the 1890s, however, a decisive number of them had concluded that nothing short of a complete break with Spain would produce an acceptable future. In the process, a new category of ethnic self-identification emerged, the *Filipino*. The term at first denoted the more politically mobilized individuals among the criollos – people of Spanish descent born in the archipelago. However, its meaning eventually expanded to provide a unifying identity for the different groups in the non-European population that launched the first national revolution in modern Asia in 1896.

SPAIN IN TURMOIL

Bourbon Spain's gradual decline became near-collapse in the course of the kingdom's involvement in the Napoleonic Wars (1808–1815). The country fell back economically, far out of step with the Industrial Revolution transforming other parts of Western Europe. The Napoleonic campaigns fought in the peninsula instead brought years of destruction and violence; afterwards, decades of political chaos further weakened the fabric of Spanish society. The European conflict set in motion colonial unrest that led to the loss of Spain's possessions in the New World, except for the Caribbean. By the late 1820s, the Spanish overseas empire had shrunk to Cuba, Puerto Rico, some Pacific island groups, a few enclaves on the North African coast and the Philippines. After Napoleon's final defeat, much of the 19th century in Spain was taken up by an inconclusive and debilitating struggle over the

Imus, Cavite, site of a key battle in the 1896 Revolution where the current Philippine flag was carried into combat for the first time. View of the main plaza with memorial to General Licerio Topacio, a leader of the Katipunan's Magdalo faction.

shape of domestic politics. This pitted moderate, progressive and radical factions of the new ideology of Liberalism against each other, and all liberals against the reactionary defenders of the old conservative order.

The Cadiz Constitution allowed Spain's colonies to send voting representatives to the Cortes, originally intended as a parliament for the entire Spanish-speaking world. The document granted full Spanish citizenship to all European-descended (criollo) *and* indigenous residents of the colonies, except for those with significant African ancestry (*negros y mulattos*). However, the criollo Ventura de los Reyes, the first Philippine delegate to the new parliament, was chosen only by his fellow criollos; in practice,

THE CONSTITUTION OF CADIZ

Liberalism, the political expression of the Enlightenment, fought to limit the power of absolute monarchy via written constitutions, sovereign parliaments and independent judiciaries. It found its first Spanish expression in the Cadiz Constitution of 1812, one of the earliest modern constitutions in Europe. This declared the transformation of feudal subjects into free and equal citizens, defined the powers and responsibilities of the government, courts and legislature, and stipulated the political and social rights guaranteed for all citizens. It ended press censorship and the Catholic Inquisition and, at least in peninsular Spain itself, gave all adult males the right to vote. The Constitution was ultimately nullified by subsequent waves of conservative reaction after 1814.

BELOW: The Cortes of Cadiz 1812, *by Salvador Viniegra (1862–1915).*

decisions about political representation in the Cortes for the Philippines were made only by inhabitants of the archipelago with European ancestry.

In theory, the Cadiz Constitution's conferral of universal Spanish citizenship rendered obsolete the Philippine version of the racial caste systems that had developed over the centuries all over the Spanish empire. These older written codes had formally stipulated the different rights and legal statuses of criollos, other Spaniards, Indio natives and Chinese, as well as the various types of mestizos (people of mixed

Spanish-Indio, Spanish-Chinese, Chinese-Indio or Spanish-Chinese-Indio heritage). Having removed these formal structures of racial hierarchy, criollo liberals and their Indio allies did not, however, get a chance to secure authentic representation for Philippine Indios or mestizos as Spanish citizens; the constitution was abolished 20 months later, soon after the return to power of the Bourbon king Ferdinand VII in 1814.

Starting in the 1820s, with the disappearance of Mexico as the imperial administrative echelon under which the Philippines was run, growing numbers of bureaucrats, businessmen, soldiers and adventurers began coming to the Philippines directly from Spain, along with fresh personnel for the powerful Catholic missionary orders. Many of these *peninsulares* regarded themselves as superior in status and prerogatives to the locally born or Mexican-born criollo people of full Spanish descent. It was in this period that a new term, *insulares* (islanders), came into frequent and often derogatory use to distinguish locally born Spanish criollos from the peninsulares.

CRIOLLOS VERSUS PENINSULARES

Peninsulares projected their prejudices about the political unreliability of all colonials (attitudes recently reinforced by the breaking away of the Latin Americans) on to the Philippine criollos, who were increasingly passed over in favour of peninsulares in appointments to official civil or ecclesiastical positions, in business opportunities and in land acquisitions. Especially as the

ABOVE
Session of the Junta of the Royal Company of the Philippines, by Francisco de Goya, 1815. The painting captures the atmosphere of demoralization and ineffective absolutism that permeated Spanish affairs in the early 19th century after the Bourbon restoration. It shows the unexpected attendance of King Ferdinand VII at a listless and demoralized meeting of the junta responsible for Philippine economic development, as that body was becoming commercially unviable and irrelevant.

DEEPENING POLITICAL CHAOS IN SPAIN

Even among those who did not call for a republic, the increasingly polarized factions among the progressive forces in Spain disagreed among themselves, sometimes violently, over the proper role of a constitutional monarch and over the conflicting economic interests of the middle classes and the masses. Other controversies included the degree of accommodation tactically necessary with conservative and feudal forces in the Church, the military and civil officer corps, the aristocracy and the landowning elites. After his restoration to the throne, Ferdinand VII exploited these divisions, enlisting the help of local and foreign reactionaries to undo liberal policies, marginalize the Cortes and eventually bring back a full absolutist monarchy in the later 1820s.

Although no single faction was quite strong enough to permanently dominate the political scene, the general trend was thus in a reactionary direction. By 1837, the Cadiz Constitution, having been abrogated and restored three times amid chronic political upheaval, was permanently replaced by a much more conservative charter. Among other things, the Cadiz Constitution eliminated the right of the remaining colonies to send representatives to the Cortes – by implication removing the status of full citizens from colonial residents, regardless of ethnic background. The exact nature of the alternative status they now had as subjects of Spanish authority was not clear.

On top of all this, the accession of Ferdinand's daughter Isabella to the throne in 1833 had divided the reactionary monarchists, the different liberal tendencies, and various non-Castilian proponents of regional autonomy into two armed coalitions: a somewhat more liberal one supporting the ministers of her various governments; and another, somewhat more conservative one supporting the claim to the throne of her uncle, Charles. The Carlists and Isabellines plunged Spain into an intermittent civil conflict for 40 years; even after Isabella abdicated in 1868 to be replaced by the first Spanish Republic of 1873–1874, the Carlist Wars dragged on until 1876.

With Spanish politics remaining extremely unstable and the country never far from ungovernability, the liberal gains of one decade were often completely undone in the next, as a succession of strongmen and dictators alternated with fragile governments under the restored Bourbons into the first half of the 20th century. The efforts at liberal reform found resonance among the educated middle classes in the Philippines, but in the end, the political chaos in Madrid mostly benefitted the reactionaries in Manila.

LEFT: Isabella II of Spain, *by Federico de Madrazo y Kuntz, 1855.*

reaction against liberal constitutional experiments in Spain set in after 1823, many of the peninsulares who had only recently arrived in the Philippines began exhibiting the kinds of reactionary tendencies that are still evident among some Western expatriate circles in post-colonial Asia and Africa today. In the Spanish Philippines, where the reach of a fragile metropolitan constitution was not clearly established, peninsulares increasingly put themselves at the top of the local colonial pecking order.

For their part, some Mexican- or Philippine-born Spanish criollos in the archipelago who had initially welcomed the reforms of the early liberal period subsequently made their peace with the subsequent waves of reactionary backlash from Spain; others remained true to liberal principles of reform and modernization. However, most criollos were united in their growing resentment of the new influx of entitled peninsulars, especially as the latter came to occupy more and more prominent positions in the colonial administration, the military and religious hierarchy.

This resentment expressed itself in various incidents of Philippine criollo unrest against Spanish rule in the 1820s. After being punished with reassignment to a backwater post in Mindanao for agitating against the favouring of peninsulares, the Mexican-born military officer Andres Novales launched a full-blown mutiny in early June 1823, intending to take over the colonial government at the head of 800 native soldiers and their criollo officers. The coup failed, and Novales and other ringleaders were executed the following day. Although contemporary with the Latin American revolutions, the Novales Mutiny ultimately more resembled earlier Philippine millenarian revolts, being driven by narrow personal grievances and not explicitly motivated by nationalism in a modern sense.

However, there was a significant moment during the brief uprising, when crowds of both criollos and Indios briefly hailed Novales as the 'emperor' of the Philippines in the streets of Intramuros. Here for the first time, the idea of a political entity spanning the whole archipelago and independent of Spain had become an explicit theme. In 1828, a policy of preferential promotion for peninsulares over criollos was extended from the military officer corps to the civil bureaucracy. This triggered the Palmero Conspiracy, another abortive attempt to take over the colonial government. Although the conspiracy was quashed before violence broke out, the large number of civilian criollo leaders implicated or suspected suggests that Novales's

Indio illustrados in Spain, 1890.

military disaffection had become that of an entire class of influential people.

Among Novales's supporters had been Luis Rodriguez Varela, a French-educated, Enlightenment-inspired criollo writer who advocated social change in the Philippines and the creation of a modern educational system, including free schools for poor Indios. He was also critical of the disproportionately large role played by 'foreign' elements – among which he counted both the Chinese and the peninsular Spaniards – in the Philippine economy. A European born in the Philippines, Varela was the first person to describe himself as 'Filipino' in print, styling himself *El Conde Filipino* ('the Filipino count'). Until then the criollos has bristled at peninsular Spaniards labelling them 'insulares' or 'Filipinos'; Varela embraced a derogatory term and used it to express the growing self-awareness of a community with its own viewpoint and interests. Eventually deported from the colony as a politically troublesome critic, Varela would leave behind this concept of a personal Filipino identity, an idea that would eventually detach itself from the narrow connotations of criollo interest in which it had originated.

THE ENLIGHTENED ONES

Varela's articulate and intellectually rigorous approach to addressing social and political problems made him a good example of an illustrado, or 'enlightened one', as educated, modernizing reformers, often from socially prominent circles, were known all over the Spanish-speaking world of the 19th century. This role of critical, reformist illustrado publicist would eventually be taken up by numerous champions of Filipino nationalism among the native principalia elite. Native illustrados – in particular some from the Tagalog-speaking regions who spent time abroad – developed their own critique, quite distinct from that of the criollos, of the shortcomings and abuses of Spanish colonial rule. Linked up by the 1870s with another, separate nativist movement to replace Spaniards with local clergy, and by 1880 with yet another in the emerging spokesmen for discontented lower classes, the rise of native illustrados was the second crucial step in the emergence of a modern Filipino identity.

POLITICS THROUGH ECONOMICS

The spread of illustrado reformism from the privileged criollos to elite natives took place against the backdrop of a gradual opening of the Philippines to global free trade starting in the 1820s. This economic shift was a reflection of solid liberal ideas about releasing entrepreneurial energy from government restrictions, and replaced the old monopolistic Manila-Acapulco galleon trade after the loss of Mexico and the onset of direct rule from Madrid. The

BELOW
The Customs House of Iloilo City on Muelle Loney (Loney Quay), named after Nicholas Loney, an English businessman and Vice-Consul who settled in Iloilo on Panay Island in 1856 and lived there until his death in 1869. Loney worked for the merchant house Kerr and Co. and helped develop the modern sugar industry on Panay and the city of Iloilo.

opening of the archipelago's ports to free trade was also an acknowledgement of uncomfortable realities; limiting the Philippines to trade only with a declining and chaotic Spain was no longer economically viable. Starting with Manila in the 1820s, and eventually extending to Cebu and Iloilo in later decades, free trade with Europe, East Asia and North America (but not with the rest of colonial Southeast Asia for the most part) finally provided the missing international market for the earlier efforts of Governor-General Basco and the Economic Society in the 1780s to develop the export potential of crops such as tobacco, sugar, abaca and coconuts.

The result within a few years was a boom in these agricultural commodities. Representatives of English and American trading houses, banks, and shipping and insurance companies soon became familiar figures in the port districts, middle-class sitting rooms, government offices and social receptions of Manila, Cebu and Iloilo, and in the agricultural back country. Spurred by this trade in coconut and tobacco, as well as sugar cane, rice and other cash crops, these cities grew quickly. Manila had something like 150,000 inhabitants by the 1850s, drawing in people from the surrounding provinces attracted by the need for factory labour and clerical staff in the export industries. Demand for artisans and household workers to provide services for the increasing numbers of well-to-do urban criollo, native and mestizo families involved in the export trade also grew. Outside Manila, the expanding cash economy also extended prosperity to the larger native landowners and the *inquilinos* of Church lands, both of whose tenants grew crops for the export market.

KNOWLEDGE IS POWER

The educational system in the colony that the new native elite classes utilized for their social rise was the product of two centuries of inconsistent, sometimes chaotic Spanish colonial policy; yet all things considered, the results achieved were significant. Despite an 1839 royal decree that aimed to put colonial school systems on a more secular basis, much of education remained firmly in the hands of the Church. Nevertheless, progress had been made by the 1840s in setting up public, non-religious vocational schools for the technical trades, and for training navigators for ships on the new routes to Europe, North America and Asia. Other schools of commercial accounting, and private academies of fine art and foreign languages such as French

THE CHINESE MESTIZOS

The wealth of the Indio elite in the countryside and towns was increasing just as new lineages were joining its ranks. Among these new families were those formed by marriage alliances between the old native principalia and Chinese entrepreneurs who had converted to Christianity. Many of these hybrid mestizo-Chinese dynasties were destined to play important roles in the future of Philippine society and politics. They combined the benefits of sitting at the top of traditional native social pyramids of rural and

RIGHT: *A display in the Bahay Tsinoy (Chinese Mestizo House) Museum in Intramuros shows a small-scale Chinese trader starting on the way to integration within his Filipino community by chatting to a likely local girl.*

BELOW: *Well-to-do Chinese mestizos in the late 19th century.*

small-town deference with the new cash injections, clan-support networks, aggressive business ethics, and effective marketing skills of the older Chinese trading tradition in rice and other commodities across the archipelago.

Over time, these mestizo-Chinese families proved to be just as aggressive as the Catholic Church in dispossessing smallholders and acquiring title to, or control over, agricultural land suitable for growing cash crops for the export market. The result was the proliferation over the course of the 19th century of haciendas, large estates in the hands of a new, relatively small, but dynamically growing, often non-European and often mestizo-Chinese land-owning class. Such families were changing the face of the formerly conformist and deferential native principalia, now claiming a more assertive position in Philippine colonial society. These people began to take on some characteristics of the bourgeois middle classes in the West, slowly outgrowing the deference their forefathers had shown to the friar-led Church and the Spanish colonial state. This rise in ambition and self-regard (*amor propio*) and awareness of larger horizons spurred a demand for improved secondary educations for the sons of these families, then further professional training in such fields as law and medicine, as a way of leveraging material prosperity into social mobility. Such hopes met the reality of continued Spanish discrimination.

and English, were founded in the same period. However, most primary and secondary schools remained underfunded, with curricula under the control of missionary friars who were mostly interested in ensuring doctrinal conformity and social deference, not independent thinking.

Another royal decree of 1863 therefore mandated a system of government oversight for this existing network of Church-controlled primary schools, introduced a system of teacher qualifications, made schools free for children aged 7–12 and regularized teachers' salaries. This was the earliest formal public school system set up by a European power anywhere in its Asian colonies, and pre-dated the Japanese national system by about 10 years. However, apart from the chronic challenges of underfunding and insufficiently trained personnel, a particularly important problem that the 1863 law left unsolved was the abysmal rate at which children in most of these schools were learning competency in Spanish – the prerequisite breakout language for exposure to the worlds of science, world literature in translation, the rest of the humanities, politics and current events.

BELOW
Standard primer on Catholic doctrine, essentially unchanged over the two centuries of its use in primary and secondary education.

Doctrina Christiana, en lengua española ytagala, corregida por los Religiosos de las ordenes Impressa con licencia, en S. gabriel, de la orden de S. Domingo
En Manila. 1593.

Even though the monarchy had instructed missionaries to teach Spanish to the natives ever since the earliest years of the colony, there was never a point when more than 10 per cent of the non-European population spoke Spanish, or read a basic text comprehensible to the average adult. This was largely the result of missionary attitudes that emphasized religious instruction in the different languages of the archipelago. The missionaries had learnt these Austronesian languages assiduously and captured their orthographies and grammar in print. However – except for selected areas of literature, drama and the like – they largely shielded their native charges from exposure to Spanish-language technical or scientific material with non-religious, possibly system-destabilizing content.

With yet another education law, the Maura decree of 1893, the Spanish state nevertheless would persist with the effort to secularize primary and secondary education in the colony. This

1893 decree relieved most community schools from compulsory inspection by clergy. At the very end of the colonial era, in 1898, a reliable estimate counted 2,143 such schools now maintained solely by the state, an increasing number offering more hours of instruction in Spanish, and teaching the other subjects in that language. This very late stage in the evolution of the colony's school system (which was to persist for another decade or so after the end of Spanish rule in 1898) was largely responsible for the last-minute emergence of a modestly sized Spanish-language reading public in the Philippines. A measure of the spread of literacy in Spanish at the end of the colonial regime is the proliferation of about 74 periodicals, newspapers or magazines at least partly in Spanish by the last decades of the 1800s. With names like *La Opinion*, *Manila Alegre*, *El Commercio*, *El Correo*, *El Catolico Filipino* and *Diario de Manila*, many of them were available in the capital as well as in the larger towns and cities of the rest of the country. Reforms in education briefly offered an archipelago-wide audience literate in Spanish for the generation of nationalists who were to preside over the revolution and the early phases of an independent Philippine state.

At the primary and secondary levels, ambitious sons of the expanding native and Chinese mestizo middle classes were singled out for preferential treatment, extra tutoring and recommendations by the local Spanish clergy

PARTIAL MODERNIZATION IN THE UNIVERSITIES

By the middle of the 19th century, the Universities of San Carlos in Cebu and Santo Tomas in Manila, and the Colleges of San Jose and San Juan de Letran, were beginning to introduce progressive elements into their curricula, adding physics, chemistry, the other natural sciences, law and mathematics to the original faculties of theology, philosophy and the humanities. Seminaries run by these religious orders also offered secondary and college preparatory instruction to paying lay students. By 1865, the Jesuits were also operating a normal school for teacher training (the first of several they established around the country), as well as the Municipal Athenaeum (Ateneo) of Manila, which was to become Ateneo de Manila University. Among the subjects on the curriculum here were algebra, agriculture, arithmetic, chemistry, commerce, English, French, geography, geometry, Greek, history, Latin, mechanics, natural history, painting, philosophy, physics, rhetoric and poetry, Spanish classics, Spanish composition, topography and trigonometry.

Although educational policy was shifting in fits and starts in a progressive, secular direction, the system was still permeated from top to bottom by an inherited emphasis on religious tutelage, and moral and political surveillance (culminating at the elite universities). In addition to serving as gatekeepers for admission to the elite universities, clergy at local and regional secondary schools were able to mould the minds of their most promising charges in conformist directions. Meanwhile, their counterparts at the universities kept a vigilant watch against anti-clerical, Masonic, excessively liberal, materialist or atheistic tendencies among the student body. Outside the educational system, public opinion was monitored and shaped by a press and book censorship board composed of appointees from state and church set up in the 1850s.

who, despite the government reforms, remained the gatekeepers to higher education. The further road to prestige and social mobility for these elite children then led to the private religious universities (mostly in Manila) that the major missionary orders had set up during earlier centuries of Spanish rule.

For the sons of both well-off members of the native principalia and the criollo insulares, however, indirect access to the more open culture and public life of the European metropole widened by the 1820s, with the introduction of a direct mail-packet service linking the colony with Spain. For those who could afford it, actual personal access to Europe received a major boost with the massive reduction in travel time and expense made possible by the opening of the Suez Canal in 1869. Even before the canal was in operation, however, a sizeable expatriate community of middle-class Indios from the archipelago already existed in Spain.

THE FRIAROCRACY

In the mid-century decades, when free trade and modernizing education first began to exert transformative effects on Philippine society, the colonial political context did not support the raised cultural and material expectations of insulares and elite Indios. In particular, the absence of any meaningful outside control over the powerful friar orders by the archdiocese of Manila or the indifferent colonial state was now taking on ominous political ramifications. Even into the late 19th century, Spanish Augustinian, Dominican and Franciscan clergy assigned as parish priests still wielded many local governmental functions – education, health measures, census and tax recording, among others. They also continued a regime of paternalistic monitoring of the character and behaviour of local inhabitants, and were decisive voices in the appointment of police and local civil administrators. They exercised censorship over amusements and public morals, and reported sedition to the civil authorities, routinely forwarding information gleaned from individual confessions and thus breaking the confidentiality of this Church sacrament.

The friar regime of surveillance and control had become so indispensable to the general maintenance of authoritarian Spanish rule that contemporary critics labelled the colony a 'friarocracy' (*frialocracia*). Well aware of the vital leadership role of the parish priest as well as the extensive prerogatives and privileges that went with the office, many natives had entered the regular diocesan priesthood – only to find their careers stymied by the friarocracy's hammerlock on parish assignments. Although the Vatican had repeatedly stipulated that parishes in fully converted countries be handed over by the missionary friar orders to indigenous diocesan priests, only 181 out of 792 parishes in the islands had Filipino priests even as late as 1871.

MILLENARIANISM

In the 1830s and '40s, the issue of native participation in religious leadership had already engendered a major politico-religious disturbance, the Cofradía Revolt. It was led by a charismatic Tagalog religious leader from the town of Lucban in Tayabas province named Apolinario de la Cruz, known to his followers as Hermano (Brother) Pule. His movement is perhaps the earliest properly documented example of the 'millenarian' tradition of Philippine revolt. Here, the language and imagery of a deeply assimilated Catholic belief system – in particular native identification with the Passion of Christ and the intermediary role of the Virgin Mary – served instead of nationalist ideology to focus the growing desperation and unrest of ordinary people.

ABOVE

Crucifixion on Good Friday in the Philippines. Sensationalist reports by foreign journalists of such events usually omit any mention of their historical function in Indio communities as a way of turning Christian narratives into symbolic language that expressed truths about power, hope and suffering, in an age before political ideology or propaganda.

Without elite educations, these people politicized religious themes of salvation, betrayal, sacrifice and love, in order to express their hopes for a better and more just society. After some success at rallying the population of several towns in Tayabas province, the insurrection was put down with military force and effectively ended with the capture and execution of Brother Pule on 5 November 1841, along with about 200 of his lieutenants and followers.

The Cofradía and its successor movements all expressed a desire to expel the Spanish and enter a vaguely defined and hybrid Promised Land. In this imaginary landscape, elements and symbols of Catholic eschatology would fuse with surviving motifs from pre-Christian animism and philosophical speculation about the ideal community, and the world as it was before the coming of outsiders. This type of mass religio-political millenarianism is alive and well in the Philippines, but is different from Filipino nationalism in the modern, ideological sense. The latter is a product of the educated urban

THE PASSION OF HERMANO PULE

A pious man who felt a vocation to enter a monastic order at an early age, Apolinario de la Cruz's repeated applications were rejected by racially prejudiced friars. His piety drove him to become a humble lay brother (*donado*) performing menial tasks at a charitable hospital in Manila. Absorbing what bits of Catholic theology and philosophy he could while in that post, he started the *Cofradía* (confraternity or brotherhood) *de San Jose*, a lay society to promote Roman Catholic devotion among Indios. From 1839 to 1840, the Cofradía recruited widely in Tayabas, south of Laguna de Bay, and the movement set up cells throughout the wider southern Tagalog area. Originally, it did not seem to have any clearly anti-Spanish or nativist political orientation. Yet its ethos of secrecy and loyalty to Brother Pule, and its barring of Spaniards and mestizos from membership without his special approval, aroused the suspicions of the authorities, who banned it as a potentially subversive organization. This move was something of a self-fulfilling prophecy, for in response Brother Pule left Manila in 1841 and gathered along the way several thousand Cofradía followers armed with rifles and *bolos* (heavy, single-bladed knives). He deployed them in the villages and hill country around the towns of Tayabas province, preaching that God would deliver the Tagalog people from slavery. Aided by local Australoid Negrito hillmen, the Cofradía defeated a punitive detachment led by the provincial governor in late October. Soon after, however, despite Pule's assurances of angels coming to the insurgents' assistance and the bullet-stopping powers of ritual amulets (*anting-anting*), a larger Spanish force took the Cofradía camp at Aritao on the slopes of Mt San Cristobal, killing an estimated 500 of its members and capturing a similar number.

Interpreting his defeat and death in Christ-like, redemptionist terms, Cofradía survivors joined the ranks of remontados, leaving their villages to live on the slopes of Mt San Cristobal and Mt Banahaw – previously long considered as holy mountains, the homes of pre-Christian folk divinities (diwatas) that lived on in traditional Tagalog culture after the Spanish conquest. After the events at Aritao, these insurgent camps evolved further into folk religious centres and destinations for religio-political pilgrimage by subsequent generations of lowland peasants. In the last decades of the 19th century, many of them lent support or refuge to the political revolutionaries fighting a war of independence against Spain. Until today, these mountains serve as refuges for various 'colorum' sects descended from the Cofradía. These reclusive religious communities continue to further cultivate the tradition of folk Christian millenarianism, now fusing to it elements from newer doctrines of Filipino nationalism that came along after Hermano Pule's death.

BELOW: *Mariang Makiling (the Maria of Makiling) is one of several ambiguous figures of folklore connected with certain mountains in Central Luzon that were venerated as the home of nature spirits and diwatas long before the coming of Christianity. The flight to the mountains of survivors of various failed millennial uprisings simply added new, Christian-influenced levels of symbolism to the existing culture of religio-political resistance to Spanish domination.*

*Altar of a present-day
millenarian cult near
Mt Banahaw that has
integrated the worship
of Filipino nationalist
heroes such as Jose Rizal
and Andres Bonifacio
into reworked versions of
Christian liturgy.*

context of Manila and the major towns – and perhaps even more, of Spain and other parts of Europe where Filipinos in exile encountered modern intellectual currents. Yet folk religion, with its proven ability to mobilize the rural masses, also tapped into the same energy of lower-class revolt that, in the form of the Katipunan (see p. 111), would reinforce the Enlightenment nationalism of the illustrados and spur a truly popular struggle, first against Spain in 1896, then against America in 1899.

The issue of friar resistance to native diocesan secularization of the clergy again came into sharp focus for the illustrados at the end of the 1850s, with the readmission of Jesuits to the Philippines after their expulsion in 1786. Among the many reasons for the original expulsion had been suspicion by the authorities of the Jesuits' readiness to educate gifted Indios in newer ways of analysis in the natural and social sciences, as well as their teaching of Spanish to non-Europeans. Their departure had opened up vacancies in a large number of parishes, which had largely been filled with secular native priests. Now, after almost 100 years, the Jesuit return in 1859 set off a chain reaction of dismissals of native clergy, in order to accommodate the

European friars of various orders being reassigned in a general shake-up of curates' posts. The evident racial bias in the official grounds for removal of many native priests from control of their own parishes embittered the diocesan Indio clergy. The rest of the 1860s saw ever more native priests embrace the nationalist cause.

THE DE LA TORRE REFORMS

In September 1868, the universally unpopular Queen Isabella II was finally deposed. The new coalition provisional government appointed General Carlos María de la Torre as governor-general of the Philippines. An outspoken liberal despite his Carlist sympathies, de la Torre quite suddenly abolished press censorship in the colony, legalized public demonstrations, and guaranteed the rights of free speech and assembly, as provided for in the latest 1869 Spanish constitution. He also broke previous protocol and fraternized with both criollos and mestizos, inviting them to the governor's palace and hobnobbing with them on official occasions. The native middle class also welcomed de la Torre warmly. Prominent Indios held a 'liberty parade' to celebrate the 1869 constitution, although the more perceptive among them noticed that, unlike Cuba, it did not give political representation in the Cortes back to the Philippines. They established a 'reform committee' to work with the governor-general in laying the foundations of

ABOVE
The reformist liberal Governor-General Carlos María de la Torre.

BELOW
Three Filipino members of the secular diocesan clergy who became early heroes of the nationalist movement: Fathers Mariano Gomez and Jose Burgos, and Brother Jacinto Zamora.

a new political, social and economic order in the colony. The Liberal Student Youth (*Juventud Escolar Liberal*) association at the University of Santo Tomas held demonstrations protesting the abuses and obscurantism of the university's Dominican friar administrators and teachers.

Among de la Torre's most avid supporters were native secular diocesan priests. The latter included Father Jose Burgos, a Spanish mestizo, whose *Manifesto to the Noble Spanish Nation* strongly criticized the peninsular officials and friars who barred Indios from the priesthood and government service. In December 1870, even the Archbishop of

Manila himself wrote to the Spanish government advocating secularization, with the warning that discriminating against native priests would destabilize Spanish rule in the colony. The political tide finally seemed to be turning against the friarocracy.

However, this brief liberal period came to an abrupt end in 1871. The allies of the missionary orders and other conservative peninsulares in Madrid succeeded in having de la Torre replaced by a far more conservative figure, Rafael de Izquierdo; upon taking his post as governor-general in April 1871, Izquierdo rescinded practically all of de la Torre's liberal proclamations and laws, and restored the censorship. The enthusiastic supporters of his predecessor now came under suspicion as subversives and threats to Spanish rule.

THE CAVITE MUTINY AND THE GOMBURZA MARTYRS

On 20 January 1872, a mutiny broke out again in the Cavite naval dockyard. Two hundred dockworkers, and eventually soldiers in the rest of the province, rose up to kill their Spanish officers, believing erroneously that a larger uprising was ongoing in Manila. The mutineers were angry about Izquierdo's revocation of their tribute and polo service exemptions, and other privileges. Although the revolt was contained and put down two days later, the jumpy authorities used the mutiny to pursue paranoid conspiracy theories linking the mutineers and prominent reformist leaders, particularly diocesan priests. Izquierdo alleged that a secret junta supported by liberals back in Madrid was getting ready to take power in Manila and overthrow Spanish rule.

After a drumhead military trial with only one coerced mutineer as a witness, the government condemned to death the three Filipino priests most closely associated with liberal reformism – the aforementioned Jose Burgos, Mariano Gomez and Jacinto Zamora – along with actual participants in the mutiny. Prominent illustrados also convicted of conspiracy were exiled to Guam and the Marianas (many escaped to continue the struggle from Hong Kong, Singapore and Europe). The Archbishop of Manila refused the governor's order that the three condemned priests be defrocked. On 17 February 1872, they were publicly garrotted to death on the Luneta field just south of Intramuros, with representatives of the foreign missionary orders in attendance. The executions had a galvanizing effect on many criollos, Indios and mestizos of both Spanish and Chinese admixture.

Gradually starting to refer to themselves as 'Filipinos', many were drawing ever closer – often reluctantly – to the conclusion that the archipelago needed to make a definitive political break with Spain.

After the repressions of 1872 and their chilling effect on public discussion in the colony, the gradual transition from reformism to a national consciousness capable of separation from Spain was particularly visible among Filipino émigrés in Spain and some cities in other parts of Europe. The most active individuals among these illustrados fell into three groups: liberals exiled in the aftermath of 1872, students who attended European universities in the subsequent decade and younger critics fleeing subsequent persecution in the colony. Together, all three contributed to the output of reformist literature and publicity known as the Propaganda Movement.

An important figure in the Propaganda Movement was Graciano Lopez Jaena, whose satire, *Fray Botod* (Friar Fat Belly), had cut short his career in the colony as an orator and publicist. In 1889, from his Barcelona exile, Jaena began *La Solidaridad* (Solidarity) a bi-weekly newspaper that

THE PROPAGANDA MOVEMENT

The movement's initial goals essentially summarized the themes of discontent that had been building up among the educated classes of Indios for the past half century. They demanded representation of the Philippines in the Spanish parliament, secularization of the clergy, legal guarantees of Spanish and Filipino civic equality, rights to free speech and association, and civil service qualifications, a public school system independent of the Catholic Church, and abolition of involuntary labour services and compulsory purchase of produce by the government. The Propagandists, however, still remained bound by their own class interests as illustrados and by their commitment to peaceful reform within the Spanish system; there were no calls for a more equitable share for the ordinary masses in the archipelago's economic life, or for clear-cut political independence from Spain as the answer to the Philippines' troubles.

RIGHT: *Three leaders of the Propaganda Movement: Jose Rizal, Marcelo H. del Pilar and Mariano Ponce.*

A formal portrait of Rizal, well known from thousands of reproductions in textbooks, on the walls of elementary schools and on boxes for a popular brand of safety matches.

BELOW
An early edition of Noli Me Tangere, circa 1887.

eventually became the house organ of the Propaganda Movement. Its contributors included Marcelo H. del Pilar, a reform-minded lawyer active in anti-friar circles in the colony. He was forced to flee to Spain in 1888, where he assumed leadership of the Filipino exile community and eventually became editor of *La Solidaridad*.

JOSE RIZAL

The most prominent figure in the Propaganda Movement, eventually to become the foremost national hero of the modern Philippines, was Jose Rizal y Mercado. Born in 1861 into a well-to-do family in the town of Calamba near Laguna de Bay, Rizal's father was an inquilino, with many tenants working the extensive friar lands he rented in the area. The young Rizal went to Manila to acquire the best possible higher education in the colony at the Jesuit Ateneo, and then the University of Santo Tomas. Although he decided on a career in the sciences, Rizal was a polymath who read widely in literature, art and the humanities. He became a practising ophthalmologist and successful novelist, and at various times was an essayist, poet, painter, playwright, educator, homesteader, historian and journalist. He also dabbled in architecture, the social sciences, cartography, the stage and martial arts.

Frustrated with the obscurantist Dominican intellectual atmosphere at Santo Tomas, Rizal left for Spain in 1882 to pursue opthalmological training. Except for one brief visit home, he stayed abroad for nine years. In this period he joined the efforts of the émigré Filipino community in Europe to draw attention to the mismanagement of the colony and petition the Spanish government for reform. But it was the publication abroad of his two best-known literary works, the novels *Noli Me Tangere* (Touch Me Not, 1887) and *El Filibusterismo* (The Reign of Greed, 1891) that constitute his lasting contribution to the nationalist cause.

In these books, Rizal built compelling portraits of people at various levels of a colonial society exposed by a feckless civil state to the domination of the powerful religious orders: Padre Damaso, a bullying, vindictive Franciscan friar with enormous power to exploit the inhabitants of the town of San Diego; Ibarra/Simoun, a once-idealistic mestizo

reformer who ultimately embraces violent revolution, and his beloved, Maria Clara, the perhaps overly melodramatic personification of the suffering country, a daughter of a prominent family targeted by the clergy. The novels gained some attention abroad but had their most powerful impact at home, where clandestine copies made Rizal enemies among civil and ecclesiastical officials.

Rizal returned to the Philippines in June 1892, partly because the Dominicans had cancelled his family's lease on the friars' estates, and partly because he understood that a base abroad could no longer serve the struggle for peaceful reform effectively. Almost immediately upon arrival, he activated his wide network of contacts and founded *La Liga Filipina*, an organization dedicated to realizing the Propaganda Movement's aims in the archipelago. This gave the clergy and their official allies the excuse needed to exile him internally to the obscure port of Dapitan in Mindanao. His deportation paralyzed the fledgling Liga, effectively silencing the voices among Filipinos who still believed in peaceful moderate reform within the Spanish system.

ABOVE

Josephine Bracken, an Irish expatriate whom Rizal met after moving to Dapitan, and who eventually came to live with him there and became his common-law wife.

OPPOSITE TOP

Andres Bonifacio on the cover of Kartilyang Makabayan, *a primer on the Katipunan and its ideology. The banner behind him carries the sun delivering the light of liberty (Liwanag ng Kalayaan) on which is imposed the Tagalog letter 'K' for Katipunan.*

The Propaganda Movement in Spain also faded away after Rizal's exile to Dapitan. *La Solidaridad* ceased operations in 1895. Disappointed at the lack of tangible results of their agitation, Del Pilar and Lopez Jaena both died in poverty in Barcelona the following year. Meanwhile in Manila, attempts to carry on the work in a revivified La Liga Filipina were stymied by a split between illustrados who continued to advocate peaceful reform (the *compromisarios*) and a less elite element that now argued for armed revolution and national independence.

THE REVOLUTION BUILDS

Eventually, increasing numbers of politically active people from all social classes rallied to a new organization, dedicated to the overthrow of Spanish rule by force – the Katipunan. Resounding with the characteristic Austronesian repeating-syllable patterns common in the Tagalog language, the organization's full name was *Ang Kataas-taasang Kagalang-galangang Katipunan ng mga Anak ng Bayan* (the Highest, Most Honourable Society of the Children of the Nation), or KKK. This KKK had no connection to the racist American organization with the same initials; the key substantive, *Katipunan* (the Society or Association) comes from the Tagalog word *tipon* (to gather).

Meanwhile, Rizal remained exiled in Dapitan from 1892 to 1896, occupying his time with writing projects, civic improvements, his ophthalmology practice, teaching in the local community school he founded, politely resisting the efforts of Jesuits to convert him back to loyal Catholicism, and collecting flying lizards and other biological specimens for his scientist friends in Europe. He had promised the Spanish Governor-General Ramon Blanco not to attempt to escape from that remote and lightly guarded outpost. Although there is evidence that he remained in touch with nationalist circles in Manila (and was elevated to honorary president of the Katipunan), it is difficult to establish from his ambiguous and sometimes contradictory statements in this period whether he came to fully support Philippine independence by armed revolution or still held fast to the project of peaceful reform.

In the same four years, the Katipunan grew steadily through secret recruitment. The organization spread gradually from Tondo, north of Manila proper, to the surrounding Tagalog-speaking provinces, with some chapters also in the rest of Luzon and small groups of sympathizers elsewhere in the archipelago. By August 1896, conservative estimates put its strength at 30,000 committed members, both men and women, plus a much larger number of auxiliaries and passive supporters. By early 1896, Manila and the surrounding areas were already rife with rumours of plots and conspiracies against the government.

The final collapse of the Spanish empire began with a revolution that broke out in Cuba in February 1895. Seeking a way to keep his word not to escape given to Governor-General Blanco (with whom he seems to have

THE KATIPUNAN

The Katipunan was founded in Manila shortly before Rizal's exile to Dapitan by Andres Bonifacio, a self-educated artisan and urban employee of relatively modest origins, together with two fellow members of La Liga Filipina. Its core objectives were full independence from Spain by any means necessary (including violence), and the erection of a Filipino republic. The KKK derived much of its aesthetic – elaborate secret passwords, initiation ceremonies and membership levels, all furnished with colourful symbols and secret formulas – from Freemasonry, which by that point had been associated with the Enlightenment revolutionary tradition in many countries for at least a century and a half. Recent scholarship has tended to modify simplistic portrayals of the Katipunan as an overwhelmingly lower-class mass organization, pointing to the relatively literate, white-collar or even property-owning elements found in its leadership. Nevertheless, the bulk of the KKK's members did come from the lower income strata, including peasants, urban employees and artisans, indicating that the nationalist movement had broadened out its base from the small community of prosperous illustrados to a truly representative cross-section of the Indio population by the mid-1890s.

RIGHT: *Among the Masonic and other secret society-type trappings of the Katipunan aesthetic was the revival of the Blood Compact as a means of sealing final membership and commitment. Exhibit at the Katipunan Museum, San Juan, Metro Manila.*

had a cordial and mutually respectful relationship), and yet get out of his exile, Rizal applied to be sent to Cuba as a Spanish army doctor. His request was granted; a recommendation letter from Blanco in hand, he left Dapitan on 1 August for Manila, from where he would prepare to leave the Philippines.

In these very same weeks, however, the KKK's secret preparations for revolution were betrayed, causing Bonifacio and the KKK leadership to trigger its premature start. On 19 August, the sister of Pedro Patiño, a low-ranking Katipunero and a typesetter at the newspaper *Diario de Manila*, confided her brother's involvement to their parish priest, who promptly informed the government. Confronted with the triple threat of imprisonment, excommunication and eternal hellfire, Patiño led the authorities to a stash of documents and other KKK material indicating an impending uprising, which proved that the worst suspicions of the friars had been realistic.

THE CRY OF BALINTAWAK AND RIZAL'S EXECUTION

With Spanish forces fanning out to secure the city and start mass arrests, the Katipunan leadership and about 50 of its supporters gathered on 23 August in the then-rural suburb of Caloocan, north-east of Manila, at a place called Pugad Lawin (Hawk's Nest) in the district of Balintawak. There, most likely at a barn owned by Melchora Acquino, a Katipunan supporter with the nickname of Tandang (Old Lady) Sora, Bonifacio and his men ripped up their government-issued *cedulas*. These were certificates of yearly poll-tax payment that had replaced the polo labour-service obligation in 1884. This action symbolized a complete break with Spain, as the assembled Katipuneros loudly declared a war of independence. The Cry of Balintawak (or Cry of Pugad Lawin) was the signal, spread by the Katipunan's internal channels as well as by the press, for previously planned attacks that commenced on 29 August against government offices, barracks, churches and other centres of colonial authority.

Remarkably, Rizal was able to leave Manila for Cuba via Spain a few days after the outbreak of the Katipunan uprising. As his ship continued on its way to Barcelona however, the revolution was spreading beyond the Manila area and the Tagalog-speaking regions around it to Zambales, Camarines and even Palawan island. Governor-General Blanco finally bowed to pressure from military officers in Intramuros and issued orders for Rizal to be arrested on the ship and brought back to Manila to face trial, accused of being a key planner of the uprising. The arrest order was received on board early enough to confine Rizal in Barcelona as soon as he landed, from where he was brought back to Manila in October.

By December 1896, Blanco had been replaced as governor-general by his adjutant, Camilo Polavieja, a hardline military officer whose promotion had apparently been sponsored by the religious orders. In a replay of the Gomburza Affair of 1872, Rizal was brought before a military court the day after Christmas on trumped-up charges of involvement with the Katipunan. A predictable guilty verdict was followed by the death sentence. This was carried out on 30 December 1896, when Rizal was executed by a firing squad at the same Bagumbayan Field on the Luneta that had already seen the killing of so many other patriots.

THE REVOLUTION FALTERS – AGUINALDO VERSUS BONIFACIO

As Rizal was being railroaded to his death, Andres Bonifacio was proving

LEFT
The Cry of Balintawak Monument.

113

ABOVE
Montjuic Fortress near Barcelona, where Rizal was briefly held after arriving in Spain before being sent back under arrest to the Philippines.

BELOW
Emilio Aguinaldo, 1898.

that the qualities that made for a good political organizer were not necessarily those required by a good military leader. A poor strategist, Bonifacio made little headway with his Katipunan forces against Spanish troops in the Manila area, and was gradually losing ground, soldiers and morale. By this time, however, the urban, illustrado-dominated wing of the revolution had found a champion in the form of Emilio Aguinaldo, the gobernadorcillo (municipal mayor) of Cavite Veijo, the modern-day city of Kawit in Cavite province just south of Manila. Coming from a well-to-do principalia dynasty prominent in Cavite Viejo for generations, Aguinaldo had already developed nationalist and Masonic sympathies before becoming town mayor in 1895. Shortly after taking office he joined Bonifacio's Katipunan. His influence over pro-nationalist groups in the area, as mayor of a strategic town with the only land approach to the nearby Spanish naval base that anchored southern Manila Bay, made him vital to Katipunan recruitment in Cavite, and to the revolutionaries' plans for the province on the start of an uprising.

Once the revolution did begin prematurely, Aguinaldo proved equally adept at quickly carrying out actual military operations without much preparation, not only bottling up the Cavite Arsenal, but also winning major set-piece engagements in Cavite province at Imus and Binakayan-Dalahikan, the earliest major Philippine victories in the war. This secured Cavite as a main staging base for the Katipunan for much of the next year, and denied much of Southern Luzon to the Spanish. It also attracted major flows of recruitment from other Tagalog provinces to safe areas in the interior of Cavite, which now posed a constant threat to Manila, tying down large numbers of Spanish troops while the revolution spread to other parts of Luzon and the rest of the archipelago.

Aguinaldo's brother, Baldomero, headed one of the two main autonomous chapters of the Katipunan active in Cavite, the so-called Magdalo faction. Much of the Katipunan base outside the major towns, however, was

under the influence of the Magdiwang faction, a chapter headed by Mariano Alvarez, uncle of Bonifacio's wife Gregoria. The factions had quickly evolved into parallel administrations in the towns that they respectively controlled, with the Magdalo noticeably more under the influence of middle-class illustrados while the Magdiwang represented a somewhat broader social cross-section. The tensions between the factions were ostensibly based on their differing ideas about the future structure of revolutionary leadership. The Magdiwang were satisfied with the Bonifacio-led Katipunan Supreme Council as the de facto revolutionary government of the future nation, while the more middle-class Magdalo line preferred the creation of a revolutionary government separate from the Katipunan structure. Behind this seemingly technical controversy also lay contrasting attitudes to the charismatic figure of Bonifacio (and to the mass non-elite support base he represented) between a more urban illustrado-dominated Magdalo and a Magdiwang with

BELOW
The first phases of the Philippine Revolution.

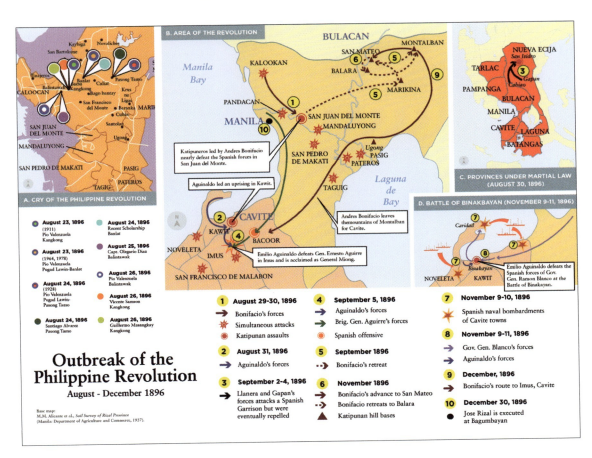

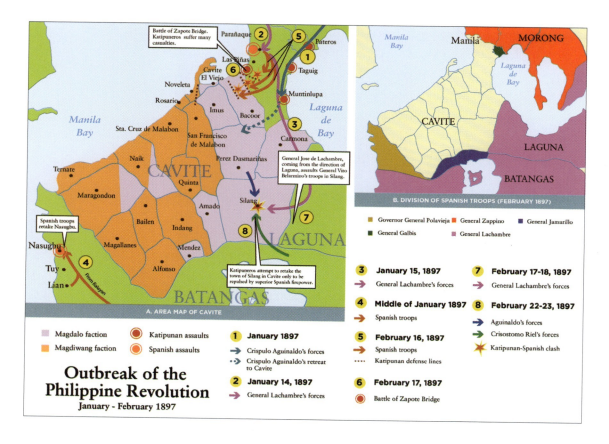

Battle of Zapote Bridge.
Katipuneros suffer many
casualties.

General Jose de Lachambre,
coming from the direction of
Laguna, assaults General Vito
Belarmino's troops in Silang.

Spanish troops
retake Nasugbu.

Katipuneros attempt to retake the
town of Silang in Cavite only to be
repulsed by superior Spanish firepower.

A. AREA MAP OF CAVITE

B. DIVISION OF SPANISH TROOPS (FEBRUARY 1897)

Governor General Polavieja   General Zappino   General Jamarillo
General Galbis   General Lachambre

■ Magdalo faction	● Katipunan assaults	**1** **January 1897**	**3** **January 15, 1897**
■ Magdiwang faction	○ Spanish assaults	Crispulo Aguinaldo's forces	General Lachambre's forces

3 January 15, 1897
General Lachambre's forces

4 Middle of January 1897
Spanish troops

5 February 16, 1897
Spanish troops

6 February 17, 1897
Battle of Zapote Bridge

7 February 17-18, 1897
General Lachambre's forces

8 February 22-23, 1897
Aguinaldo's forces
Crisostomo Riel's forces
Katipunan-Spanish clash

1 January 1897
Crispulo Aguinaldo's forces
Crispulo Aguinaldo's retreat
to Cavite

2 January 14, 1897
General Lachambre's forces

Outbreak of the Philippine Revolution
January - February 1897

ABOVE

*The progress of the
revolution into 1897.*

more personal links to Bonifacio.

Soon after the reinforcements brought in from Spain by Governor-General Polavieja retook much of Cavite by early 1897, Bonifacio was requested to mediate the disputes among Katipunan factions at the Tejeros Convention, called to assess the progress of the revolution in Cavite in March of that year. The meeting quickly turned into a general debate about the structure of revolutionary leadership, and the Magdalo position prevailed; its delegates were able to convince the entire meeting to vote on the spot for the presidency, vice-presidency and cabinet of a new revolutionary government, operating outside the Bonifacio-dominated Katipunan structure itself.

Aguinaldo, off fighting a field campaign and thus unable to attend, was nevertheless elected president. Bonifacio provisionally accepted the results that elected him vice-president of the revolutionary government, on condition of a vote recount. In a tense exchange with Magdalo partisans, he perceived what to him were insulting comments suggesting that only candidates with law degrees were qualified for the offices. He angrily invoked his authority as supreme leader of the Katipunan and the revolution, declared that the election results were void and the convention had no authority, and left with most of his followers.

The remaining delegates to the convention held another round of voting that ratified the original choice of Aguinaldo as president, and replaced Bonifacio with Mariano Trias as vice-president, along with a full roster of cabinet members. Historians mark the event as the first presidential election in Philippine history. However, the Tejeros Revolutionary Government was only elected by an internal Katipunan vote, not a general popular election. It did not have a constitution, a functioning administration, or even a definitive constitutional form as a republic, monarchy, unitary state or any other form of government. Its main significance was to mark a decisive shift of power from the early Katipunan – a secret underground society with a Bonifacio-dominated supreme council and a marked urban and mass base – to the later fighting organization and political apparatus led by better educated, upper middle-class illustrados and principales who would henceforth dominate the revolutionary government.

The Tejeros decisions did not immediately result in the emergence of a unified revolutionary movement or army. Similar to other Katipunan leaders in other parts of Luzon such as Emilio Jacinto and Artemio Ricarte, Bonifacio continued to operate autonomously as increasingly isolated KKK 'Supremo' from his base in the town of Naic. He called on Katipunan units to form a new military government under him, independent of the Tejeros government, and for the arrest of the latter as traitors to the revolution.

Upon hearing that Bonifacio had not only issued the Naic Agreement but had started burning towns whose leaders refused his commands and

ABOVE
Flags used during the revolution.

117

RIGHT

Progress of the revolution up to Biak-na-Bato.

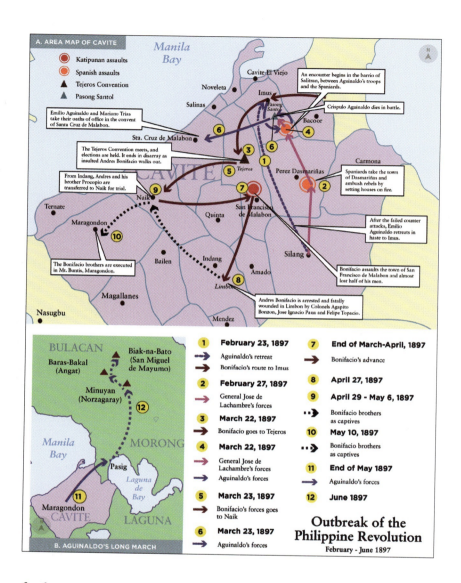

food requisitions, Aguinaldo in turn ordered Bonifacio arrested and placed on trial. The forces under Aguinaldo (including Magdiwang units disturbed by Bonifacio's actions) acted faster to neutralize the other side; Bonifacio was arrested by late April, tried for sedition and treason before a military tribunal composed mainly of Aguinaldo supporters, and executed on 10 May.

THE TREATY OF BIAK-NA-BATO

Although the revolution was now under more stable and effective leadership, the Spanish reinforcements pouring into the country and the aggressive tactical approach of Governor-General Polavieja were making themselves felt. Leaving an exposed Cavite, Aguinaldo and forces under his command first retreated south into Batangas province, before moving northwards into Bulacan, rallying other Katipunan groups all over Luzon. At the town of Biak-na-Bato (Broken Rock), he declared a Philippine republic in July of 1897. On 2 November 1897, the revolutionary forces drew up a constitution for the new state.

Behind the scenes, however, the Spanish and Filipino sides were both looking for a way out of a conflict that they both were finding unwinnable. On 15 December 1897, the two sides signed the Treaty of Biak-na-Bato, whose terms required Aguinaldo and his cabinet to go into foreign exile on payment of $400,000 plus $900,000 in compensation for Filipino civilians who had suffered loss or injury during the fighting. With the indemnity partly paid, Aguinaldo and his government left for Hong Kong on 27 December. Sources disagree on his intentions – some suggest that the funds immediately went to the purchase of large quantities of arms and ammunition for a later phase of the struggle, while others pointed to signs that the Filipino side had slowly been regaining the upper hand on the battlefield at the time, to suggest that the Biak-na-Bato agreement was nothing more or less than a sell-out. In any case, both sides hardly respected the terms of the treaty. The Spanish did not pay out all the promised funds, and continued their reprisals and counterguerrilla activities, while the uprising went on in a decentralized fashion in Luzon without Aguinaldo's central authority.

What future direction the revolution might have taken without any other external intervention is unknowable. The war in the archipelago was about to get caught up in a larger conflict between Spain and the United States, one that would spell the end of Madrid's role as an overseas power. America's rise to globalism in the coming century would include an intervention in Asia that changed the course of the unfinished Philippine revolution.

BELOW
Philippine revolutionary exiles in Hong Kong, early 1898.

5

THE TRIALS OF 'BENEVOLENT ASSIMILATION'

The Philippines as America's Only Colony, 1901–1950

In 1890, the American strategist Alfred Thayer Mahan published his work *The Influence of Sea Power upon History*. Mahan noted how Britain's rise to global empire underscored the importance of a powerful navy to any serious concept of national strength. The small US Navy of the age of sail had been an occasional presence around the world, but it had almost disappeared from neglect and underfunding after the American Civil War. By the 1880s, a new 'Steel Navy' of armoured, steam-driven ocean-going ships with quick-firing high-calibre guns in rotating turrets was under construction; Mahan's book advocated acquisition of overseas possessions to complement this new blue-water fleet.

There were many reasons for Mahan's enthusiastic reception in the US of the last decade of the 19th century. Theories about biological competition and natural selection were misapplied by Social Darwinists to social conflicts at home and geopolitics abroad. A belief in Protestant Anglo-Saxon superiority that deserved to dominate the world was widespread among Americans of longer-settled Western European stock. Economic imperialists sought captive colonial markets for the industries of their country, as well as an exclusive source of raw materials, agricultural products and cheap labour. Many Americans believed that international rivalry enhanced the vitality of a nation, preventing decadence and domestic conflict in an age of labour unrest against capitalism.

THE FIRST TEST OF STRENGTH

Conflict with Spain, now the weakest by far of the original imperial powers, would be a first chance to apply these ideas. The catalyst was the

ABOVE
The US Atlantic Fleet, 1907.

OPPOSITE
An aerial view of American Manila in the 1930s, with the Post Office building and the Jones Bridge over the Pasig River.

THE CIVILIZING MISSON OF AN EXCEPTIONAL NATION

Along with some Britons, American cheerleaders for empire believed that a self-appointed 'White Man´s Burden' obligated English-speakers to do lesser peoples a favour by taking control of them and educating them in the ways of modern civilization. Many Americans were convinced that the exceptional circumstances of their country's history had uniquely gifted them with a universally valid set of political and cultural values that needed to be shared with the rest of the world: democracy, republican forms of government, individualism, personal liberty and dignity, egalitarianism and laissez-faire free-market capitalism. From this perspective, any US intervention abroad served universal human progress, freedom and justice, not narrow American self-interest.

Cuban Revolution (1895–1898), proceeding parallel to the Philippine one but only 90 miles off the Florida coast. Reports about atrocities by Spanish forces against the Cuban population were already stirring up Americans when the armoured cruiser USS *Maine* exploded and sank while on a visit to Havana in February 1898. The exact cause of the explosion was unclear. Nevertheless, many Americans were incensed at the ship's sinking, tipping the balance between pro- and anti-war voices in the public debate. President William McKinley signed a Congressional authorization for war with Spain on 21 April.

Even before the sinking of the *Maine*, Washington had ordered Commodore George Dewey's US Asiatic Squadron to Hong Kong for further orders and reinforcements. After both arrived in late April, Dewey steamed to Manila Bay, where on 1 May 1898 his armoured cruisers and gunboats engaged and destroyed the Spanish Pacific Squadron, while sustaining only one American death (from heatstroke). This marked the end of Spanish hopes of retaining the colony. With the ground forces required to take Manila still under way from the US, however, Dewey began a blockade of the harbour and gathered more information about the overall situation. He noted the vulnerability of most Spanish positions against the Philippine revolutionary forces, now revitalized after the Spanish naval defeat.

BELOW
Illustration from 1903 showing Civilization condemning Russian barbarism while representatives of other powers (including the US, lower right) look on.

AGUINALDO'S RETURN

On 19 May, Emilio Aguinaldo arrived back in the Philippines on board the USS *McCulloch* and quickly regained the loyalty of most Katipunan units. The American envoy in Singapore had spoken to Aguinaldo in the preceding months, offering mixed signals implying that the US supported a resumption of the revolution. Dewey was equally ambiguous, at first welcoming Aguinaldo but afterwards distancing himself on instructions from Washington. Meanwhile, Aguinaldo publicly acknowledged the US as a sort of benevolent, sponsoring big power for the ongoing Philippine liberation struggle. Both sides seem to have chosen to downplay the long-term incompatibility of their respective viewpoints, in favour of

ABOVE
Contemporary artist's depiction of the Maine *explosion.*

BELOW
The armoured cruiser USS *Olympia, Dewey's flagship at Manila Bay, now preserved as a museum ship docked at Philadelphia, PA.*

the immediate benefits to both sides from Aguinaldo's return. On 9 June, Aguinaldo proclaimed himself dictator of a provisional government for the country until a constituent assembly could ratify a formal constitution. Meanwhile, American troops and equipment were pouring off transports from California; by late July, 12,000 US soldiers were in Manila, with many more on the way.

Aguinaldo now took further steps to clarify his ultimate goal of independence. On 12 June, to the strains of a new national anthem, he unfurled a new Philippine flag (essentially the current anthem and flag of today's republic) at his ancestral house in Cavite, and declared the independence

APOLINARIO MABINI

A crucial role in these months fell to Apolinario Mabini, a lawyer of peasant stock, Freemason, member of La Liga Filipina and former correspondent for *La Solidaridad*. Now Aguinaldo's chief political adviser, Mabini convinced his improvisation-prone boss to back-pedal from a dictatorship to the presidency of a provisional revolutionary government. He drafted decrees reinforcing the central government's control over local administrations and distant field commands. Known to subsequent generations of Filipino schoolchildren as 'The Brains of the Revolution', Mabini's other title, 'The Sublime Paralytic', alluded to a crippled lower body that did not affect his ability to respond quickly to a rapidly evolving political and military situation, thus maintaining the revolution's impetus.

LEFT: *Apolinario Mabini, date unknown.*

of the Philippines from Spain. The declaration ambiguously mentioned the 'protection' of the US and Dewey had been invited to the occasion, but he begged off with the excuse of too much paperwork and correspondence. Aguinaldo followed up the ceremony with a series of appointments to a provisional cabinet.

THE PLAY-ACTED SURRENDER OF MANILA

By August, Katipunan units or sympathizers were in control of most population centres in Luzon, and Aguinaldo's forces could easily cut off water and supplies to Intramuros. To avoid the unbearable humiliation of capitulating to their erstwhile Filipino subjects, the Spanish commander, Fermin Jaudenes, began secret surrender negotiations with Dewey. For the sake of Spanish prestige, Dewey and Jaudenes agreed to schedule a mock battle for Intramuros on 13 August, as a prelude to the orderly turnover of its garrison to the Americans. Intentionally or not, six Americans and 49 Spaniards were killed in the firefight that duly ensued.

Spanish honour satisfied, American troops moved in to secure Intramuros and much of central Manila. They denied entry into the city to Aguinaldo's army, citing fear of Filipino reprisal killings against their Spanish captives. Overnight, the Americans had shifted from ambiguous semi-allies of the Filipinos to collaborators with the Spanish in preventing Filipinos from gaining control of the situation. With the intentions of the Americans to take over the colony now more evident, Aguinaldo quickly tried to secure diplomatic recognition for his government from other states, although

LEFT
The Aguinaldo Shrine at Kawit, Cavite, site of the Philippine Declaration of Independence.

BELOW
American soldiers guarding a bridge over the Pasig River near Intramuros on the afternoon of the Spanish surrender. The vendor walking past them is carrying a tiffin box, perhaps hoping to sell a late lunch.

Felipe Agoncillo, the Aguinaldo government's representative, was excluded from the negotiations that began in Paris in late September between the US and Spain to formally end the war.

THE MALOLOS REPUBLIC

Meanwhile, Aguinaldo, his adviser Apolinario Mabini, and the Katipunan leadership convened a revolutionary congress on 15 September to draw up a constitution for the new republic. Delegates elected by local councils met at Malolos, a town in Bulacan province 32km (20 miles) north of Manila.

A draft constitution was approved on 29 November, and promulgated on 21 January 1899. Two days later, Aguinaldo was inaugurated as President of the Philippine Republic.

Not a single foreign power recognized the Malolos Republic as a legitimate Philippine national government; the direct transfer of sovereignty over the archipelago from Spain to the US had been finalized in the Treaty of Paris, signed on 10 December 1898. This formally ceded colonial political

125

ABOVE
Emilio Aguinaldo (seated at centre) and other delegates to the Assembly of Representatives that passed the Constitucion Politica de la Republica Filipina in Barasoain Church, Malolos, Bulacan.

BELOW
American unit rushing a bridge in the Manila suburb of Santa Cruz at the start of the Filipino-American War.

authority from Spain to the US under international law. (Spain also gave up Guam and Puerto Rico to the US; Cuba had technical independence but was hedged in with special arrangements that tied it closely to the US.) The Americans paid Spain US$20 million to leave its overseas possessions.

The more radical elements in Malolos led by Mabini and Antonio Luna prepared for war, and the new constitution was amended to give Aguinaldo sweeping emergency powers. On 21 December, US President McKinley announced a Philippine policy of 'benevolent assimilation' under American rule. Aguinaldo immediately issued a counter-proclamation condemning the 'violent and aggressive seizure' of the archipelago by the US. Without any formal declaration of war from either side, the practically inevitable hostilities erupted on 4 February 1899, when two American privates of the Nebraska Volunteers on a night patrol in a Manila suburb encountered and killed three Filipino soldiers.

THE FILIPINO-AMERICAN WAR

The Filipino-American War (or Philippine Insurrection) officially lasted about three years, but fighting in one form or another continued for almost a dec-

ade afterwards. A total of 126,000 American soldiers were deployed, with perhaps 5,000 killed by the end of the conflict. Reliable estimates of losses on the other side are more difficult to make; 16,000–20,000 Filipino regular soldiers died in action, out of about 80,000–100,000 total regular army effectives. An unknown number of Filipino irregulars and civilians died from direct or indirect war-related causes, with estimates ranging from an improbable low of 34,000 to equally imprecise highs of around a million, of which perhaps 200,000 were due to disease.

For the Americans, the war started well with the expulsion of Filipino troops from the Manila suburbs by late February and the capture of Malolos, the revolutionary capital, on 31 March 1899. Aguinaldo and his government fled Bulacan and set up a new capital at San Isidro, in Nueva Ecija province. As the Filipinos suffered these early setbacks, the Americans were already preparing a stable post-war colonial order. Even before the fall of Malolos, a fact-finding commission under Jacob Schurman, President of Cornell University, arrived in Manila, announcing 'that the United States is ... anxious to establish in the Philippine Islands an enlightened system of government under which the Philippine people may enjoy the largest measure of home rule and the amplest liberty'.

ABOVE
Fighting in the Manila suburb of Caloocan, February 1899.

127

ABOVE
General Gregorio del Pilar.

BELOW
Trinidad Pardo de Tavera, co-founder of the Federalista Party.

In response, moderates in the Malolos government, now on the run from one temporary capital to another in central Luzon, attempted to end the independence struggle and strike a compromise. They proposed a three-month armistice during which representatives of both sides would arrange terms for the settlement of the war. President McKinley authorized an offer of a government consisting of 'a Governor-General appointed by the President; cabinet appointed by the Governor-General; [and] a general advisory council elected by the people'. The illustrado-dominated revolutionary congress voted unanimously to accept peace on this basis, and on 8 May replaced the cabinet headed by Mabini with a new 'peace' cabinet headed by Pedro Paterno and Felipe Buencamino. At this point, however, General Antonio Luna, now field commander of the entire revolutionary army, arrested Paterno and most of his cabinet. A vacillating Aguinaldo quickly withdrew his support from the 'peace' cabinet, and Mabini returned to power. McKinley now threatened to 'send all the force necessary to suppress the insurrection if Filipino resistance continued'.

Despite the *anting-anting* (magical amulets) many carried, Aguinaldo's soldiers were no match for American troops in conventional combat. Apart from a small number of captured Spanish artillery pieces and early machine guns, probably only half were armed with modern rifles of varying quality; the rest only with bolos, spears and home-made firearms. However, Filipinos were formidable opponents in guerrilla warfare throughout the entire war. Unable to hold fixed lines as the Americans moved deeper into northern Luzon, Aguinaldo dissolved the regular army structure in November 1899 and replaced it with a decentralized network of guerrilla commands in separate military zones. In a self-sacrificing rear-guard action at the Battle of Tirad Pass in December 1899, picked troops under the 24-year-old General Gregorio del Pilar (nephew of Marcelo H. del Pilar, late of the Propaganda Movement) managed to delay pursuing American forces. Aguinaldo was able to escape into the mountains of eastern Isabela province, from where he attempted to coordinate the guerrilla war for 14 more months.

THE POLICY OF ATTRACTION

Meanwhile, the Schurman Commission was canvassing for support among the illustrado and principalia elites now returning to Manila who had dominated the suppressed Malolos Congress. Many were quickly appointed to judgeships and posts in the new colonial administration organized under the aegis of the US military. This successful co-optation of the Filipino elite was called the 'policy of attraction'. Such wealthy, educated and conservative people had been reluctant revolutionaries, suspicious of the mass-based Katipunan, and willing to compromise with either Spain or the US to maintain their position and prerogatives in Philippine society. They established the Federalista Party in December 1900, as a political association advocating full American statehood for the islands. Most Americans scoffed at this Federalista goal but nevertheless valued the party as a source of pliable and cooperative figures to install in the selected public posts of the new colony that were opened to Filipinos. Despite a claimed membership of 200,000 by May 1901, however, the Federalistas were never able to gain much support among Filipinos for their proposal to make the islands an American state.

ABOVE
Philippine Commissioners General Luke E. Wright, Governor-General William Howard Taft and Judge Henry C. Ide.

In 1901, Federalista leaders such as T. H. Pardo de Tavera and Benito Legarda joined high American officials in the ranks of the new Second Philippine Commission (or Taft Commission), a permanent body set up to carry out the Schurman Commission's recommendations. The commission wielded executive power as the highest council of the Insular Government under its chair, the first American Governor-General William Howard Taft.

At the same time, the Taft Commission also had legislative functions and began developing the local government system in areas 'pacified' by American troops. As the first Filipino members of the Commission, de Tavera and Legarda enabled the appointments of numerous other Federalistas to provincial governorships, the new insular Supreme Court and positions in

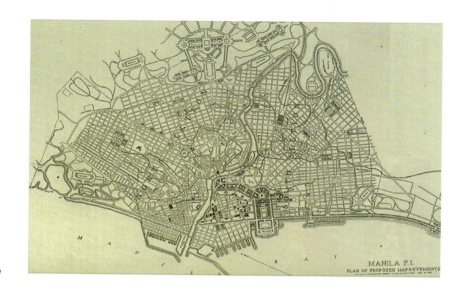

RIGHT

The Burnham plan for the development of Manila, 1905. Daniel Burnham was a prominent landscape architect and urban planner associated with the Progressive-era City Beautiful movement who designed the centrepiece parks and expansions of major American cities around the turn of the century. The American authorities in the Philippines, eager to harness architecture and city planning to the colonial civilising mission, envisioned a massive new metropolis beyond the original Spanish harbour city. The new American city was intended to radiate far out into the surrounding countryside via rationally planned avenues and transportation junctions, around which a careful mix of commercial and residential neighbourhoods was intended to develop, anchored by imposing civic monuments and administrative buildings. A modest fraction of this agenda was realized before the Second World War, not only in Manila, but also in other cities such as Cebu for which development plans were also drawn up. The war destroyed most of this work, except for a few representative buildings and avenues, disarticulated from their planned grids and now almost lost under a new kind of postcolonial urban sprawl.

the new civil service. Alongside the establishment of state institutions, the Taft Commission intended economic development and education to be the other two pillars of the US mission to uplift the Philippines.

US Army units had begun holding English-language classes around Manila even as the Spanish were being driven out of the country. In August 1901, the transport ship *Thomas* brought about 540 American teachers and some of their families to the Philippines to help establish the public-school system mandated by the Taft Commission. Although other batches also arrived, this particular contingent was the largest, and all American teachers in the early colonial Philippines came to be known after them as the Thomasites. Their threefold objective was to educate new generations of Filipinos in an American-style basic curriculum, spread English – first as the medium of instruction, then as the language of daily life – and train new generations of Filipino teachers.

THE GUERRILLA WAR TURNS UGLY

At the same time that the Thomasites were beginning the education process, Aguinaldo's shift to a guerrilla war was inaugurating the era of American counter-insurgency warfare around the globe. It was in the Philippines that US soldiers first learnt what it was like to carry the conflict to an enemy concealed within a civilian population. As an inevitable consequence, civilians caught between Americans and Filipino guerrillas suffered severe reprisals.

AMERICA'S ENGLISH-LANGUAGE EDUCATION POLICY

The Thomasites and the Filipino cadre they trained would eventually staff a nationwide system of public elementary and secondary schools built on the modest start inherited from the Spanish era. The Thomasites also reopened the Philippine Nautical School, originally established by the Spanish in 1839, and established the Philippine Normal School (now Philippine Normal University) as the country's flagship teacher training college. Hundreds of thousands of people among the two generations of Filipinos to have direct contact with Thomasites as children or young adults would achieve native-speaker levels of proficiency in the English language. Although it has been a struggle to maintain that proficiency in later generations, the American educational effort begun in the early 1900s would eventually transform the Philippines into the third-largest English-speaking nation in the world.

BELOW: *A burial plot in a Manila graveyard reserved for some of the original Thomasites who stayed on to settle in the Philippines after their teaching contracts ended.*

RIGHT
American troops in the
Philippines man an
entrenched firing position,
1898–1900, location
unknown. As with many
images from this period and
context, there is a possibility
that this photograph was
posed.

As the fighting ground on, more and more atrocities would be committed by both sides. US troops applied a method of interrogation called the 'water cure' to Filipino insurgents, an ancestor of the early 21st-century practice of 'waterboarding'. Other atrocities committed by both sides included the burning or shelling of entire villages, indiscriminate killing of civilians caught in security zones, the display of decapitated heads or other body parts in prominent locations to intimidate the opposition, and summary mass executions of military prisoners.

THE END OF THE MALOLOS REPUBLIC

In March 1901, after his long retreat through the uplands of Luzon, Aguinaldo was captured at Palanan in Isabela province by a clandestine operation under General Frederick Funston, using the Macabebe Scouts, pro-American auxiliaries pretending to be revolutionary reinforcements. In the latest of several ambiguous and disorienting reversals of position in

THE MACABEBE SCOUTS

The Macabebe Scouts were among the most prominent, loyal and effective of numerous auxiliary combat forces that the Americans recruited to their side during the Filipino-American War. They had already served in the Spanish Army against their own countrymen during the original revolution, and carried over this anti-revolutionary stance to service with the Americans. In retaliation, their hometown was attacked by the army of the First Philippine Republic. Under the command of General Frederick Funston (disguised as their prisoner) and dressed in revolutionary army uniforms while posing as reinforcements sent to aid Emilio Aguinaldo, the Scouts were instrumental in Aguinaldo's capture at his headquarters in Palanan in a remote part of Isabela Province in April 1901.

his long political career, Aguinaldo quickly pledged allegiance in April to the US and its military government in the Philippines, formally ending the existence of the First, Malolos Republic. He then urged Filipino forces to lay down their arms. Nevertheless, Aguinaldo was never fully on board among the many illustrados and former members of the Malolos Congress who sought to actively collaborate with the Americans. He retreated instead into a wary semi-retirement from which he would emerge in later decades whenever a chance to advance the nationalist cause seemed to present itself. The war itself would not end with Aguinaldo's call for a Filipino surrender – even though the Republic had ceased functioning, its army was still effective

LEFT
Memorial to the Macabebe Scouts in Macabebe, Pampanga.

ABOVE
Aguinaldo in captivity boarding the gunboat USS Vicksburg for shipment back to Manila, 1901.

enough for some members of the dispersed military leadership to continue the fighting autonomously.

The levels of mutual atrocity escalated even higher after Aguinaldo's surrender. In the Balangiga Massacre of the same year, about 50 American soldiers stationed in this town in Samar province were killed by knife-wielding guerrillas and vengeful townspeople. In response, Samar's American sector commander issued orders for the execution of all inhabitants above the age of 10 who could not give a satisfactory account of their presence in designated killing zones. Although some of his subordinates refused to carry out such measures, other units did, and went a considerable distance towards turning the island, in his words, into a 'howling wilderness'.

By July, Taft felt that the situation was stable enough to declare the 'insurrection' officially over, although fighting still raged in many areas until 1903. Soon after, a general amnesty was declared for all Filipinos who had laid down their arms by that summer, with the die-hards who kept fighting now classified not as belligerents but as 'bandits'. Particularly outside the larger towns, sporadic fighting would go on for years.

RECONCENTRADOS

In the southern Tagalog provinces, the Americans attempted to cut off the die-hard Katipunan General Miguel Malvar from the support offered by rural villages by introducing a Spanish policy from Cuba of *reconcentrados*, later to reappear in the Malayan Emergency and the Vietnam War as 'strategic hamlets'. Reconcentrados herded rural populations into large, open-air detention areas with only the most basic sanitation, supplies and shelter, surrounded by no-go free-fire zones. Villagers were only able to leave them to tend to their fields or animals with special permission. Conditions deteriorated so badly that possibly 100,000 civilians died in four southern Tagalog provinces as a direct result. Reconcentrados proved to be effective enough; Malvar's forces surrendered in April 1902, one of the last organized republican armies to do so.

THE ORGANIC ACT

The official end of the war was accompanied by the passing in the US Congress of the 1902 Organic Act of the Philippine Islands, which served as the de facto constitution of the new colony until 1916. The Act sent two Filipino Resident Commissioners to serve as the colony's representatives in Washington. Alongside economic provisions friendly to US investment, the Act ratified the already started educational system and provided for a judiciary, prison, police and legal system that blended the common-law US and civil-law Spanish traditions. It regularized elections in local government units (the larger municipalities and cities continued to have appointed governments). The Act also affirmed the separation of church and state already pioneered in the First Republic's Malolos Constitution, disestablishing the Catholic Church as the official religion.

Finally, the Act also authorized an elected Philippine Assembly to serve as a lower legislative house to the upper house of the appointive Philippine Commission. A system of property and literacy qualifications initially limited voting to an estimated 5 per cent of the male population. Despite (or

BELOW

Bilibid Prison, Manila, in 1928. Penology was one of the many areas where the Americans introduced tropicalized versions of the latest practices in public administration. Opened in 1866, Bilibid had been the main Spanish prison for serious criminals as well as political prisoners. The Americans refurbished it according to the standards of state penitentiaries like New York's Sing Sing, including the only functioning electric chair ever deployed outside the United States.

THE PHILIPPINE INDEPENDENT CHURCH

During the revolution, the original nationalist grievances concerning the frailocracy and European suppression of the native clergy produced efforts to break away completely from the authority of the Vatican and foreign missionary orders, while still preserving the essentials of the Catholic culture and faith. By 1902, this had resulted in the creation of the Philippine Independent Church (*Iglesia Filipina Independiente*, IFI). In the manner of the Anglican Church, the IFI preserved most of the forms of Catholicism, but was no longer in communion with Rome (the IFI was to indeed join the worldwide Anglican/Episcopal union in 1960).

ABOVE: *Father Gregorio Aglipay.*

The IFI was a joint initiative of Isabelo de los Reyes, a prominent revolutionary politician, and Gregorio Aglipay, a nationalist Catholic priest very much in the mould of the Gomburza martyrs of 1872. Apart from the IFI, another reason for this lasting tension between devout Catholics (*catolicos cerrados*) and adherents of the nationalist tradition was the American decision to allow the Church to bring into the country new European or American clergy (many of them Irish or Irish-American) to replace departing Spanish missionaries, rather than filling the empty positions or mission fields with native priests.

Despite their role in maintaining and revitalizing the foreign, mostly white, missionary presence in the Philippines, the Americans did agree with the Filipino nationalists that neither the friars from the old Spanish missionary orders who still tarried in the Philippines, nor the new foreign clergy, could retain their vast property holdings. The Vatican, which represented the orders diplomatically, agreed to sell the friars' estates and promised to gradually phase in Filipinos and other non-Spanish priests in place of the friars. Actual withdrawal of personnel of the old religious orders from the islands would proceed very gradually. In 1904, the US administration bought most of the friar lands, amounting to some 166,000ha (166km²), for about $7 million dollars. Half of them in the vicinity of Manila, these lands were eventually resold to Filipinos, a few of them tenants, but the majority existing owners of large estates.

perhaps because of) this, the political and administrative system created by the Organic Act eventually proved an effective vehicle for reconciling most of the urban, educated illustrados and the old principalia elite to the new reality of American rule. These people occupied the broad middle zone between die-hard military resistance from Katipunan remnants still fighting in the field on the one hand, and the ultra-collaborationists pushing for American statehood and permanent US control of the Philippine society and economy on the other. Most elite politicians maintained a formal commitment to ultimate independence, but were willing to cooperate with the Americans for the foreseeable future in the practical tasks of colonial governance – incidentally guaranteeing their careers and continued prominence in Philippine society.

As the more educated or middle-class members of the nationalist movement gradually surrendered and/or began to collaborate within the colonial structure prepared for them by the Americans, the insurgent impulse fell back on the population base of ordinary Filipino peasants who had nurtured it before the political turn to the revolution in the 1890s. With the formal cessation of hostilities in 1902, the US Army withdrew from the anti-insurgency campaign, leaving behind a new organization, the Philippine Constabulary, as an archipelago-wide paramilitary police force to control brigandage and deal with the remnants of the insurgent movement.

A NEW POLITICAL ELITE

In 1905, the Federalista party revised its programme over the objections of its leaders, abandoning the goal of American statehood, calling for 'ultimate independence' and changing its name to the National Progressive Party (*Partido Nacional Progresista*). The Federalista/Progresista rebrand could not remove popular perceptions of the party as opportunistic, elitist or even traitorous; it would instead be the new Nacionalista Party, established in 1907, that would dominate Philippine politics until after the Second World War. The Nacionalistas were led by a new generation of politicians who did not come from elite illustrado backgrounds, but were also by no means radical representatives of the masses. They reflected the rise of newer,

THE MORO WARS

Alongside the Philippine-American War itself, the US Army was also fighting a parallel and slightly later armed conflict in Mindanao. In August 1899, an agreement had been signed with the Sultan of Sulu, Jamal-ul Kiram II, pledging an American policy of non-interference. In 1903, however, the US authorities set up a 'Moro Province' administration, outlawed slavery, set up schools with a non-Muslim curriculum and sidelined the authority of traditional community leaders with new local governments. A new civil code replaced the sharia, or Islamic law. Armed resistance grew, and the Moro province remained under US military rule until 1914, by which time the major Muslim groups had been subjugated. This campaign involved the Massacre of Bud Dajo of 1906, during which American troops laid siege to about 1,000 men, women and children of an insurgent faction from the Tausug people who had set up a mountain stronghold inside an extinct volcanic cone on the island of Jolo. Only six Moros were left alive after the engagement, a kill rate of over 99 per cent, leading to predictable outcries in the Manila press and the US itself.

ABOVE
Manuel L. Quezon.

BELOW
Sergio Osmeña.

middle-class urban elements anxious to join the existing mainstream of Filipino politics. Unlike many in the illustrado generation, these people had made a point of mastering the public use of English at the start of their adult careers. In July 1907, the first elections for the Philippine Assembly were held, and it opened its first session on 16 October 1907. The election results began the uninterrupted domination of the Assembly for its entire existence by two Nacionalista leaders, Manuel Quezon and Sergio Osmeña.

An officer in Aguinaldo's army, Quezon took a post-war law degree, entered provincial politics and became governor of Tayabas province in 1906. His public-speaking skills and charisma attracted the support of influential Americans and helped elect him to the Philippine Assembly the following year. His partner and sometime rival in the Nacionalista leadership was Sergio Osmeña, a college-educated scion of a mestizo-Chinese clan from the Visayas who had made an early name for himself in provincial journalism. Like Quezon, Osmeña had served as a provincial governor (of Cebu) before being elected to the Assembly. At the age of 29, he was elected as its first speaker.

The Nacionalistas' official platform called for 'immediate independence'. However, most Americans understood that the party used this demand only to appeal to an electorate where nationalistic sentiment still ran strong. In practice, both leaders were quite prepared to cooperate with the Americans for the moment to block any attempt by the radical nationalist wing of the party to force a confrontation over the issue. Personally, Osmeña and Quezon, who became the dominant figures in Philippine politics until the Second World War, were genuinely committed to independence. The failure of Aguinaldo's revolution, however, encouraged in them an attitude of conciliatory gradualism that was to have major social and political effects.

As the acknowledged representatives of this system at the national level, Osmeña and Quezon were not genuinely interested in tackling the many social issues that had emerged in Philippine society over the last several generations of haphazardly modernizing late Spanish colonial rule. Serious problems involving land ownership, tenancy and the highly unequal distribution of wealth were largely ignored. The Nacionalista Party's hammerlock on legislative and executive power under American sponsorship, particularly in the period after 1916 when it gained almost complete control of a bicameral Filipino legislature, prevented the expression of non-elite interests in the political system. With Americans reluctant to intervene in Philippine socio-economic relations, Nacionalista dominance ensured that the status quo in landlord and tenant relationships in the countryside – where the bulk of Filipinos remained employed – would be maintained, even if certain of its traditional aspects were destabilized.

The elite and the cultivators began living increasingly separate lives culturally and geographically, as well as economically. Many more of the provincial elite became absentee landlords, leaving estates in the hands of frequently abusive overseers. As landlords used profits from the sale of cash crops to support their new urban, Americanized life-styles or to invest in other kinds of enterprise, interest in tenants' welfare waned. Cultivators accused landowners of being shameless and forgetting the humanizing feudal principle of *utang na loob*, demanding services from tenants and no longer offering the protective if patronizing noblesse oblige – such as free schooling for their children, assistance at funerals and help with hospitalizations – of the former feudal system.

In 1913, the Philippine Commission had a Filipino majority for the first time. Part of the Nacionalistas' success in this institution during the crucial early decades of American colonial rule lay in their good working relationship with Governor-General Francis Burton Harrison (1913–1921). Harrison's approach to colonial affairs reflected the liberal stance of Woodrow Wilson's Democratic Party. He authorized the setting up of key institutions such as the Philippine National Bank and the Manila Railroad. Harrison also pushed for the 'Filipinization' of the civil service.

ABOVE
Coat of Arms of the American colonial state in the Philippines.

THE RISE OF THE TRADITIONAL POLITICIAN ('TRAPO')

Much of the Nacionalistas' success came from the careful grafting of modern political institutions on to traditional social structures and practices. This required the party leadership to sponsor the integration of local-level elite groups into the new political system. In many cases the descendants of the *principalía* of Spanish times, these local elites now controlled modern electoral constituencies tied to them in traditional patron-client relationships. Although issues around independence took centre stage in politics at the national level, the keys to popular support were more often local, particularistic issues than ideological concerns. Although the extension of voting rights to all literate males in 1916, the growth of literacy and the granting of women's suffrage in 1938 increased the electorate considerably, the elites continued to monopolize the support of the newly enfranchised according to these traditional patterns. A genuinely populist, issues-based alternative to the status quo never really emerged.

THE JONES LAW

American critics accused Harrison of being the 'plaything and catspaw of the leaders of the Nacionalista Party'. On his watch, a major step was taken in the direction of independence when the US Congress passed the Jones Law, or the Philippine Autonomy Act of 1916, which replaced the 1902 Organic Act as the colony's de facto constitution. It mandated the granting of Philippine independence as soon as a stable government was established, but did not give a specific date. A new, largely popularly elected Senate replaced the appointive Philippine Commission as the upper house of the legislature, and the lower house was renamed the House of Representatives. However, the legislature's actions were subject to American veto, and its laws could not affect the rights of US citizens. The executive was still firmly under the control of an appointed governor-general, and most Supreme Court justices, who were appointed by the US president, were still Americans in 1916. With the continued Nacionalista hegemony, Quezon was elected president of the Senate, and Osmeña continued as speaker of the House.

Although the Jones Act had brought the legislative branch under permanent Filipino control, Harrison's successor, General Leonard Wood

BELOW
Provincial Capitol building in Malaybalay, Bukidnon, Mindanao – a concrete sign of the colonial state's expansion into Mindanao, following the inflow of new settlements of Christian settlers.

(1921–1927), was an authoritarian throwback who had been the commanding general of the Moro region during the Massacre of Bud Dajo. Right before becoming governor-general, he was part of a fact-finding mission sent by the new Republican administration to assess progress in the colony. He reported that the Filipinos were not ready for independence, and was convinced that US withdrawal from the islands would be as disastrous for the Filipinos as it would be for the interests of the US in the Western Pacific. He angered the Nacionalistas by using his veto power 126 times during six years in office, prompting Quezon's memorable quote: 'I would prefer a government run like hell by Filipinos than one run like heaven by Americans.'

During the 1920s, Muslims perceived the rapid Filipinization of the civil service and US commitment to eventual independence as serious threats. An independent Philippines would be dominated by Christians. Already, immigration of Christian settlers from Luzon and the Visayan Islands to the relatively unsettled regions of Mindanao was encouraged, and the new arrivals began supplanting the Moros in their homeland. There was no legal recognition of Muslim customs and institutions. Any suggestion of special status for or continued US rule over the Moro regions, however, was vehemently opposed by Christian Filipino leaders.

A STATE OF LINGUISTIC CONVENIENCE

Such social and political tensions were not the only reason why popular identification with a strong, homegrown state remained difficult. Although it had fought and bled in the name of a new and synthetic 'Filipino' identity, the revolutionary nationalism of the Katipunan period had been an overwhelmingly Tagalog-speaking phenomenon. However, *non*-Tagalog-speaking groups collectively formed more than three-fourths of the archipelago's lowland Christian population. Particularly in the Visayas region in the middle of the archipelago, some of these other ethnolinguistic groups had strong and separate cultural identities, rough numerical parity with Tagalogs and modernizing elites of their own.

Nevertheless, there was a marked tendency among both the Tagalog-speaking leaders of the revolutionary tradition and the later moderate nationalists of the American period – even including elite Visayans among the latter – to minimize these differences for the expedient purpose of wishing into being a new nation with a single official native language, Tagalog

Map labels:
Ivatan
Cordileran Languages
Western Ilocano
Pangasinense
Eastern Ilocano
Kapampangan
Bulacan Tagalog
Tanay-Paete Tagalog
Bataan Tagalog
Tayabas Tagalog
Tagalog
Lubang Tagalog
Central Bicolano
Pandan Bicolano
Sorsogon Bicolano
Batangan Tagalog
Romblomamon Languages
Aklanon
Waray
Kinaray-a
Hiligaynon
Palawan Hilltribal Languages
Bohol Cebuano
Surigaonon Cebuano
Cebuano
Subanon
Mindanao Hilltribal Languages
Mindanao Maguindanao
Chavacanon
Davaoeno Cebuano
Mindanao Hilltribal Languages

0   100 km
0   50 miles

N

ABOVE

The main languages of the Philippines.

relabelled as 'Filipino'. This, however, confused wish with reality. Tagalog simply had not made any significant inroads into daily use in the rest of the country. In comparison with the nearest relevant case, multiethnic Indonesia's search for a national language was simplified by the fact that a widely understood trade language – Malay – already existed in most population centres without being associated with the most dominant ethnolinguistic group, the Javanese. Except for the numerically non-dominant Malays, learning Malay-based Bahasa Indonesia put a more equal burden of effort on all other ethnolinguistic groups. In the Philippine case, a serious and sustained dialogue between Tagalogs and non-Tagalogs over the complicated relationships between identity, language and national feeling did not really occur. The result was a suppressed (and to Tagalogs inconvenient, and therefore unacknowledged and incomprehensible) resentment among non-Tagalogs that emerged from the casual conflation of 'Tagalog' and Tagalog-ness with 'Filipino' and Filipino-ness. This resentment was fanned by many Tagalogs' embrace of the frequent American dismissal of other Filipino languages as mere 'dialects'. These linguistic tensions continue to haunt and potentially destabilize the Philippine state and society until today.

THE COMMONWEALTH ROAD TO INDEPENDENCE

The diverse political interests in the US in favour of Philippine independence were unlikely but welcome allies for the Filipino nationalists. American agricultural lobbies in the sugar-beet, tobacco and dairy industries wished to keep out low-tariff Philippine competitors, in the deepening depression of the early 1930s. West Coast labour unions wanted to exclude Filipino labour. Some American geopolitical observers and strategists saw the Philippines as an unsustainably exposed potential flash point in the face of a potential Japanese 'southern resources' push, and argued for a withdrawal of military resources from the archipelago back across the Pacific to Hawaii.

Responding to these changes in American domestic politics, Osmeña and Manuel Roxas – the latter a rising star in the Nacionalista Party – successfully campaigned for the Hare-Hawes-Cutting Independence Bill, which was approved in early 1933 by the US Congress. Quezon, however, opposed the bill, ostensibly because provisions regarding trade, the exclusion of Filipino immigration to the US, persistent American bases on Philippine soil and the prerogatives of an envisioned US High Commissioner compromised independence. A more fundamental reason was Quezon's reluctance to support anything that might raise the political profile of his rival, Osmeña, in the Nacionalista power hierarchy. The bill was defeated in the Philippine legislature by an unlikely, Quezon-organized coalition that ranged from anti-independence sugar interests from Negros Island to pro-independence activists who did not think the bill went far enough. Quezon

THE DEMISE OF THE SPANISH LANGUAGE

Despite the straightforward wish for political separation that the revolution had represented, the fate of the Spanish language posed another cultural and political problem for Filipinos during the American colonial period. Along with Tagalog, Spanish had been the language of the Philippine Revolution, and the only official language of the First Malolos Republic. It had been the language of commerce, law, politics, business and the arts during the colonial period, and remained so well into the 20th century. It was the main language in which most illustrados and many revolutionary leaders had publicly expressed themselves. During the early part of the American period, Spanish education was widespread and command of the language was relatively well maintained among the urban and educated classes.

As the first generations emerged from the English-language primary and secondary schools of the new American system into adult life, however, a gap began to grow between them and the revolutionary-nationalist heritage, which was expressed mostly in Spanish. Although the generation of Quezon and Osmeña that had switched to English in adulthood experienced no such gap, the cohorts that came after were increasingly cut off from the written record of the emergence of Filipino nationalism, as well as the outpouring of cultural work produced by the illustrado generation. The result was a culturally shallow generation unmoored from the original sources of Filipino national identity except for superficial renderings of it in English-language schoolbooks. Surveying the Philippines at the end of the 20th century, the historian Benedict Anderson concluded: '... almost no one other than a few scholars understands the language in which the revolutionary heroes communicated among themselves and with the outside world – to say nothing of the written archive of pre-20th-century Philippine history. A virtual lobotomy has taken place'.

ABOVE
*Colourized image of a
Manila street scene, 1936.*

himself then went to Washington and negotiated the Congressional passage of a revised independence law with essentially the same provisions, the Tydings-McDuffie Act of March 1934. This time, the Filipino side ratified it, angering Osmeña and threatening a potentially fatal split in the Nacionalista Party.

The Tydings-McDuffie Act laid out a 10-year transition path to full independence, during which a Commonwealth of the Philippines under US protection would be the country's political form. With an accredited American High Commissioner replacing the governor-general, the Commonwealth would have a constitution and be self-governing in domestic matters; its foreign policy would remain in the hands of the US. Laws affecting immigration, foreign trade and the currency system had to be approved by the US president. Only 50 Filipino immigrants were allowed into the US annually, while American entry and residence in the islands were unrestricted. The act allowed for five years' free entry of Philippine goods during the transition period, and five years of gradually steepening tariff duties thereafter, reaching 100 per cent in 1946, whereas US goods could enter the islands unrestricted and duty free during the full 10 years. The US would retain only a naval reservation and fueling stations, and promised to negotiate with foreign governments for the neutralization of the islands.

The Philippines' first fully functioning constitution (the Malolos document had not been implemented across much of the country) was the result of a constitutional convention that first assembled in July 1934. Approved by plebiscite in May 1935 with an overwhelming majority, it established the political institutions for the 10-year Commonwealth period that began that year. Upon the dissolution of the Commonwealth after the end of the Second World War, its constitution would soldier on after cosmetic changes as the constitution of the independent Republic of the Philippines until 1973. Elections for the new Philippine Congress and most executive governmental posts were held in September 1935. Manuel Quezon and Sergio Osmeña had patched up their disagreements and reunited the Nacionalista factions to run on a Coalition Party ticket, and were elected president and vice-president, respectively.

ECONOMIC AND SOCIAL DEVELOPMENTS

The 1901 Taft Commission had argued that tariff relief was essential if the islands were to be developed. In 1913, the Underwood Tariff Act removed all restrictions on free entry to the US of all Philippine products. The archipelago became increasingly dependent on American markets; between 1914 and 1939, the portion of Philippine exports going to the US rose from 50 to

LEFT
Signing the Constitution of the Philippine Commonwealth, 23 March 1935.

145

85 per cent, and in return, 65 per cent of imports came from the US. By the 1930s, a generation of Filipinos educated in the public school system had not only learnt to appreciate writers and poets as varied as Edna St Vincent Millay, Theodore Dreiser and Ralph Waldo Emerson, but had also developed a preference for imported American goods (known in the archipelago as 'stateside' items) over any available local counterparts, just as the imperial metropole was developing the world's first full-blown consumer society.

As ambitious Filipinos with higher academic degrees won at American universities returned to the archipelago to build a new professional elite, they re-encountered countrymen who in the meantime had become a mass audience for Hollywood films, Madison Avenue hard-sell techniques, and children who dreamt of white Christmases full of snow and reindeer underneath the sweltering tropical sun. Not only did industrialization fail to take off because of the availability of US imports and the structural disincentives to local investment in anything but agriculture, but much of Philippine mass popular culture in the coming decades would became a derivative copy of the American one, with numerous Frank Sinatras or Elvis Presleys of the Philippines belting out their versions of 'My Funny Valentine' or 'Heartbreak Hotel'.

Perhaps appropriate in the decade of the worldwide Great Depression, this Americanization was proceeding without a stable middle class in both the cities and the countryside. In 1918, there were roughly 2 million farms, of which 1.5 million were operated by their owners; by 1939, these figures had declined to 1.6 million and 800,000, respectively, as individual proprietors became tenants or migrant labourers. Disparities in the distribution of wealth grew. By 1939, the wealthiest 10 per cent of the population received 40 per cent of the islands' income. This growing socio-economic inequality brought with it a new wave of mass unrest.

The resurgence of traditional messianic millenarianism in the 1910s was in its turn gradually giving way to more secular and at times leftist-revolutionary movements. The most important of these were the Sakdalistas, led by Benigno Ramos, a former Nacionalista Party member and associate of Quezon who broke with him in 1933 over the issue of American collaboration. The Sakdal Party (*sakdal* means to accuse) contested the 1934 election with a programme of complete independence by the end of 1935, land reform and an end to landlord oppression. Sakdalistas won some seats in the legislature and provincial posts. By 1935, the party may have had as many as 200,000 members. Sakdalistas eventually took up arms and attacked government offices in a number of locations on 2–3 May 1935. The response by the constabulary killed approximately 100 people and sent Benigno Ramos into exile in Japan.

THE SECOND WORLD WAR AND THE FALL OF THE PHILIPPINES

Forced to open its doors to the world by the Americans in the 1840s, and conscious of nearby China's ongoing humiliation by the West, a rapidly industrializing Japan had concluded by the 1890s that the only safety in a world of predatory military imperialist powers was to become a predatory military imperialist power itself. By the 1920s, Japan had acquired Korea, Taiwan, parts of the Russian Far East, and various Pacific island groups that Germany had previously purchased from Spain in 1898. By the 1930s, Japanese armies were deep in a massive and brutal land war in China, eventually putting their empire on a collision course with the Western powers.

Allied with the Nazis by 1940, Japan had taken over French Indochina

ABOVE
Japanese soldiers in China, 1930s.

BELOW
The Japanese aircraft carrier Kaga, 1928.

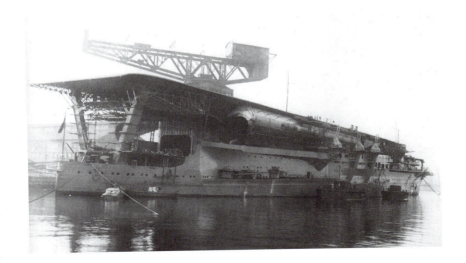

ABOVE
Douglas MacArthur at a Philippine Army Air Corps commissioning ceremony, August 1941.

BELOW
A car bedecked with Japanese flags and welcome signs during the entry of Japanese forces into Manila, May 1942.

from a compliant Vichy government, and imperial land, air and sea forces were in a position to threaten the resource-rich British colony of Malaya as well as the Dutch East Indies. The American-controlled Philippines lay along the path of any future Japanese move south, and Quezon's Commonwealth government cooperated in reinforcing Washington's available forces in Southeast Asia. Quezon had a close relationship with General Douglas MacArthur (son of the second military governor of the Philippines), appointing him Field Marshal of the Philippine Commonwealth Army after his retirement from US Army service in 1937. Although MacArthur was recalled to active duty in 1940 to command the reinforced US Army Forces in the Far East (USAFFE), strategists in Washington were fully aware of the Philippines' exposed position and the slim chances of proper reinforcement in the event of a serious Japanese attack.

With USAFFE and Commonwealth forces in various states of unreadiness, this attack came by surprise on 8 December 1941, nine hours after the Japanese attack on Pearl Harbor. Air strikes on airfields, naval depots and other targets were followed by landings of ground troops both north and south of Manila and in Davao on Mindanao. MacArthur had been slow to respond to news of the Pearl Harbor attack. Most aircraft under his command were caught on the ground and destroyed, naval forces were dispersed to avoid getting trapped in Manila or Subic Bay, and reinforcement and resupply routes from the US for his forces were cut off. Unable to hold their lines against superior Japanese forces, the USAFFE withdrew to the Bataan Peninsula and to the island of Corregidor in Manila Bay. Manila, declared an open city to prevent its destruction, was occupied by the Japanese on 2 January 1942. The Philippine defence under General Jonathan Wainwright continued until the surrender of USAFFE forces on Bataan in April 1942, and on Corregidor in May. Most of the 90,000 or so prisoners-of-war captured went on the infamous Bataan Death March to prison camps in Tarlac province. About 20,000 of them died before reaching their destination. Quezon and Osmeña were able to escape to the US, where they set up a government in exile. MacArthur left via Mindanao for Australia, where for the next two years he prepared his promised return to the Philippines.

Although the Japanese had promised independence for the islands after occupation, they directed civil affairs through an appointed executive until October 1943, when they declared the Philippines an independent republic in an effort to mobilize the country more effectively for the demands of total war. This Japanese-sponsored Second Philippine Republic was headed by President José P. Laurel, elected by a National Assembly hurriedly convened as prescribed by an equally

ABOVE
Allied propaganda poster featuring the Bataan Death March.

MOBILIZING FOR THE JAPANESE EMPIRE

The Japanese created mass organizations to replace the political party landscape of the Commonwealth. The Association for Service to the New Philippines (*Kapisanan sa Paglilinkod sa Bagong Pilipinas*, KALIBAPI) was announced as a network of neighbourhood groups to help in food distribution, to supply labour drafts and to provide a focus for mass rallies. In reality, it also served as a national surveillance network tightly controlled by the Japanese political police. The hooded informers and armed auxiliary militia of the Patriotic Society of Filipinos (*Makabayang Katipunan ng Pilipino*, MAKAPILI) assisted the imperial occupation forces in identifying and eliminating members of the underground anti-Japanese resistance, or simply those with anti-Japanese attitudes.

KALIBAPI was headed by Benigno Aquino, the father of the future Senator Benigno Aquino, Jr, main opponent of the 1970s and '80s Marcos dictatorship. The leader of the MAKAPILI was none other than Benigno Ramos, the former head of the Sakdal movement of the 1930s, who had gone into exile in Japan before the war. Another notable exile returnee from Japan was Artemio Ricarte, a former general of the original Katipunan noted for being one of the few revolutionary veterans never to have sworn loyalty to the Americans. Both Ricarte and Emilio Aguinaldo were trotted out by Japanese propaganda specialists at times deemed appropriate – with radio addresses, the flag raising at Laurel's inauguration and so on – to imbue the puppet state with nationalist legitimacy. However, it was clear that both men no longer had meaningful political followings. Aguinaldo would survive the war and be pardoned for his wartime activities, while Ricarte would evacuate Manila in 1945, only to die of dysentery in northern Luzon while on the run with the retreating Japanese army after the American re-invasion in 1944.

第七卷
第三號

東洋文化協會

ABOVE
Japanese tanks passing the Rizal monument, 1942.

OPPOSITE TOP
Douglas MacArthur's invasion forces land in Leyte, 1944. President Sergio Osmeña is at the far left of the picture, in pith helmet and sunglasses.

OPPOSITE BELOW
General Tomoyuki Yamashita being brought back to his cell during war crimes trials in Manila, 1946.

quickly written constitution. Philippine collaboration in Japanese-sponsored political and administrative institutions – which later became a major domestic political issue – had a variety of motives. Among them was mitigating the harshness of Japanese rule (an effort that Quezon himself had advocated), protection of family and personal interests, and a Pan-Asian interpretation of the future of Philippine nationalism. Many collaborated to pass information to the Allies.

The brutality and arrogance of the Japanese occupation of the Philippines enabled its most remarkable achievement: making the Americans far more popular than they ever had been before 1941. The new face of pro-Americanism was visible in the increasingly effective and widespread guerrilla warfare led by stay-behind Filipino and American officers of the USAFFE, as well as nationalist underground groups and leftist guerrillas that temporarily cooperated, with varying degrees of enthusiasm, with the pro-US forces. An estimated 260,000 people were active guerrillas, supported by even larger numbers of people passively resisting the Japanese occupation. The major element of resistance in the Central Luzon area was furnished by the Huks (*Hukbong Bayan Laban sa Hapon*, or the People's Anti-Japanese Army), organized in early 1942 under the leadership of Luis Taruc, a communist party member since 1939. The Huks armed some 30,000 people and extended their control over much of Luzon.

Prevailing over alternative plans to seize Formosa and bypass the Philippines, Douglas MacArthur's Allied forces landed on the beaches of Leyte on 20 October 1944, after the largest sea battle in history offshore saw the destruction of the remaining striking power of the Imperial Japanese Navy. MacArthur was accompanied by Sergio Osmeña, who had succeeded Manuel Quezon as Commonwealth president after the latter's death in American exile on 1 August 1944. Subsequent landings on Mindoro and Lingayen Gulf began the drive towards Manila, while Cebu, Iloilo and Mindanao were also gradually cleared of Japanese troops.

Fighting was fierce, particularly in the mountains of northern Luzon, where General Tomoyuki Yamashita and the Japanese high command for the Philippines had retreated, and in Manila, where naval troops under Admiral Sanji Iwabuchi ignored Yamashita's orders to leave the capital an open city. Instead, Iwabuchi's stand triggered a month of intense urban fighting, as well as the separate programme of reprisal killings and atrocities known as the Manila Massacre. Fighting between the Japanese and Filipino guerrilla units together with American regular forces continued in upland regions of the Visayas and Luzon until Japan's formal surrender on 2 September 1945. The ensuing Manila Tribunal war crimes trials found high-ranking Japanese officers such as Yamashita and Masaharu Homma guilty of war crimes by command responsibility; the two, along with several others, were executed in the Philippines in 1946.

6

SHOWPLACE OF DEMOCRACY IN ASIA?

The Third Philippine Republic and the Post-war world, 1946–1972

The Philippines saw some of the heaviest fighting in the Second World War. Manila was one of the Allied cities regularly cited as second only to Warsaw in the extent of its destruction by urban combat, but other cities like Cebu and Iloilo saw similar levels of devastation. In many smaller communities across the country, three and a half years of neglected and damaged infrastructure, hunger and disrupted supply systems also left their mark, along with the trauma of Japanese detentions, summary killings, random brutality and mistreatment, confiscations and the effects of population displacement. American bombardment and infantry attack, along with the counterviolence of guerrilla warfare and reprisals against the Japanese and their collaborators, as well as the degeneration of many guerrilla units into banditry and score settling, also contributed to the shredding of the social fabric. On top of all this, the air-dropped supplies and discarded logistics bases of the American campaign to retake the country (or Liberation, as Filipinos of that and later generations learned to describe it) left the country flooded with thousands of unregulated firearms.

Many of these weapons soon fell into the hands of people or groups with little or no connection to the wartime resistance. These were now rapidly evolving into the private political armies, community vigilantes, warlord militias, simple bandits and random goons for hire that have so lovingly preserved the power of the gun in Philippine public life until today. More than a million

OPPOSITE
American sailor on Manila shore leave at a fruit stand.

BELOW
The ruins of Manila's walled city of Intramuros, May 1945.

ABOVE
Philippine guerrillas, 1945.

BELOW
A Willys 'Jeep' restored to its 1943 configuration.

people were initially reported missing, with up to another million estimated dead. The country's export trade had ceased. An estimated 80 per cent of school buildings and their equipment, supplies, and facilities had been damaged or destroyed. Most bridges, roads, harbours, housing, and industrial or commercial premises were either destroyed or in dire need of repair and maintenance. This unprecedented level of material devastation, and the social breakdown that accompanied it, permanently interrupted the somewhat artificial, perhaps unsustainable, but certainly orderly colonial development pattern that had started in the pre-war American and Commonwealth periods. What replaced it was often a material culture of makeshift improvisation, exemplified by the spread of jerry-built, but eventually permanent, 'squatter' settlements on waste lots in the middle of urban areas. Another manifestation of this pattern was the conversion of cast-off American light military vehicles as the early prototype for the minibus-like private 'jeepneys' whose descendants still dominate post-war Philippine roads. In many ways the Philippines has never really recovered from the Second World War.

THE MATERIAL COST OF THE WAR

Initial estimates of the material damage, expressed in the claims the Philippine government eventually laid on Japan, amounted to $4 billion in 1945 dollars (around $48 billion in 2018). Part of this amount was recovered from Japanese assets sequestered in the post-war period inside the country, or in the form of industrial equipment seized in Japan and sent to the Philippines as reparations by Douglas MacArthur, who had moved to Tokyo as the head of the American military occupation government there. The intensifying Cold War soon eliminated the American desire to punish Japan with large reparations, however, in favour of cultivating its industrial strength and prosperity as a bulwark against communism in a US-dominated ring of vassal states in littoral East Asia.

The US itself was the other source of rehabilitation funds. In its case the release of these funds was tied to the compliance of successive Philippine

ABOVE

Sixty years after the end of the Second World War, the classic reconfiguration of a military design into a low-end people mover – a fully loaded jeepney at Carbon market in Cebu City, 2005.

155

TRADE AND AID

Even as Japan's Asian victims protested, the recovery of Japan's economy by the 1950s allowed Tokyo to begin negotiating bilateral agreements for reparations with countries it had occupied during the war; in return Japan once again got access to these countries' internal markets as targets of investments and exports. It can be argued that these arrangements in the end brought more benefits, at least of the material kind, to both sides than the initial one-way reparations demands. By 1956, Japan had agreed to a 10-year schedule of payments to the Philippines of $500 million annually in goods and materials, $30 million in technical assistance and services, $20 million in payments to widows and orphans, and $250 million in long-term loans at advantageous terms. The value in the longer run to the Japanese of regaining access to the Philippines as an investment and export market, and the ultimate consequences for the Philippines of a return to an import-dependent consumer economy, are much harder to quantify.

governments with the priorities of post-war American policy. This link was implicit in the conflicting pressures MacArthur and the administration of President Harry S. Truman exerted on the restored Commonwealth government over three key issues. These were wartime collaboration, access to the Philippine economy for US investors and entrepreneurs, and the role of the Philippines in America's Cold War military and diplomatic posture.

THE ISSUE OF JAPANESE COLLABORATORS

The presence of collaborators among the population was a potentially explosive social and political issue in the early post-war period. Accusations of collaboration, whether founded or unfounded, were instrumentalized in the competition among those who were now jockeying for positions of power and influence in post-war Philippine society and politics. The collaboration issue threatened to become a source of permanent conflict and embitterment that would have damaging effects on the country's ability to recover from the war. Proven or provable Japanese collaborators included prominent social elites, businesspeople and politicians.

Many of these people had also enjoyed close personal ties to MacArthur going back to the Commonwealth period. Although Sergio Osmeña had been duly installed as

BELOW
The destroyed Legislative Building, Manila 1945.

President of the Commonwealth in 1944 after Manuel Quezon had died
in exile, real power lay in the hands of MacArthur as supreme American
commander, the only authority with the means, men and materiel to bring
to the task of restoring order and government in the country. Even after
MacArthur himself left the Philippines for his next post as supervisor of the
occupation of Japan, his policies and preferences continued to set the tone
of Philippine affairs. Osmeña did not have a smooth working relationship
with MacArthur, who considered him too old, uncharismatic and insufficiently compliant with American priorities.

Osmeña, however, was under pressure from Truman and most of the
US Congress to ensure a serious reckoning with collaborators, both because
of evident popular sentiment and because they believed that such a process
would provide a solid foundation for the rule of law in the post-war period.
Truman's cabinet made the release of US rehabilitation funds dependent on
an evaluation of each collaboration case, for which Osmeña set up a special
'People's Court' in Manila. MacArthur, however, subscribed to a different
philosophy, also evident in the Cold-War-driven decisions of US occupation

157

officials in Germany and Japan, to quickly cease serious denazification and demilitarization efforts in those enemy countries except for the most egregious war criminals. About 5,000 accused collaborators were supposed to be tried before the Manila People's Court, but only 15 judges and 25 prosecutors were available to handle this caseload, and they were meant to wind up their work within six months. Even before the court began its proceedings, MacArthur had already pre-emptively exonerated the prominent politician Manuel Roxas, the American general's personal favourite for future Philippine leader over Osmeña, from the collaboration charges likely over his wartime record.

MANUEL ROXAS

Roxas had already enjoyed a successful pre-war political career. Born in 1882 in the province of Capiz on Panay island into a prominent principalia family that claimed Spanish mestizo connections, Roxas was appointed Governor of Capiz by the colonial government in 1919. From 1921 to 1938 he was one of the province's representatives in the colonial Philippine Legislature, where he replaced Osmeña as Speaker of the House from 1922 to 1933. He was active in the drafting of the 1935 constitution, and was Quezon's Secretary of Finance when the war broke out. He had also been elected to the Senate in 1941, but the war prevented him from serving. Mobilized as a lieutenant colonel, he developed a good working relationship with MacArthur as liaison officer between the Commonwealth Government and the USAFFE. He had been designated as emergency head of state should Quezon and Osmeña not have made it safely to Australia.

After being captured in Mindanao and refusing pressure to collaborate for a year, Roxas started working with the Japanese occupation on issues of food supplies for the population. Jose P. Laurel, the President of the Japanese-sponsored Second Republic, briefly appointed Roxas to head the Economic Planning Board and the National Rice Authority (*Bigasang*

Bayan), agencies responsible for coordinating food and logistics to cope with the requisitioning needs of the Japanese military.

After the retreat of the Japanese army to northern Luzon, Roxas resumed contact with the incoming US military. MacArthur publicly embraced him, reappointing him again as a general to his personal staff and vouching for his patriotism. Roxas quickly took up his deferred seat in the Commonwealth Senate, which promptly elected him Speaker. MacArthur, however, wanted presidential elections held as early as possible before the scheduled termination of the Commonwealth in 1946. He sought a pliable, pro-American candidate, one strong enough to beat Osmeña in time for the negotiations that would determine the basis of the political, military and economic relationship between the US and the soon-to-be-independent Philippines.

Roxas, however, was still a member of the Nacionalista Party (as were most mainstream Filipino politicians), which was fielding the incumbent Osmeña as presidential candidate in 1946. Roxas broke away from the Nacionalistas early that year to found the Liberal Party, the country's second-oldest, still-functioning political party, and ran as its candidate for president.

INDEPENDENCE – A REAL TWO-PARTY SYSTEM?

Although the Liberals technically provided the modern Philippines with a major opposition party – an essential element of electoral democracies – there was little to distinguish the Liberal from the Nacionalista platform; the electoral contest was *ostensibly* over who could achieve broadly similar goals more effectively. On an even more fundamental level than mere policy, however, the real purpose of the Liberal Party was to act as a vehicle for Roxas's personal political ambitions. By founding a whole new party as a vehicle for this career move, Roxas was setting a precedent for many future post-war Filipino politicians. Many Nacionalistas began crossing over to him, scenting the direction the political winds were blowing.

The Commonwealth elections of April 1946 brought victory to Roxas and his vice-president, Elpidio Quirino. Apart from ending the political career of Sergio Osmeña, by that time truly the 'grand old man' of Philippine politics, and breaking the almost half-century-long Nacionalista monopoly on power, the victory also brought useful majorities for the Liberals in the House and Senate of the new Philippine Congress. Three months afterwards,

BELOW
Manuel A. Roxas.

159

on 4 July 1946, the long-promised handover of sovereignty from the US to an independent Republic of the Philippines took place on schedule, marked by ceremonies at the Luneta. There, at the monument to Rizal, flanked by the walls of old Spanish Intramuros and the battle-scarred reminders of just-ended American hegemony in the Manila Hotel, the Army and Navy Club, and the Embassy, the Stars and Stripes were lowered for the last time. Roxas, the last president of the Commonwealth, became the first president of the Third Philippine Republic, as the flag raised during Aguinaldo's proclamation of the First Republic in 1898 unfurled over the crowd.

The true meaning of this independence still needed to be worked out via the diplomatic, military and trade agreements that were struck between the US and the Philippines during Roxas's time in office. In Japan, MacArthur was making genuine efforts to reform the social structure and political system in order to stabilize a new Cold War American ally, with measures such as authentic land reform, effective labour unions and the break-up of the

BELOW
An independent Philippine Republic is inaugurated, 4 July 1946.

giant *zaibatsu* corporations central to the pre-war Japanese military-industrial complex. In the newly independent Philippines, the means to the same end were different. MacArthur had supported Roxas's rise to power because of the Filipino politician's readiness to quickly move past the collaboration issue and reunify the old, elite (and reliably anti-communist) pre-war establishment in the Philippines. As in previous political environments, these people had a vested interest in the continued influence and power of the US over the young republic, as a guarantor of their own dominant political and economic position in a deeply unequal society.

AMERICAN CONDITIONS

In the months around the independence proclamation, two important pieces of American legislation were presented for ratification to the Philippine Congress. The Philippine Rehabilitation Act (PRA) set an upper limit of $1.24 billion in cash and materiel that the Americans would pay out for the estimated $4 billion in total war damage claims. Additional funds were earmarked for the new Philippine Army, on condition that outstanding pension benefits promised in 1941 to Filipinos who fought alongside US forces were withdrawn (it would take 60 years of agitation against this injustice until a modest lump-sum payment was finally awarded to the few aged survivors in 2009).

While the Liberal-dominated Philippine Congress quickly ratified the PRA, the Philippine Trade Act (or Bell Act) was more problematic. In exchange for a 30-year timetable for the phasing in of full tariffs for Philippine exports to the US, the Act restricted the Philippines indefinitely from manufacturing products that might compete with a schedule of American goods, thus providing an unfair advantage for these 'stateside' imports. It also gave the US Treasury the power to peg the Philippine peso at a fixed exchange rate to the US dollar. But the section of the Act that drew the most ire in Manila was its so-called 'parity rights' clause, which gave US investors the same rights to develop the country's resources and operate public utilities as Filipinos. This ran counter to a provision in the 1935 Commonwealth constitution that required at least 60 per cent Filipino ownership of all corporations formed to develop or exploit the country's national resources. The issue had to be resolved by a special 'parity rights' plebiscite that authorized the Philippine Congress to amend the constitution to allow the PTA's provisions for American ownership. After the nationwide plebiscite was carried out in 1947, the amendment passed by a single vote, and only because the Roxas administration and its allies among the Liberal Party delegates successfully prevented seven representatives and three senators from the opposition who had spoken out against the change from voting, via trumped-up charges of electoral fraud.

By early 1948, Roxas had also issued a blanket amnesty for all accused wartime collaborators and pardoned the 156 convicted out of the more

ABOVE

All over the Philippines, plaques like this, often obscured under later layers of paint, can still be found on older public buildings, indicating their restoration or replacement in the 1940s and '50s with American funds after wartime damage.

MILITARY TIES

Two more bilateral agreements in 1947 perpetuated the powerful American military presence in the Philippines, and ensured that the country would remain a platform for projecting US hard power across all of Asia. The Military Bases Agreement (MBA) extended the leases on two of the largest American military installations in the world – Clark Air Base and Subic Bay Naval Base – and about 21 other smaller bases and facilities all over the country, to 99 years. Accompanying the MBA was the Military Assistance Agreement (MAA), which attached a Joint US Military Assistance Group (JUSMAG) to the Philippine Armed Forces and provided for advanced training of Filipino military officers in the US. Much of JUSMAG's training, logistical support and advisory oversight was geared towards the Philippine military's role in identifying and combating internal security threats from the Filipino population itself, and not outwards national defence against foreign aggressors.

BELOW LEFT: *Aerial photo of Clark Air Base at a later phase of its history, in 1989. McDonnell Douglas F-4E and F-4G Phantom II fighter-bombers, Lockheed C-130 Hercules transports and a single Lockheed C-141 Starlifter heavy transport are visible parked around the runways.*

BELOW RIGHT: *Subic Bay Naval Base, 1981.*

than 5,000 such cases that lay pending, essentially removing any possibility of extending the operations of the People's Court. The amnesty brought reassurance for the powerful landlords and elites who made up much of Roxas's base that there would be no internal conflicts among them over their wartime activities that might weaken the dominance of their class as a whole over Philippine society. The marriage of convenience between elite and American interests represented by many of the policies of the Roxas administration would, however, have its own destabilizing consequences.

CORRUPTION, OLIGARCHY AND STIFLED DISSENT

The first point of contention was the perpetuation of a post-war culture of massive corruption, already prefigured in wartime profiteering on the black market. The Americans, dependent on the old oligarchy to maintain stability, were ready to ignore the blatant misappropriation of funds, war surplus and relief material made possible by the weak oversight of the central state throughout the rehabilitation period. The pattern quickly spread from those with authority over post-war relief and rehabilitation resources, and soon pervaded much of the rest of the underpaid government bureaucracy. In departments such as highways, customs and many others, an institutional culture of bribes and kickbacks emerged in the late 1940s Philippine civil service, which has persisted until today.

The second, even more grave, consequence of the American readiness to rely on a conservative oligarchy for stability in their client state was the continued absence of ways to address legitimate social and economic discontent from the broad population within the bounds of acceptable mainstream politics. In the context of a global Cold War, any criticism of the prevailing system of power and wealth distribution was immediately tagged as 'subversive' by a ruling elite that knew how to play on America's preoccupation with communism to stay in power. Among other ways this conflict would play out was the government's response to the resurgence by the later 1940s of the Huks. This serious armed insurgency in the post-war Luzon countryside, born out of wartime leftist guerrilla resistance to the Japanese, was an inconvenient and embarrassing reproach to American efforts to portray the Philippines as a showcase of their style of democracy in Asia.

ABOVE
US Department of State anti-Huk propaganda in Ilocano, a northern Philippine language.

THE HUK REBELLION

The Huk leadership finally decided to resume armed struggle against the government after the Democratic Alliance representatives to Congress were prevented from voting on the Parity Amendment to the constitution. The Huk Rebellion was led by Luis Taruc, a former wartime guerrilla fighter and one of the Democratic Alliance representatives excluded from

THE HUKS IN THE POST-WAR PHILIPPINES

During the war, Hukbalahap units had cautiously co-operated with pro-American guerrilla forces in the common anti-Japanese struggle, and communist forces controlled many areas in rural and small-town Luzon at the end of hostilities. The Japanese occupation had only put a temporary hold on the pre-war push for social justice in the countryside. Returning landlords who had fled to urban areas during the fighting returned to the villages in late 1945, employing military police and their own armed bodyguards to demand back rent. However, guerrilla veterans among the tenant farmers were not as willing to be intimidated by landlords as they had been before 1942. The Japanese surrender after

MacArthur's return had been the signal for US Army units and the reconstituted Philippine Constabulary to begin eliminating and suppressing Huk units they came across in the countryside, even if the latter had cooperated with them in the anti-Japanese struggle. Echoing tensions between left and right in wartime anti-fascist insurgencies that escalated into post-war civil conflicts in Greece, Yugoslavia, China and Vietnam (and to a lesser degree in Indonesia, France and Italy), the early post-war period witnessed the swift disappointment of the Huk leadership's hopes of being able to transition from armed conflict to a share in peaceful political decision-making in the new republic.

BELOW

One of the last photographs of Roxas on a visit to Clark Air Base, where he died in 1948.

the parity vote. Issuing an ultimatum to Roxas, Taruc went underground and began rebuilding the Huk combat structure, changing the name of the HUK movement from the People's Anti-Japanese Army (*Hukbong Bayan Laban sa Hapon*) to the People's Liberation Army (*Hukbong Mapagpalaya ng Bayan*). It numbered 15,000 armed individuals by 1950, as the Huk leadership got busy re-establishing the infrastructure of alternative local

governments, taxation, arbitration courts and community services in rural areas that had lapsed after the war. Roxas alternated between negotiation and harsh suppression in his policies towards the Huks. He set up an Agrarian Commission and mandated 70 per cent of the harvest earnings to go to tenants, although this was extremely difficult to enforce. The Huks demanded reinstatement of the Democratic Alliance in Congress; disbandment of the military police and the pullback of the constabulary; and a general amnesty that left them with their weapons. In March 1948, Roxas instead declared the Huks an illegal and subversive organization, and threw more resources and armed units into the counter-insurgency push. He would not see the full extent of the resulting civil conflict, or its outcome, dying on 15 April 1948 of a heart attack while a guest of the US on a visit to Clark Air Base. His vice-president, Elpidio Quirino, also from the Labour Party, served out the remainder of Roxas's term and was elected president in his own right in 1949.

The Huk rebellion peaked around 1950. Quirino had been elected president on the Liberal ticket, amid much violence and intimidation at rural polling places. This drove even more farmers to the Huks, who had 11,000–15,000 armed fighters by the following year. Although their heartland remained in Central Luzon, active Huk operations began in the rest of the island, and in some agrarian areas of the Visayas and Mindanao.

ABOVE
President Quirino receiving Luis Taruc and other Huk leaders at Malacañang Palace.

MAGSAYSAY AND THE QUIET AMERICAN

By 1951, better-trained, US-equipped and -advised Philippine Army soldiers and constabulary units, and more generous assistance to peasants from the Quirino government, were only two of the factors in the successful roll-back of the insurgency. A further crucial contribution was the combined efforts of the Filipino politician Ramon Magsaysay and Colonel Edward Lansdale, Magsaysay's CIA handler. Magsaysay was a member of Congress from Zambales Province and veteran of a non-Huk guerrilla unit during the war who became Quirino's secretary of defence in 1950. Under Lansdale's tutelage, he pursued a sophisticated counter-insurgency campaign to defeat the insurgents militarily, and at the same time win popular support for the government. Along with techniques such as targeted assassinations, generous welfare and community assistance, and disinformation, Lansdale's experience as an advertising executive led to innovative approaches such as the use of traditional folk beliefs in psychological warfare, and blanket media coverage of Magsaysay as a charismatic, constantly smiling, larger-than-life champion of the ordinary man, blessed with the common touch.

ABOVE
Edward Lansdale.

RIGHT
Cosmopolitanism, Cold-War style in Manila. The 1953 International Fair featured a live performance of Arthur Koestler's anti-communist play Darkness at Noon *by a Filipino repertory company at the Catholic pavilion.*

BELOW RIGHT
The Magsaysays and Eleanor Roosevelt in the 1950s.

BELOW
Ramon Magsaysay.

Quirino grew increasingly wary of Magsaysay's popularity as defence secretary and possible rival, and coordination of anti-Huk policy suffered. To insure continuity of the counter-insurgency campaign, Magsaysay bolted the Liberals and was nominated as the Nacionalista Party's presidential candidate in the 1953 elections. He won almost two-thirds of the vote, against the best efforts of Quirino's publicists. Once in office, Magsaysay turned up the intensity of his persona as a man of the ordinary people ('the common *tao*', as his own publicists put it). He opened the doors of the presidential Malacañang Palace to thousands of peasants and labourers (adding that bare feet were always welcome) and encouraged people to send him telegrams, free of charge, with their complaints.

The capture and killing of Huk leaders, the dissolution of Huk regional committees, and finally the surrender of Taruc in May 1954 marked the waning of the Huk threat.

GARCIA AND DISCREET NATIONALISM

At the height of his popularity and power, Magsaysay died when his aircraft crashed into a mountainside

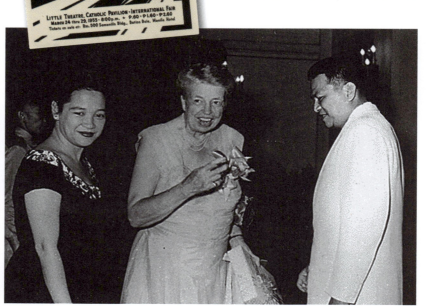

HOMESTEADING INTO CONFLICT

With American aid, small-scale but highly visible projects – the building of bridges, roads, irrigation canals and artesian 'liberty wells', special courts for landlord-tenant disputes, agricultural extension services and credit for farmers – were given favourable press coverage. The CIA-sponsored Economic Development Corps (EDCOR) project settled some 20,500 Huk families on government-purchased land on Mindanao. A continuation of similar homesteading projects on the large southern island from the Commonwealth period, EDCOR promoted the settlement of poor people from the Christian north in traditionally Muslim areas. Although it relieved population pressures in insurgency-prone Luzon and Panay, like similar *transmigrasi* projects from overpopulated Java to other parts of contemporary Indonesia, it also exacerbated centuries-old hostilities between different religious communities in Mindanao for the rest of the 20th century.

north of Cebu City in March 1957. His vice-president, Carlos P. Garcia, was immediately sworn in as his replacement. In the same year, Garcia won election in his own right to a whole presidential term. Garcia maintained the essential aspects of the Philippines' role as a reliable ally of the US, but took a more nationalist tone in relations with the Americans, including a more nativist approach to economic management. He renegotiated the military bases agreements with the US in 1959, taking back control of large base areas no longer required for their operation. After a heated and prolonged public debate, the Congress finally approved a bill outlawing the Communist Party of the Philippines (PKP), and Garcia signed the bill into law on 1 June 1957. Garcia also instituted an austerity programme to reduce rice imports to a minimum, overhaul the transport system to reduce the importation of petrol and spare parts, achieve more progressive distribution of the tax burden, restrict government imports to essential items and intensify food production.

In an effort to achieve whatever economic sovereignty was possible, Garcia introduced a 'Filipino First Policy'. He implemented the tax incentives and the controls on access to foreign exchange and repatriation of earnings abroad already envisioned by nationalists as far back as the Quirino administration, to counteract the advantages enjoyed in the Philippines by

ABOVE
One of the last photos of Ramon Magsaysay, on the eve of his departure from Cebu City. The flight the next day would crash into Mt Manunggal outside the city, killing all on board except for one journalist. Cebu City mayor Sergio Osmeña, Jr and his father, former President Sergio Osmeña, are on either side of the smiling Magsaysay.

ABOVE
Vice-President Carlos P. Garcia cut short his trip abroad to SEATO allies to fly back home and take over the presidency after Magsaysay's death.

US businesses. Garcia's critics charged that the post-war plague of public corruption that began with the management of rehabilitation funds and war surplus had now found a new form in the unofficial patronage networks and kickback systems that developed to cope with the regulations of the foreign exchange and import control bureaucracies. Garcia's more nationalist allies also pressed for pro-Filipino changes in laws governing retail trade that greatly affected the 'Chinese' business community. The latter reacted by deepening their patronage links with the political dynasties perceived to be non-Chinese, accelerating an ongoing process of intermarriage and blended cultures among many middle-class families, and challenging the government's definition of who was Filipino.

Despite Garcia's efforts to preserve some autonomy vis-à-vis US trade and military policies, the Philippines of the late 1950s probably also reached the country's high-water mark of receptiveness to American popular and high culture – and not just among the urban, better-educated elements in the population. Those of the generation that had gone to elementary schools in towns and countryside during the Commonwealth period were now entering the adult phases of their lives armed with a working knowledge of colloquial 1930s American English. Although the quality of English instruction in schools began to degrade somewhat (to reach a crisis point by the 1970s), Filipinos' command of the language was nevertheless constantly reinforced after 1945 by the ever-expanding range of high-, middle- and especially lowbrow offerings in journalism, literature and non-fiction writing that became available on the mass market. Meanwhile, film and radio coverage and the new medium of television were projecting the output of the American popular-culture industries into the ears and retinas of most Filipinos around the clock. In addition, the availability of consumer products and other manifestations of American material culture was reaching a new level of intensity during this decade.

RESTORING THE FREE MARKET AND FIGHTING CORRUPTION

The 1957 election had for the first time produced a vice-president, Diosdado Macapagal, who came from a different political party than the president. In the 1961 elections, Macapagal ran for president and won in his own right as the candidate of the Liberal Party. The accusations of corruption in Garcia's Filipino First Program played a large part in Macapagal's successful campaign to portray himself as 'The Incorruptible'. Decades before neo-liberal efforts to dismantle the regulatory state in most other parts of the free world, Macapagal promised a full commitment to free and private enterprise. Exchange controls were lifted, and the peso was allowed to float on international exchange markets. It promptly devalued from 2.64 pesos to the US dollar and stabilized at 3.80 pesos, with a downwards trend until the end of the 20th century.

ABOVE

Diosdado Macapagal on the bridge of the USS Oklahoma City, *1962. All Filipino presidents have had myriad photo opportunities showing them visiting American representatives, many of the latter military.*

Yet a semi-official programme providing for some level of government involvement in the direction of the economy was formulated by private economists and business leaders, who came up with the socialistic-sounding 'Five-Year Socio-Economic Integrated Development Program'. In this scheme, the government would no longer intervene in currency controls or import/export quotas, but it would promote key private industries, particularly those that required capital infusions too large for businessmen to put up by themselves. Among the enterprises selected for active government promotion were integrated steel production, fertilizers, wood pulp and paper products, meat canning and processing, and tourism. Supported by a $300 million stabilization loan from the International Monetary Fund, Macapagal was able to achieve steady economic progress, and annual GDP growth averaged at 5.53 per cent for 1962–1965.

Like Magsaysay, Macapagal made much of his humble origins as a 'poor boy from Lubao'. Unlike the perpetually grinning and charismatic Magsaysay, however, Macapagal had very little popular appeal due to his stiff personality. Nevertheless, he made a serious effort to tackle the perennial problem of rural tenancy and inequality with the Agricultural Land Reform Code of 1963, which encouraged the purchase of private estates for division among landless tenants on easy terms of payment. In an effort to get around the loopholes that had stymied earlier land-reform efforts, it lowered the maximum retention limit to 75ha (0.75km²), whether owned by individuals or corporations, removed the term 'contiguous', established a legally defined system of leaseholding, and prohibited the sharecropping or *kasama* system. It assured agricultural workers the right to self-organization and a minimum wage.

The law was, however, predictably watered down by powerful landowning lobbies in Congress. Major exemptions were added: plantations with large levels of capitalization established during the late-Spanish and American periods, fishponds, salt beds, and land primarily planted to valuable tree crops such as citrus, cacao, durian, coffee, coconuts and other similar permanent trees. Landholdings converted to residential, industrial, commercial or other similar non-agricultural purposes were also exempted, fuelling an early speculative boom in subdivisions and suburban developments around Manila, Cebu and some other cities. The 75ha limit proved to be impracticably large for encouraging land distribution. Congress originally allotted only 1 million pesos for the implementation of this code and only raised this by small increments yearly, when at least 200 million pesos a

RIGHT

Macapagal's version of the cult of the common tao (common man) included the government's subsequent decision to preserve his boyhood home – a modest house walled and roofed with dried nipa fronds – as a national cultural property.

THE SABAH CLAIM

During Macapagal's administration, a historical dynastic claim to sovereignty over the territory of eastern North Borneo (now Sabah) was ceded by the heirs of the Sultanate of Sulu to the Philippine government. The Philippines then took the view that this cession gave it the full authority to pursue a claim to eastern Sabah in international courts. After a British-guided independence process had seen the Sabah population vote to join a new federated Malaysia in 1963, the Philippines broke off relations with the new Malaysian state. Although succeeding Philippine administrations have placed the claim on the back-burner in the interest of pursuing cordial economic and security relations with Kuala Lumpur, an opposite and parallel undertone of irredentism, persistent legal challenge and occasional armed provocation had persisted in unofficial Philippine circles regarding the Sabah issue. Even as the Sabah issue was emerging, Macapagal sought closer relations with the neighbouring Southeast Asian countries, proposing a loose regional federation called MAPHILINDO, after the first syllables of Malaysia, the Philippines

ABOVE: *Sabah politicians declare accession of the state to Malaysia, 1963.*

and Indonesia, promoting it as a realization of Rizal's vision of linking the Malay peoples. However, the continuing armed confrontation between Indonesia and newly established Malaysia, the Philippines' unresolved claim to Sabah, and suspicions of Manila's role as a base for clandestine CIA armed interventions in Indonesia all ensured that MAPHILINDO never really got off the ground.

year from the enactment and 300 million in the next three years was needed for the programme to be successful. By 1972, the code had benefited only 4,500 peasants covering 68 estates, at the cost of 57 million pesos to the government.

FERDINAND MARCOS, AND THE REPUBLIC IN CRISIS?

Ferdinand E. Marcos, the Nacionalista candidate in the 1965 elections, won and succeeded Macapagal as president. Marcos would dominate Philippine politics for the next two decades as an elected president in 1965 and 1969, then as a dictator after his proclamation of martial law in 1972. He was born into the usual locally prominent circumstances in Ilocos Norte province in northern Luzon, a relatively poor, hilly region also reminiscent in other ways of pre-modern Scotland, with its high rates of emigration, clannish politics and a perhaps undeserved reputation for tight-fistedness. Marcos was a brilliant law student who successfully reversed his own murder conviction

A NEW/OLD INDEPENDENCE DATE

In an effort to attract more nationalist support to his administration, in 1962 Macapagal shifted the commemoration of Philippine Independence Day from 4 July, the date it was granted by the Americans in 1946 (it is also the date of American Independence Day), to 12 June 1962, in commemoration of the declaration of independence from Spain on that date in 1898. In the same way that encouraging a nationalist cult around the non-violent Rizal over that of the revolutionary Bonifacio had suited the priorities of the American colonial regime, the shift of independence date was a relatively effortless way to move the chameleon-like Aguinaldo and the fratricidal revolutionary Katipunan from their ambiguous positions in historical Philippine politics into the mainstream of official national memory. Linked to Macapagal's nation-building challenge to fight the 'Unfinished Revolution', the change became permanent in 1964 with the signing of Republic Act No. 4166, which coincided with Aguinaldo's death that same year after a long, Zelig-like life. Years later, Macapagal shared with American journalist Stanley Karnow a more personal reason for the change: 'When I was in the diplomatic corps, I noticed that nobody came to our receptions on the Fourth of July, but went to the American Embassy instead. So, to compete, I decided we needed a different holiday.'

before the Philippine Supreme Court in the late 1930s, after being convicted of shooting a political rival of his father. He fought in the 1942 Battle of Bataan, then claimed, spuriously, to have led a distinguished guerrilla unit, the Maharlikas. Marcos was elected to the House of Representatives in 1949 and to the Senate a decade later. His marriage to Imelda Romualdez in 1954 brought him a glamorous partner, one with family connections to a powerful regional political dynasty from Leyte in the Visayas.

RIGHT
President Ferdinand Marrcos and his wife Imelda in a private conference in Manila with US President Lyndon Johnson, 1966.

LEFT
*Heads of state of the
South East Asian Treaty
Organization in front of
the Philippine Congress
building, 1966.*

BELOW
*A member of the Philippine
Civic Action Group
distributes medicines in
South Vietnam, 1966–1967.*

In a foretaste of developments during his later dictatorship, Marcos's first elected term was marked by well-publicized public-works projects – roads, bridges, schools, health centres, irrigation facilities and urban beautification schemes – intended to improve the quality of life while also funnelling benefits to his friends. However, he hewed to an older pattern already in place in previous administrations, of periodically announcing ambitious plans every few years to finally do something about land reform, but never seriously implementing any of them for fear of alienating the powerful landlord lobbies in Congress.

Marcos actively sought economic and military aid from the US, but unlike Magsaysay during the Korean conflict, resisted pressure from President Lyndon Johnson to become militarily involved in the Second Indochina War. The Philippines contribution was limited to a 2,000-member Civic Action Group sent to South Vietnam between 1966 and 1969. Under Marcos, the Philippines became a founding member of the Association of Southeast Asian Nations (ASEAN) in 1967. The dispute over Sabah with fellow ASEAN member Malaysia

ABOVE
Student protesters outside the Old Legislative Building where Marcos is delivering his State of the Nation address, 1970.

continued, however, and relations between the two countries remained strained after discovery of special units being trained by the Philippine army to infiltrate Sabah.

Marcos was re-elected as president in 1969, the first president in the independent Philippines to gain a second full elected term. However, the optimism that characterized his first years in power had largely dissipated. Economic growth had slowed. Ordinary people, especially in urban areas, experienced a deteriorating quality of life, and a spiral in crime rates and random violence. A new and different type of communist insurgency replaced that of the Huks and the old PKP. A new 'Communist Party of the Philippines-Marxist Leninist', usually referred to as the CPP, was founded in 1968 along Maoist lines in Tarlac province north of Manila. The CPP's military arm, the New People's Army (NPA), soon spread from Tarlac to other parts of the archipelago. In the south, violence between Muslims and Christians, the latter often recent government-sponsored immigrants, was escalating. In response, the insurgent Moro National Liberation Front (MNLF) was organized on Malaysian soil and supported by some Islamic states such as Libya.

The reaction to Marcos's second inauguration into office reflected general dissatisfaction with one of the most dishonest elections in the history of the Philippines, along with concern that Marcos might manipulate changes to the 1935 constitution to maintain himself in power. On 30 January 1970, the 'Battle of Mendiola' (a street in front of the presidential Malacañang

CONSTITUTIONAL CHANGE

A broad consensus had emerged across all political groupings that the American-authored 1935 constitution ought to be replaced by a new document that would enable thorough-going reform of the political system. In 1967, a bill had passed mandating a constitutional convention; delegates to the convention were elected three years later. The convention first met in June 1971. The 1935 constitution limited a presidency to two terms. Fearing that a proposed change to a parliamentary system would allow Marcos to stay in power indefinitely, opponents prevailed on the convention to adopt a provision banning the incumbent Marcos and his family from further eligibility under whatever arrangement was finally established. Marcos, via bribes and intimidation, got the ban nullified the following summer.

LEFT
Plaza Miranda in 2011. The square has been renovated since the 1971 explosion. The obelisk with a figure on top is a memorial to the event.

BELOW
Headline of a Marcos-controlled newspaper, 24 September 1972.

Palace) saw student demonstrators trying to enter the palace clash bloodily with riot police, kicking off a three-month period of intense and often violent street demonstrations known among leftists as the First Quarter Storm.

At this point, random bombings officially blamed on communists but possibly set by government agents provocateurs, began to inflame the atmosphere even more in Manila and other large cities. Grenade explosions during an opposition Liberal Party legislative election rally at Plaza Miranda on 21 August 1971 killed nine people and wounded 100 more, eight of the latter Liberal Party candidates for the Senate. Marcos blamed communists, and suspended habeas corpus. The exact responsibility for the blast has remained unclear.

Even if Marcos could have run again in 1973, however, pundits expected a likely defeat by an arch-rival, Senator Benigno 'Ninoy' Aquino. That election would take place, but under circumstances very few would have expected, and without Aquino's participation. On 23 September 1972, Ferdinand Marcos proclaimed a state of martial law over the entire archipelago. The proclamation document was actually dated 21 September, which is the date historians use as the official start of the authoritarian regime under which Marcos would rule the Philippines for the next thirteen and a half years. It would take Aquino's death, the deaths of thousands of others and the suffering of many thousands more in an increasingly impoverished country to end it.

7

THE 'NEW SOCIETY' AND ITS AFTERMATH

The Marcos Dictatorship, Its Victims, and the Aquinos, 1970–1992

The incident that provided the pretext for the coming of dictatorship to the Philippines was an attempt, allegedly by communists, to assassinate Marcos's Secretary of National Defense, Juan Ponce Enrile. As Enrile himself admitted after Marcos's downfall in 1986, it was a faked excuse; his unoccupied car had been riddled by machine-gun bullets fired by his own men on 22 September, the night after the official date of Proclamation 1081, the Declaration of Martial Law (Marcos had signed it on the 17th and proclaimed it on the 23rd). The document contained six 'general orders' regarding its implementation. In them, Marcos affirmed his sole and complete control of the government and armed forces. The entire civil administrative system from national to local level, and all provincial, district and local governments, were to continue their routine functioning. The regular courts were also to operate as normal – except for a running list of cases that the government took out of their control.

The military, as in normal times, was under the command of the president through his defence secretary. However, the latter was now authorized to arrest and hold indefinitely a revolving list of persons provided by the president's office. The entire country lay under a curfew from midnight to four o'clock in the morning; anyone then out of doors had to have a specific authorization, or risked arrest and detention. Strikes, demonstrations, rallies and all other forms

OPPOSITE
Cory Aquino in 1992.

BELOW
Associated Press wire report from the very first hours of martial law.

Philippines Defense **Chief Escapes Shooting**
A police officer inspects the car of Philippine Defense Secretary Juan Ponce Enrile after it was peppered with bullets by unidentified gunman in a suburb of Manila late Friday. Enrile, who was in another car, escaped unhurt. Uniformed Philippine police took over the offices of the Manila Times and The Associated Press according to informed sources, and press communications were cut off. The development took place a few hours after the assassination attempt on Enrile.

Top commanders of the military, police and security forces at a briefing for President Marcos. Such images projected public messages that the country was in safe and capable hands while the demolition of democratic structures and processes was still going on.

of mass assembly or 'group actions' in public and in private places were prohibited. Finally, a firearms ban was imposed over the whole country. In the coming months and years, Filipinos would grow accustomed to a higher military and police presence on the streets, checkpoints and censorship of news, as well as periodic anti-jaywalking campaigns with violators doing push-ups on the streets, soldiers walking around with scissors ostentatiously cutting off the hair of long-haired males and other efforts at symbolic social discipline.

In the special programming in the weeks and months after September 1972 that replaced regular television, newspaper stories and radio programming, the regime's spokesmen – many of them military – spelt out the goals of martial law. It would eliminate the threat of a violent overthrow of the republic from both left and right, end corruption in government and law enforcement, bring back peace and order, minimize violent crime, revitalize the country's economy, and restore public trust and confidence in the government. Particular targets singled out were the private armies controlled by traditional politicians, regional warlords and radical political organizations, and the general culture of firearms and violence that pervaded the country.

Critics pointed out, however, that existing laws already gave the president enough power to address all these issues; he did not need martial law to do so. What the declaration uniquely enabled was an interruption in the normal operations of government, including regularly scheduled elections, for the duration of the declared emergency. The office of vice-president was abolished; although the courts were mentioned and enjoined to maintain their normal duties and cooperate more fully with the executive, the Congress was shut down, its facilities occupied by the military and many of its members placed under arrest. Marcos assigned himself the power to legislate by presidential decree.

Marcos termed his governing approach 'constitutional authoritarianism', and glibly deployed more jargon from the then-fashionable ideology of developmental technocracy to give his regime a veneer of legitimacy and

REPRESSION

The arrests began with prominent political opponents such as senators Benigno Aquino, Jose Diokno, Sergio Osmeña, Jr and Eugenio Lopez, Jr – the last from the same Lopez clan as Marcos's vice-president. The Lopezes were of particular interest because of their prominence as a symbol of the old oligarchical structure, as well as their widespread holdings in the media. Shortly before Enrile's fake ambush and the declaration of martial law, Aquino had presented before Congress evidence of a military campaign to stage provocative incidents and blame radical organizations for them as a justification for martial law. Marcos denied this, but Aquino nevertheless found himself under arrest on charges of sedition and illegal firearms possession. By 1977, he had been sentenced to death by a military tribunal, although this was not carried out for fear of creating a martyr. He was later allowed to leave the country for medical treatment. Diokno had been secretary of justice under Macapagal, and had made numerous enemies during his anti-corruption investigations. Released from military custody in 1974, he quickly became a champion of the estimated 30,000 politicians, social activists, journalists, community leaders, regime critics, actual insurgents and anti-democratic extremists, and others caught up in the initial wave of arrests and arbitrary open detentions, as well as the many further thousands of others subsequently arrested and held without trial in the subsequent 14 years of the Marcos regime.

effectiveness. He made frequent allusions to such successfully authoritarian places as Singapore, Taiwan and South Korea (with their very different Confucian cultural heritage and colonial histories) as models for his national renewal project. Although the regime also had obvious similarities with the packaging and contents of the contemporary 'guided democracy' under Suharto in neighbouring Indonesia, Marcos preferred to proclaim that the Philippines was embarked on the building of a 'New Society', echoing Lyndon Johnson's Great Society programme.

In numerous ghostwritten books with titles like *Today's Revolution-Democracy, Progress and Martial Law* and *The New Philippine Republic – A*

LEFT
Police deployed against student demonstrators on the University of the Philippines campus during the martial law years.

Third World Approach to Democracy, Marcos and his propaganda specialists under information minister Francisco Tatad sketched a reinvigorated polity saved from extremism by the commitment, discipline, and sacrifice of its patriots and its youth. While breaking up the entrenched power and corruption of the old elites and ensuring social justice for a newly mobilized and disciplined population, the regime would hold the line with its security forces to crack down on conservative warlords and their private armies, as well as a radical left that abused its civil liberties to destabilize the country. In an effort to replace the old oligarchical political parties as well as the leftist mass movements, the regime created its own 'spontaneous' mass political base in the New Society Movement (*Kilusang Bagong Lipunan*,

GUARDIANS OF THE AUTHORITARIAN STATE

The main bases of support for the dictatorship were the military and police. The Armed Forces of the Philippines (AFP), which had inherited a tradition of apolitical professionalism and respect for civilian primacy from its parent, the US military, became in the Marcos years a powerful political actor in its own right. Marcos enabled this shift from the military's original non-partisan ethos by ensuring that key senior appointments went to officers from the Ilocos region, his home province. Shared regional origins and personal loyalty to Marcos counted more than talent or a distinguished service record in promotion and command assignments. A prominent example was Fabian Ver, formerly a chauffeur and a childhood friend of Marcos who became AFP chief-of-staff and head of the regime's internal security apparatus. While the Philippines did not develop the kind of full-blown, military-owned sector of the economy – with proprietary farms, property holdings and factories – as was the case in Turkey, Pakistan and Indonesia, military personnel received upgraded salaries and generous housing, welfare and

other amenities. The number of active-duty generals appointed to run or sit on the boards of various civilian businesses, foundations, non-governmental organizations, regional development bodies and the like increased considerably. The armed forces increased from about 58,000 personnel in 1971 to 142,000 in 1983. The higher ranks of staff officers, including Ver, played an important policy-making role in issues beyond security and defence, such as community affairs, broadcasting and censorship. Beneath the national level, local or regional commanders were well placed to exploit economic advantages and establish networks of personal clients dependent on their patronage, as the civil representatives of the dictatorship and the military establishment evolved a new kind of ruling system, insulated from popular ratification or control.

ABOVE: *General Fabian Ver, the military leader most loyal to Marcos, chief-of-staff of the armed forces, head of presidential security and intelligence services, and chief enforcer of the regime.*

KBL), which found willing recruits in most localities by enlisting the political machines of old-style politicians who had chosen to back Marcos.

CONSOLIDATION

Soon after declaring martial law, Marcos repurposed the ongoing Constitutional Convention, which since 1971 had been conveniently meeting to draft a replacement for the American-vetted 1935 Commonwealth Constitution. By 1973, his partisans in the Convention had bullied and manipulated the assembly into instead formalizing a structural and legal framework for his dictatorship. The resulting 1973 constitution rubber-stamped the Declaration of Martial Law, removed term limits to presidential tenure, authorized rule by decree, set the country on a transition from a presidential to a parliamentary system of government, and theoretically allowed Marcos to be president and prime minister at the same time. It was supposed to have been ratified by a nationwide referendum; instead it was rubber-stamped by ad hoc 'citizen's assemblies' packed with Marcos loyalists.

ABOVE

Giant bust of Marcos, carved into a mountain in Northern Luzon. In a typically Filipino allusion to the busts of US presidents carved into Mt Rushmore, the Marcos bust site was nicknamed 'Mount Cash-no-more' in the regime's waning years, as fiscal problems and deepening poverty became entrenched.

This type of regime propaganda was complemented by a cult of personality built around Marcos as the saviour and heroic leader of the Filipino people. Films about his supposed wartime exploits as an anti-Japanese guerrilla leader were soon joined by imposing statuary and hagiographical portraits, culminating in an enormous stone bust hewn out of a stone mountainside in his home region of Ilocos, à la Mt Rushmore in the USA. As time went on, he and his wife Imelda succumbed to a mounting urge for even more megalomaniacal self-representations. Regime propagandists unashamedly promoted idealized semi-nude images of them as the mythical couple, *Malakas* (the Strong One) and *Maganda* (the Beautiful One) from Tagalog mythology, born fully formed out of a split bamboo to be the rulers of creation. Other larger-than-life paintings of the Marcoses and their family in

ABOVE
An illustration of the First Man and First Woman, with whom the Marcoses were identified by regime propagandists.

poses reminiscent of royalty looked out on to receptions held in the increasingly ornate interiors of regime-owned guesthouses, hotels and pavilions around the country and in Malacañang Palace itself.

REALPOLITIK

The 1970s and '80s were good decades to be an anti-communist dictator seeking US support; alongside Suharto, Marcos belongs to this classic vintage that includes Augusto Pinochet of Chile, the Shah of Iran, Park Chung-Hee in South Korea, Suharto in Indonesia and the military junta in Argentina. Distracted by the Watergate scandal at home, American government officials were reluctant to say or do anything that might further destabilize the Philippines, especially after the fall of South Vietnam made the archipelago even more important as a linchpin of US military and security policy in Asia. Both Marcos and Henry Kissinger, the American Secretary of State, knew that any Philippine president would have to present himself to the Filipino people as a nationalist who defended the country's prerogatives, while being prepared nevertheless to serve as a loyal American subaltern when it really counted.

Marcos did nothing to alter the existing agreements allowing the US to use its military bases and individual American businesses to pursue their investments in the Philippines. The Philippine military continued to benefit from a steady stream of supplies, equipment, funding and training via the Joint US Military Assistance Group (JUSMAG). The local US business community made its approval clear, as big multinationals such as Exxon Mobil, Caltex, Ford, Goodyear and Union Carbide continued to increase their market share and access in the Philippines. The country experts and intelligence officers in the State Department, Manila embassy and CIA always had the information and ability available to make realistic assessments of the Philippine situation, but regardless of their often disturbing findings and recommendations, all US presidents from Richard Nixon to George Bush continued to treat Marcos as a valued and respected personal ally. In the mid-1980s, Ronald Reagan and his Secretary of State, Jeanne Kirkpatrick, were particularly welcoming of Marcos's anticommunism. Reagan's vice-president George Bush notoriously gushed during a 1981 state visit: 'we love your adherence to democratic principles'.

It is conceivable that Bush truly believed what he said; earlier that year, Marcos had issued Proclamation 2045, formally ending martial law. Some controls were loosened, but the ensuing New Republic proved to be an only superficially liberalized version of the dictatorial New Society. Marcos had made sure that all the technical arrangements were in place in the 1973 constitution to ensure that he could retain real control indefinitely. Predictably, Marcos won an overwhelming victory in the subsequent June 1981 presidential election, after it had been boycotted by all the main opposition groups.

BELOW
Marcos on a visit to Clark Air Base in 1979.

ABOVE

Imelda Marcos as the optical highlight of a meeting with American ambassador Stephen Bosworth and other people in earth tones or neutrals, Leyte, 1984.

IMELDA MARCOS

The Marcos critic Primitivo Mijares (who disappeared sometime during the Marcos years, probably in the US, and whose son's mutilated body was also found afterwards) published a book of revelations, *The Conjugal Dictatorship*, whose title grasped something fundamental about the nature of the regime. To the chagrin of most Filipinos, Imelda Marcos (in conjunction with her collection of thousands of designer shoes) is probably still the immediate, almost knee-jerk, free-associational image that occurs to most foreigners whenever the Philippines is mentioned. Cory Aquino's saintly profile, Manny Pacquiao's pugilistically populist pauper-to-prince pugnaciousness and Rodrigo Duterte's penchant for shooting every person associated with the drug trade might give Imelda some competition, but the ongoing spectacle of Marcos's wife, the 'Iron Butterfly', has arguably become *the* permanent Philippine contribution to world popular culture.

An aspiring singer and beauty queen from the prominent Romualdez clan of Leyte, Imelda had met Ferdinand Marcos during his rise to political prominence in the mid-1950s. She developed a charismatic public profile during his 1960s presidential campaigns, with the expected beautification drives and less predictable but highly popular appearances at rallies, singing sentimental ballads and in general adding a touch of glamour that strongly resonated with the average masses. Although always influential, she truly built her own power base during the martial law years. With her husband's support, she became Governor of Metro Manila and created a whole new holistic government agency, the Ministry of 'Human Settlements', with her as minister to pursue her urge to act as a salvific mother figure to the Filipino people. She also created a new 'University of Life' to indoctrinate new generations in Marcos's developmental-authoritarian pseudo-ideologies and technocratic propaganda.

REPRESSION AND MURDER

Four years after the initial arrests of 30,000 people upon declaring martial law, the Marcos government was still holding at least 6,000 political prisoners, according to a 1976 Amnesty International report. Many of these people were subjected to torture, with female detainees routinely sexually molested or raped. In addition to those detained, independent observers such as the human rights group Task Force Detainees Philippines (TFDP) and the historian Walter McCoy have documented the unexplained disappearances and probable or verifiable deaths of about 3,257 more people from 1973 to 1985. Of these, 2,225 of their often mutilated or tortured bodies were later dumped or displayed in public places or roadsides, intimidating warnings about the consequences of criticizing or opposing the regime. The colloquial term for such episodes of extrajudicial killing in Filipino English was 'salvaging', evoking associations with *desaparecidos* in contemporary Latin American dictatorships, the 'evacuated' during the Germans' Final Solution

BELOW
The Main Theatre (Tanghalang Pambansa) of the Cultural Center of the Philippines Complex, completed in 1969. The yellow-and-black no-parking zone markings on the kerb, added sometime at the end of the 20th century, detract from the intended minimalism of the design. By the 1990s, the dignified restraint of mid-20th-century (and therefore colonialism-tainted) urban signage and design standards were often overlaid with such well-meaning but unsightly traffic markings (as talismans of robust independent technocratic progress) on the roadways of much of Southeast Asia.

ARCHITECTURAL OBSESSIONS

Even before martial law, Imelda Marcos had already shown an interest in leaving a permanent mark with her 1966 project for a Cultural Center of the Philippines, a showcase for the performing and fine arts. This developed into an obsession with expensive and increasingly inappropriate signature building projects during the years of dictatorship. In 1974, she added the 10,000-seat Folk Arts Theater to the Cultural Center Complex to host the 1974 Miss Universe Pageant. Elsewhere in Metro Manila, the Philippine Heart Center was erected as a pioneering specialty hospital of its kind in Southeast Asia, in a country where malnutrition was a primary health problem.

In the coming years, the CCP continued to be ground zero for more of these oversized, unnecessary and instantly recognizable structures associated with the pretensions of the regime. In their own overbearing way, such building projects sought to provide 20th-century Manila with the kind of core post-Spanish civic representational space that had never been achieved, because previous American or Commonwealth-era plans for such official districts had not been fully realized, or had been blown to rubble in 1945.

Many of these buildings were designed with sweeping elevated entry ramps by the Marcos regime's court architect, Leandro Locsin. Their style combined Le Corbusier, Albert Speer-tinged brutalism and – particularly as their groundskeeping suffered under later budget cuts and regime changes – eventually Late Mayan Jungle Temple. Rushed to completion to serve as the venue for the first Manila Film Festival of 1982, the Film Center was only finished using 40,000 workers working three shifts straight through 24 hours, and 1,000 workers constructed the lobby in 72 hours, a job originally estimated to require six weeks. In the course of the construction, an accident happened on 17 November 1981. Scaffolding collapsed and several workers were trapped under quick-drying wet cement. Rescue teams took nine hours to get to the building, held back by a security cordon and news blackout thrown over the whole area by the regime. Estimates of the number of dead, most of whom were asphyxiated under the cement, range as high as 169 people. Persistent rumours of the dead workers haunting the building, requiring exorcisms to be removed, have become part of modern Philippine popular culture.

BELOW LEFT: *A close-up of the current somewhat deteriorated state of another Imelda building in the Cultural Center Complex, the Folk Arts Theater (Tanghalang Balagtas). It has recently been rented from the public authorities by an American-style Christian mega-Church revival ministry. The potential for an overgrown-Mayan-temple type situation (or the emergence of the permanent headquarters of another typical Philippine millenarian religious cult) at this site is evident. Possibly to forestall such outcomes, the building has been slated for demolition as part of a general remodelling of the Cultural Center complex.*

BELOW RIGHT: *The Manila Film Center, 1982.*

and other such euphemisms for political murder. All told, reliable research tallies 35,000 individual cases of torture and 70,000 incarcerations for political reasons in the almost 13 years of the dictatorship.

PUBLIC ORDER AND NEW INFRASTRUCTURE

With their better observed traffic rules, more reliable refuse collection, fewer guns in private hands, less street crime visible, and a drop in corruption and bribery in government offices, the first years of martial law were to some degree a honeymoon period between the regime and the majority of the non-politically active mainstream population. This seemed the case not only in terms of an improvement in general conditions of public order (admittedly from an abnormally destabilized baseline at the end of the 1960s), but also in the economy. Improved tax collection and stricter auditing resulted in more government revenue, which joined increases in international borrowing and receipts from tourism as public order improved. A noticeable amount of new infrastructure got built or improved – schools, roads and massive flagship projects like highways and bridges. The most spectacular of the latter was the San Juanico Bridge linking the islands of Samar and Leyte and bringing a north–south national highway network

ABOVE
Edgar Jopson, one of the best-known dissident victims of the Marcos regime, in a photo from his days as a student activist.

PRO-STATE ARMED MILITIAS

Along with the constabulary, police and military units involved in human rights abuses and repression, government-sponsored part-time auxiliary vigilante groups also operated in many rural communities, working closely with the full-time security forces. Known as Civilian Home Defence Forces (CHDFs), these militias were sometimes recycled from the private landlord or politician armies proliferating after the war. If they could not be fully eradicated, they could be co-opted by the Marcos regime. Like their more casual predecessors during the Huk insurgency, CHDF vigilantes hunted leftist activists, recalcitrant local farmers and anyone else who might represent opposition to the government in their community. There was also some overlap in personnel, ethos and mission between them and more unpredictable, less controllable fanatic quasi-religious paramilitary cults with names like Tad-Tad ('Chop-Chop') that had their own separate pedigree – ironically the tradition of resistance to oppression dating back to the revolutionary period, or even further back into 19th-century peasant millenarianism.

within reach. Progress was made in such industries as vehicle assembly, textiles, consumer electronics, food processing and furniture construction.

PROSPERITY?

Marcos's appointment of talented technocrats such as Cesar Virata to financial and economic planning posts in the early martial law period encouraged confidence in foreign investors and lenders. Even through the oil crisis of the mid-1970s, both the inflation rate and the gross national product were within satisfactory ranges. Oil imports were kept under control via domestic finds and one of the world's most ambitious geothermal energy

programmes. Marcos announced measures intended to give land titles to 184,000 farming families by late 1975. Implementation was as, usual in the Philippines, riddled with loopholes and exceptions, and in the end did not change the fundamental relationships between powerful local landowning elites and landless peasants, who remained desperately poor.

By the late 1970s, it was becoming clear that whatever wealth was being created was not being distributed according to the regime's stated objectives of transcending

class and political divisions and forging a resilient new national community through technocratic management. Instead, by the beginning of the 1980s, real wages had declined by 20 per cent overall, with up to 40 per cent in some sectors. Prices of basic commodities like rice, oil and salt had increased by 200 per cent. Income distribution, already skewed considerably in the direction of the top earners in society and away from the bottom majority, had got much worse since detailed record keeping began in the American period. The dictatorship's policies had increased, not shrunk the gap between rich and poor; by the end of the Marcos regime, more than 50 per cent of the population was living below the statistically adjusted poverty line. There had always been large and decrepit slums in the major cities, at least since 1945, but in the 1970s they finally lost the character of stubborn post-war improvisations; entrenched and ever expanding, they reflected the ballooning numbers of unemployed and dispossessed people streaming out of the countryside into urban areas looking for work.

As hundreds of thousands of the truly destitute migrated domestically

ABOVE

The Lucky Plaza shopping centre on Orchard Road in Singapore. It has become a favourite weekend gathering place for many of the thousands of Filipinos employed in Singapore, often in menial or housekeeping positions. Many of the illuminated signs underneath the main entry awning advertise services or products geared to the Filipino market.

into the cities, others joined the working and professional classes who left the country permanently or temporarily. The later 1970s and '80s witnessed the beginnings of a huge new global labour market in the oil-rich states of the Middle East. In lieu of educating (and perhaps dangerously mobilizing) their own highly subsidized and barely literate populations, the autocratic rulers of these countries could suddenly afford to import trainable (and more controllable) non-white workers from the rest of the developing world who spoke basic global English, in order to build up national infrastructures and service economies in the Gulf and other regions. Filipinos, culturally primed by earlier waves of healthcare and sex-work migration to post-war Japan and the US, responded to Middle Eastern recruiters, at first in modest numbers, then in major human flows by the 1980s.

FLIGHT ABROAD

Whatever immiseration, brutality and repression the Marcos dictatorship was responsible for at home, it was not the kind of totalitarian regime that completely blocked departure abroad as a response to the worsening domestic economy. Instead, the regime made departure a monetizable privilege granted by the state, in the guise of looking after worker welfare. Recognizing a safety valve against social unrest, Marcos's Labour Ministry set up agencies for the regulation, promotion and monitoring of working-class Filipinos employed abroad on fixed-term contracts in the building, hospitality, industrial and other trades. Meanwhile, university-educated doctors, accountants, nurses, engineers and other professionals (not so often lawyers or social scientists) continued older forms of less-regulated or monitored 'brain drain' migration for career and personal-lifestyle reasons, mostly to the USA and other Western countries. The rich or well connected of course also continued to travel without hindrance – except for those with political or economic problems with the regime.

The steady slide into poverty of an ever-growing majority that drove this emigration had several causes, among them excessive foreign borrowing, mismanagement of macroeconomic policies, the usual kinds of administrative and political corruption, and class warfare over land. But perhaps the most visible major cause, certainly the one that drew the most public ire, was the signature Marcos-era phenomenon dubbed 'crony capitalism'. Diverting earnings or funding from government or quasi-public programmes or projects became a source of massive direct cash income for the dictator, his family and a select circle of friends, political allies and other trusted associates. Old-style oligarchs had varied in the percentage of their riches they chose to invest back into the economy, on their own lavish lifestyles or into improving social capital. The new Marcos cronies tended to keep far more of the cash they looted, and often expatriated their winnings. They also ran their allotted economic fiefdoms in unsustainable ways for the sake of getting rich quickly.

A CRONY ECONOMY

Chasing massive kickbacks, a crony named Herminio Disini lobbied the Marcoses through his Herdis Group to shift the already inflated contract for the earthquake fault-situated Bataan Nuclear Power Plant from General Electric to Westinghouse, turning the project into the most expensive of its kind in the world. The Lopez family's empire of major newspapers, a broadcasting network and the country's largest electric power company was broken up and distributed to Marcos loyalists, including Imelda Marcos's brother, Benjamin 'Kokoy' Romualdez, and another loyal crony, Roberto Benedicto. Huge monopolies and semi-monopolies emerged in manufacturing, construction and banking, protected from failure by government subsidies in the hundreds of millions of pesos.

The most destructive impact of crony capitalism, however, was in the traditional cash-crop sector, vital to the livelihoods of millions of ordinary Filipinos in the countryside. Distribution and marketing monopolies for sugar and coconuts under the control of cronies like Benedicto and Eduardo Cojuangco were established. Farmers were paid on scales pegged to sink far below whatever the world market rate was for their crops, and were the first to suffer when world commodity prices dropped. The enormous profits from these monopolies were diverted into overseas bank accounts, property deals, and purchases of art, jewellery and antiques. Meanwhile back on the island of Negros, farm tenants and sharecroppers suffered from degrees of malnutrition unusual outside Africa.

BELOW LEFT: *The mothballed Bataan Nuclear Power Plant. One of the most expensive projects of its kind in the world, it has not generated a single watt of electric power for the Philippines.*

BELOW RIGHT: *A coconut tree at the height of its productive capacity.*

RIGHT
Anti-communist propaganda broadsheets in Tagalog.

RIGHT
Anti-communist propaganda broadsheets in Tagalog.

INSURGENCY

A military whose commanders, with some exceptions, were rewarded for loyalty rather than competence proved both brutal and ineffective in dealing with the resulting growth of a new communist insurgency, the New People's Army, or NPA. This communist insurgent force was founded by university educated Maoists from the new Communist Party of the Philippines who felt that the old PKP and Huk generation was no longer militant enough. After some reverses in the 1970s, the NPA grew quickly in the early 1980s, particularly in some of the poorest regions of the country. Further south, the Muslim separatist movement had reached a violent peak in the mid-1970s, then declined greatly, because of divisions in the leadership of the movement and reduced external support brought about by the diplomatic activity of the Marcos government in Arab countries.

SPECIAL RELATIONSHIP

Relations with the US remained the most important foreign affairs issue for the Philippines in the 1970s. Although the fundamental asymmetry of a dependent neo-colonial relationship remained intact, the special relationship between the two countries underwent significant modification; trade, investment and defence ties were all redefined. The Laurel-Langley

Agreement defining preferential US tariffs for Philippine exports and parity privileges for US investors expired on 4 July 1974, and trade relations were governed thereafter by the international General Agreement on Tariffs and Trade (GATT). During the martial law period, foreign investment terms were substantially liberalized, despite official rhetoric about foreign 'exploitation' of the economy. A policy promoting 'non-traditional' exports such as textiles, footwear, electronic components, and fresh and processed foods was initiated with some success. Japan increasingly challenged the US as a major foreign participant in the Philippine economy.

ABOVE
Japanese Emperor Hirohito on a state visit to the Philippines, 1966.

The status of US military bases was redefined when a major amendment to the Military Bases Agreement of 1947 was signed on 6 January 1979, reaffirming Philippine sovereignty over the bases and reducing their total area. At the same time, the US administration promised to make its 'best effort' to obtain congressional appropriations for military and economic aid amounting to US$400 million between 1979 and 1983. The amendment called for future reviews of the bases agreement every fifth year. Although the administration of President Jimmy Carter emphasized the promotion of human rights worldwide, only limited pressure was exerted on Marcos to improve the behaviour of the military in rural areas and to end the death-squad murders of political opponents. Pressure from the US, however, did play a role in gaining the release of Benigno Aquino in May 1980; he was allowed to go to the US for medical treatment after spending almost eight years in prison, including long stretches of time in solitary confinement.

'NINOY' AQUINO

Benigno 'Ninoy' Aquino was, like his life-long rival Ferdinand Marcos, a consummate politician, Philippine style. Born in 1932, he interrupted his college studies to pursue a journalistic career, first in wartime Korea, then in Vietnam, Malaya and other parts of Southeast Asia. He bolstered his

popularity by claiming credit for negotiating the May 1954 surrender of Huk leader Luis Taruc. Aquino became the governor of Tarlac Province in 1963, and a member of the Senate in 1967. His marriage to Corazon Cojuangco, a member of one of the country's richest and most prominent Chinese mestizo families was, like Marcos's marriage to Imelda Romualdez, a great help to his political career.

Allowed to go into American exile in 1980, ostensibly for medical reasons, Aquino became a major leader of the opposition. The steady deterioration of the economic and political situation and Marcos's worsening health led Aquino to return home, hoping either to persuade the president to step down or to continue building an effective opposition. He wished to avoid the worst possible outcome – a post-Marcos regime led by Imelda, backed by the military under Ver.

On 21 August 1983, Aquino was shot in the head and killed as he was escorted off an arriving flight at Manila International Airport by soldiers of the Aviation Security Command (AVSECOM). The government quickly identified the assassin as a lone communist gunman, Rolando Galman, conveniently killed on the airport tarmac by AVSECOM. Marcos appointed a commission headed by jurist Corazon Agrava, which concluded in late October 1984 that a military conspiracy lay behind the killing. The Sandiganbayan, a court charged with prosecuting criminal officials, ignored Agrava and upheld the government version of events, acquitting Ver

HINDI KA NAG-IISA

and 25 alleged other co-conspirators in December 1985 (another court decision in the 1990s would reverse these findings and convict the accused of murder). Most domestic and foreign opinion in 1983 already believed, however, that Imelda Marcos and Fabian Ver wanted Aquino assassinated. His funeral became the largest mass demonstration in Philippine history, focusing popular indignation against a corrupt regime. It marked the birth of the People Power movement, which bore fruit in the ousting of Marcos on 25 February 1986.

THE PEOPLE DEFEND THE SOLDIERS

People Power included a broad spectrum of the non-communist segments of Philippine society, but was primarily, although not exclusively, urban based; another name for it was the EDSA Revolution, from the main roadway through Metro Manila (Epifanio de los Santos Avenue), which was the setting for its most sustained mass demonstrations. Although it drew millions of rural, working class, middle-class and professional supporters, its leadership was solidly from the middle classes – the Roman Catholic hierarchy, career military and civil officers, and members of the business community. These groups would not have willingly acknowledged any particular partisan ideology or class interest, but in the personalistic manner of almost all Philippine politics, were united by their sympathy for Aquino's widow, Corazon, and their disgust with the Marcos regime. In the end, it is clear that they were all driven by an essentially centrist-conservative impulse.

ABOVE
The People Power monument along Epifanio de los Santos Avenue, marking the site of the 1986 Revolution.

SNAP ELECTION AND MARCOS'S OUSTER

An indirect reminder of the importance of American support for his regime was Marcos's 1985 decision to announce 'snap' presidential elections on a US television talk show, *This Week with David Brinkley*. Setting 7 February 1986, a year before his six-year presidential term ran out, as the date for the election, Marcos believed that another rubber-stamp victory would solidify American support, silence critics in both countries and perhaps end the pall the Aquino assassination had laid over his regime. However, this move proved to be a monumental blunder.

Right after her husband's assassination, Corazon 'Cory' Aquino had taken on a symbolic role as martyr's wife and emotional focus of the opposition in an emotional country. This eventually became a substantive leadership role in the year before Marcos's downfall in late February 1986, as she became the main opposition presidential candidate. Cardinal Sin brokered an

FROM COLLABORATION TO OPPOSITION

During the Marcos dictatorship, the Catholic Church had become the country's strongest and most independent non-governmental institution. Influenced by the conveniently timed 'liberation theology' movement sweeping parts of the so-called Third World in the 1960s and '70s, its colonial, anti-nationalist heritage and traditional alignment with conservative landed elites underwent a partial shift during the martial law years. Parish priests and nuns witnessed the suffering of the common people and often became involved in political activism, generally of the leftist kind. Although Pope John Paul II had instructed clergy not to engage in direct political struggle, the Pope's own commitment to human rights and social justice encouraged both the rank and file and the Philippine Church hierarchy to criticize the dictatorship's abuses. Following Aquino's assassination, Jaime Cardinal Sin, Archbishop of Manila and leader of the Catholic Bishops Conference of the Philippines, redefined the hierarchy's stance from one of 'critical collaboration' to open opposition.

The Aquino assassination happened as the Philippine economy was reeling from years of crony mismanagement and unfavourable international conditions. Business leaders outside crony circles feared a collapse of the economy if things continued on their current path. Inflation and unemployment were soaring. The country's GNP, stagnant by 1983, contracted by -6.8 per cent in 1984, and -3.8 per cent in 1985. There was a steep decline in both domestic and foreign business confidence and investment. As much as US$2 million a day was flowing out of the country via various channels in the panic following Aquino's death. The banks, brokerage houses, luxury hotels and upper-class homes of Makati, Manila's business hub, became centres of vocal resistance to the Marcos regime.

The demoralizing effects of involvement in brutal repression, and the obvious corruption in the command structure of the armed forces, spurred the growth in the early 1980s of a politically active dissident faction of young military officers, mostly graduates of the elite Philippine Military Academy. Known as the Reform the Armed Forces Movement (RAM), these officers advocated a return to the apolitical 'professionalism' of the pre-martial law period. They found a powerful if discreetly ambiguous ally in the Minister of National Defence himself. Juan Ponce Enrile was a long-time Marcos loyalist, but had become increasingly unhappy with the effects of Fabian Ver's ascendancy over the armed forces.

alliance between Corazon Aquino and Salvador Laurel, who had previously announced his own candidacy but now agreed to run as Aquino's vice-presidential hopeful. Aquino's immense popular support and Laurel's organization skills and contacts in the world of traditional electoral politics made for a spirited campaign. The Church hierarchy abandoned any pretence of neutrality and committed its considerable resources to support to the opposition ticket. In a classic bit of seminarian's sophistry, Cardinal Sin spoke out to poor people who could not refuse bribe money offered for votes. Aware that the ethic of moral obligation, or *utang na loob*, demanded that they vote for the briber, Sin reminded voters that an immoral contract was invalid, and that they should vote according to their consciences anyway.

On the day of the election, NAMFREL and international observer teams reported significant irregularities. US Senator Richard Lugar of Indiana, a member of a US delegation, claimed that 10–40 per cent of voters' names had been removed from registration rolls in highly contested areas. The government's Commission on Elections (COMELEC) predictably reported Marcos leading, whereas equally predictable NAMFREL figures showed a majority for the Aquino-Laurel ticket. The next day, COMELEC computer operators, noting discrepancies between their internal figures and those officially announced, walked out in protest on live television, at some risk to their lives. About a week later, the Marcos-dominated National Assembly proclaimed him the official winner. Despite the Reagan administration's continued official support for Marcos, a consensus of policy makers in the White House, Department of State, Pentagon and Congress was emerging to advise the withdrawal of support from Marcos.

On 22 February, Enrile and General Fidel Ramos, commander of the Philippine Constabulary, citing fears of their own arrest, issued a joint statement demanding Marcos's resignation. They set up a command post for what was swiftly developing from a mutiny into a full-blown rebellion inside the adjoining military bases of Camp Aguinaldo and Camp Crame in Metro Manila, supported by several hundred rebel troops. When Marcos sent loyal units to suppress the uprising, the Catholic-run Radio Veritas appealed to the people to supply and feed the rebels. Cardinal Sin reminded listeners to use non-violence in efforts to block pro-Marcos troop movements.

In the tense days that followed, hundreds of thousands of clergy, students, ordinary citizens and children joined and surrounded the rebel camps, peacefully confronting the tanks and machine guns of government troops. Many of the latter defected, including the crews of seven helicopter gunships from the 15th Strike Wing of the Philippine Air Force seemingly preparing to attack the massive crowd on 24 February. Instead, the gunships landed in Camp Crame and announced their support for People Power. There was little or no violence. No Filipino soldiers were ready to wage war on their own people.

A surreal inauguration ceremony at Malacañang Palace on 25 February, boycotted by almost the entire diplomatic community, was the last defiant gesture from the Marcoses. Paul Laxalt, a US senator with close ties to Reagan, advised Marcos to 'cut, and cut cleanly'. By that evening, the Marcoses were on their way via Clark Air Base to exile in the US. Hundreds of ordinary

Marcos's defiant final inauguration ceremony, early 1986. His eldest son Ferdinand, Jr ('Bongbong') is puzzlingly dressed in a green active-duty military field uniform, off to the right of the picture.

people ran into Malacañang Palace to view evidence of the Marcoses' extravagance (including those hundreds of shoes that will be forever associated with Imelda). That same day, 25 February, Corazon Aquino had been sworn into office by Justice Claudio Teehankee at the Club Filipino resort as the seventh president of the independent Republic of the Philippines.

CORY AQUINO

Corazon Aquino's assumption of the presidency signalled the end of the first episode of authoritarian rule in an independent Philippines. Damage control and amelioration were to be key themes of her administration. The peaceful change of regime made the Filipino experience of February and March 1986 an example for similar democracy movements worldwide in the last decade of the 20th century. In a more ambiguous legacy to the future, memories of its undoubted populist legitimacy also instituted the mass demonstration and the armed coup as increasingly thinkable and routine methods to change *any* Philippine government, alongside the legitimate elections provided for in the written constitution.

Corazon Sumulong Cojuangco was born in 1933 in Tarlac province, the sixth of eight children of Jose Cojuangco, a former congressman and business entrepreneur, and Demetria Sumulong, a pharmacist. Aquino's grandfather, Melecio Cojuangco, had been a member of the Malolos Congress. Her mother's side of the family were also politically influential;

LEFT
The inauguration of Cory Aquino at the Club Filipino, Manila, February 25, 1986.

Juan Sumulong ran against Manuel L. Quezon for the Commonwealth presidency in 1941.

Aquino went to elementary and high school at exclusive Catholic girls' academies, where she absorbed the devoutness and piety of the conservative elite Catholic milieu (*catolica cerrada*). Afterwards, she and her family went to the US, where she graduated from the College of Mount Saint Vincent in 1953, with a major in French and minor in mathematics. She then returned to the Philippines and studied law at Far Eastern University. After meeting Ninoy Aquino, she discontinued her law education and married him in Our Lady of Sorrows Church in 1954. The couple raised five children as Ninoy went through the various phases of his political career, until his arrest, flight into exile and return to his death at the Manila International Airport in 1983.

Aquino, president of a revolutionary government by virtue of people power, had the political momentum to unilaterally repeal the repressive laws of her predecessor, decree the restoration of civil liberties, abolish the 1973 'Marcos Constitution' and dissolve the Marcos-dominated National Assembly. She immediately created a Constitutional Commission to draft a new constitution. Another one of her first steps on taking office was the creation of the Presidential Commission on Good Government (PCGG), whose mission it was to recover the ill-gotten wealth of the Marcos family and its cronies. After her term in office, however, the PCGG itself was also, somewhat predictably, implicated in corruption scandals.

ABOVE
Cory Aquino at the International Rice Research Institute, Los Baños, Laguna, 1986.

DAMAGE CONTROL

Aquino inherited an economy that was bankrupt and debt-ridden. Her administration was quickly able to dismantle most of the monopolies that had been set up by Marcos's cronies during his time in power. Instead of repudiating the estimated $26 billion in international debt incurred in the Marcos years, Aquino chose to honour all the debts that were incurred previously under different administrations, defending this highly unpopular decision as crucial for regaining investor confidence in the Philippine economy. The Aquino government paid off $4 billion of the country's outstanding debts to regain good international credit ratings and attract the attention of future markets. However, the administration also borrowed an additional $9 billion, increasing the national debt by $6 billion within six years after the ousting of Marcos in 1986.

Nevertheless, the Aquino administration also sought to trim down the government's budget deficit that had grown massively during Marcos's rule. The method was privatization of government services and deregulation of vital industries. The economy grew by 3.4 per cent during Aquino's first year in office. But as her government began to encounter one armed coup attempt after another, investor confidence fell and the economy became stagnant. When Aquino left office, inflation had reached a worrying 17 per cent, and unemployment over 10 per cent, higher than in the Marcos years.

THE MENDIOLA MASSACRE

Aquino's family and class background as a privileged daughter of a wealthy and landed clan became the focus of criticism against her land-reform agenda. Three weeks after the 1987 Constitution was ratified, agrarian workers and farmers marched in Mendiola Street near Malacañang to demand genuine land reform. The demonstration became violent when Philippine Marine Corps soldiers started firing at farmers who broke through designated demarcation lines set by the police. Twelve farmers were killed and 19 injured. The event came to be known as the Mendiola Massacre, and led some members of Aquino's Cabinet to resign their positions. Though Aquino did not have any personal and official involvement with the drastic actions taken by some police elements, her family's retention of its own landholdings (including the giant Hacienda Luisita) until 2006 cast Aquino's land reform efforts in an unflattering light.

COUP D'ETAT

In the year and a half after People Power, there were six plots to overthrow the government. Indicating the long-term danger to democratic stability of accepting military assistance in deposing an earlier authoritarian regime, a significant number of soldiers involved in these attempts came from the Reform the Armed Forces Movement (RAM) led by Gregorio 'Gringo' Honasan, while others were Marcos loyalists. Two of the attempts – in November 1986 and July 1987 – were quashed before getting under way. Only the August 1987 coup attempt, which left 53 people dead, resulted in significant violence.

However, an even more worrying development took place during a much more serious coup attempt on 1 December 1989, when RAM members joined forces with soldiers loyal to Marcos. Metro Manila was shaken by significant fighting over broadcasting stations, military camps, hotels and office buildings in Makati. At one point, the rebels almost captured all of Malacañang Palace. The coup was completely defeated by Philippine Government forces on 9 December 1989. With her government forces hard-pressed by the rebels, Aquino requested humiliating assistance from the US military based at Subic Bay and Clark Air Base. American airpower cleared the skies of rebel aircraft and allowed the Philippine military to consolidate their forces, while two American carrier battle groups took stations offshore. The coup cost the lives of 99 people (including 50 civilians), and left 570 more wounded.

LEFT: *'Gringo' Honasan in his post-RAM career as an establishment politician and senator, 2016.*

RIGHT: *F-4E Phantom II fighter-bomber of the USAF's 3rd Tactical Fighter Wing based at Clark Air Base, 1980s.*

REBUILDING DEMOCRACY

Immediately after assuming the presidency, President Aquino promulgated the provisional 1986 Freedom Constitution, pending the ratification of a permanent new constitution by the people. This allowed Aquino to exercise both executive and legislative powers until the establishment of a new Congress in 1987. Aquino's changes to the government structure received criticism from Defence Secretary Juan Ponce Enrile, Vice-President Salvador Laurel and many other government officials. Doubting her competence, Enrile and Laurel subsequently resigned from Aquino's government. On 2 February 1987, the new Constitution of the Philippines, which put strong emphasis on civil liberties, human rights and social justice, was overwhelmingly approved by the Filipino people. The ratification of the new

ABOVE
Eruption of Mt Pinatubo as seen from Clark Air Base, 1991.

BELOW
Ash from the Pinatubo eruption blankets Subic Naval Base.

constitution was followed by the election of senators and congressmen that same year and the holding of local elections in 1988.

MILITARY INTERVENTIONS

Dealing with the fallout from the Marcos years would have been challenging enough for any successor administration. As if that was not enough, the greatest danger to the Aquino government's mission of national recovery and stabilization came from the continuous series of mutinies, uprisings and full-blown coup de état attempts directed at her government from her own armed forces – the same ones that had helped install her in power in the first place. The Philippines had now joined a long list of countries that have experienced military interventions in the political process during particularly difficult moments in the modernization experience – Cromwellian England, 1930s Japan, 1920s Germany, most of the rest of the Hispanic world, modern Greece and Turkey, neighbouring Indonesia, Pakistan, Thailand, and most of Africa, to name a few. In almost all these cases, the military tended to remain a player in the political arena afterwards.

THE END OF THE BASES

After a dormant period of 500 years, Mt Pinatubo volcano erupted on 15 June 1991. Located just 32km (20 miles) from the US naval base at Subic Bay and about 16km (10 miles) from Clark Air Base, Pinatubo was the second most powerful volcanic eruption of the 20th century. At the same time, heavy rain, lightning and thunder fell from a typhoon passing over Luzon. The damage to the Philippine economy and infrastructure was estimated at 12 billion pesos. Despite the successful evacuation of about 60,000 people from the thickly settled areas around the volcano, about 850 people were killed, with 200,000 left homeless, and much prime agricultural land and forest habitat destroyed.

By the next day, the naval base at Subic lay buried under a foot of rain-soaked, sandy ash. Clark Air Base, much closer to Mt Pinatubo, was declared a total loss, and plans for a complete closure were started. In the year immediately

before the Pinatubo eruption, intense negotiations between the governments of the US and the Philippines had resulted in a draft Treaty of Friendship, Peace and Cooperation between the two countries that would have extended the lease of the American bases. On 13 September 1991, the Philippine Senate rejected the ratification of this treaty. After abortive talks in December to extend the withdrawal of American forces for three years, Aquino issued formal notice for the US to leave by the end of 1992. With Clark Air Base already inoperable, the shutdown of Subic Bay proceeded in the following several months.

A SYMBOL TO THE END

Towards the close of Aquino's presidency, advisers and friends told her that she was still eligible to seek the presidency again in the upcoming 1992 elections, never having been elected before. She strongly rejected the suggestions, in light of the damage to the Republic's democracy caused by her predecessor's attempts to prolong his time in office. She threw her support behind the candidacy of her defence secretary and EDSA Revolution hero, General Fidel V. Ramos, who had loyally defended her government from the various coup attempts and rebellions. Her withdrawal of support from Ramon Mitra drew criticism not only from her more liberal and leftist supporters, but also from the Roman Catholic Church, suspicious of Ramos since the latter was a Protestant. Ramos eventually won the 1992 elections, albeit by a narrow margin, and was sworn in as the twelfth President of the Philippines on 30 June 1992.

In full view of a generation that had never experienced an orderly democratic transition of power, Aquino attended Ramos's inauguration at the Quirino Grandstand in Manila. Her final act as president was to ride the presidential limousine to the event and leave later in a modest Toyota sedan, a gift from her siblings, to return to private life as 'Citizen Cory', still a source of hope and inspiration to many until her death in 2009.

BELOW
Cory Aquino's funeral, 2009.

8

NEW FORMS FOR OLD CHALLENGES

*The Fifth Republic and the Future of the Philippines,
1986 to the Present*

Fidel Ramos was part of the first generation of Filipino military officers who built their careers within the framework of the Philippines' post-colonial, client-state relationship with the US. Born in 1928 into a prominent family from the province of Pangasinan, he was distantly related on his mother's side to Ferdinand Marcos. His father had been a member of Congress and Secretary of Foreign Affairs. After studying at the Philippine Military Academy, Ramos graduated from its prototype, the US Military Academy, in 1951. He rose through the entire army hierarchy, fighting alongside American forces in the Korean War and later leading the non-combatant Philippine Civic Action Group in Vietnam. In 1972, Marcos appointed Ramos as commanding general of the Philippine Constabulary. Obviously in an ideal position to know about, or be involved in, the dictatorship's numerous human rights abuses and atrocities, Ramos has never been personally implicated in any of them. Whatever degree of command responsibility should have fallen on him became politically irrelevant when the RAM officers, defence minister Juan Ponce Enrile and Ramos himself began the military rebellion against Marcos that joined up with People Power to sweep Cory Aquino to the presidency in 1986.

Like his predecessor Enrile, Ramos continued to display the traits of a consummate political survivor after being appointed Secretary of National Defence in the Aquino cabinet. While protecting Cory from seven separate coup attempts, he retained the respect of both the loyal majority

OPPOSITE
Gloria Macapagal-Arroyo with American marines deployed in disaster relief in the Philippines, 2006.

BELOW
Fidel Ramos visits the Pentagon, 1998.

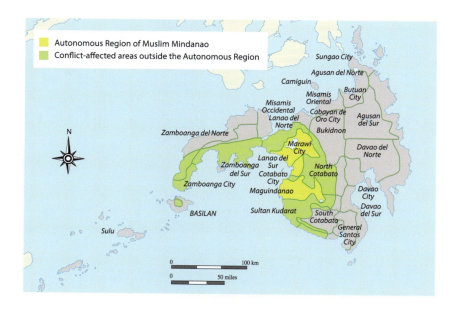

of the Philippine military and its discontented, rebellion-prone black sheep. Aquino's endorsement of his candidacy as her successor in the presidential elections of 1992 was certainly invaluable in his eventual victory, but his own reputation for level-headedness and his professed respect for civilian government supremacy over the military had already earned him the sobriquet 'Steady Eddie'. In his time in office, the country experienced a smooth and legitimate political transition to relatively better economic times. This contributed significantly to the restabilization of democracy in Philippine society after the traumas of dictatorship and constitutional breakdown.

TIGER CUB?

Once in office, Ramos quickly announced his signature development strategy, 'Philippines 2000'. Placing economics at the forefront of national policy, it envisioned a place for the archipelago among the newly industrialized countries, perhaps even as one of the burgeoning 'tiger'-type economies proliferating in Asia, the European periphery and Latin America. After the West's victory in the Cold War, Ramos recognized a window of opportunity for the country to catch up with the opportunities missed during the Marcos years. Riding the seemingly irreversible triumph of globalized neo-liberal capitalism, a revitalized Philippine private sector would be the partner of a capable managerial/technocratic state. The latter would assert the collective national interest in the face of lobbies, oligarchies and special interests, while remaining responsive to democratic oversight.

A good part of this agenda was realized in the six years of Ramos's tenure. Significant steps were taken to deregulate and revitalize key industrial sectors such as civil aviation, shipping, telecommunications and energy, which had suffered most from the cronyism and bureaucratic stasis of the Marcos years. The easier regulatory climate and improved peace and order situation encouraged foreign capital investment, which in turn encouraged an export-driven model of technology-based manufacturing. Significant growth in the overseas diaspora and its remittances home also contributed its share to increasing the material security of large sections of the population, while exposing more and more Filipinos to foreign realities, attitudes and ways of life.

The deregulation of telecommunications (including computer services and networks) away from the Philippine Long Distance Telephone Company resulted in a lively market of more than a dozen companies offering

BELOW
Geothermal sources of energy expanded in the 1990s. The Philippines derives about 17 per cent of its energy needs from geothermal sources, and is the second largest producer of geothermal energy in the world. This is a view of the Palinpinon geothermal plant near Dumaguete, Negros Island.

EXPORT PROCESSING ZONES

Ramos's administration was active in the development of export-processing zones (EPZs) where foreign investors could open facilities offering thousands of new jobs for the surrounding region under less stringent government oversight. Alongside sites in Metro Manila and the former American naval base at Subic Bay, a particularly successful EPZ developed in Cebu. Together with a surge in property development and in new international air links in that island province, this EPZ drove a decade of rapid growth in the Central Visayas' economy known as 'Ceboom'.

LEFT: *The skyline of Cebu City, early 21st century.*

BELOW: *The former US naval base at Subic Bay has evolved into a successful special economic development zone since the Ramos administration.*

competitive rates by the late 1990s. The Ramos government's reputation for effective technocratic approaches combined with a commitment to economic liberalization was further enhanced by its decisive handling of the chronic energy and water infrastructure problems that had long plagued Manila and other cities. Rolling electrical outages, or 'brownouts', lasting up to 12 hours had become so frequent as to become a deterrent to effective investment. Similarly, Metro Manila's water-supply system was woefully inadequate and often unsanitary. The Ramos government, armed

ABOVE
A special power-generating barge of the National Power Corporation for delivering electricity to vulnerable areas during peak demand periods.

with emergency powers and funding from Congress, solicited bids from independent contractors able to commit to delivering service-ready electric power plants in two years. By 1994 the crisis in power generation had been resolved, although prices remained comparatively high. Manila's water-supply system was also vastly upgraded by a consortium of foreign and domestic contractors, with funding from the World Bank.

The 1997 Asian economic crisis obviously had a major impact on the Philippines, with growth being near zero for the next couple of years. However, the general consensus among economists was that the country weathered it effectively, and emerged in comparatively better shape than some regional neighbours. This was partly due to effective management of the peso's unavoidable downturn in value, which kept Philippine exports competitive while trying to mitigate the worst impact of layoffs and plant closures. Another reason was that in comparison to the Asian tigers, the Philippines of the 1990s was not so deeply integrated into the capital flows of international financial markets. This may have hindered previous growth, but it also reduced exposure even as those fluctuating markets dictated massive increases in the ratio of foreign debt to GDP for many other Asian nations. Growth returned to the Philippines in 1999, and at an encouraging rate of 3 per cent.

OVERSEAS FILIPINO WORKERS

One other reason for the relative mildness of the 1997 economic downturn was the almost $6 billion in remittances per year faithfully sent home

by the approximately 10 per cent of the entire native-born population that lived or worked abroad as permanent residents or as overseas Filipino workers (OFWs) by the end of the millennium. Having grown to an estimated 10 million people by 2010, overseas Filipinos made up one of the largest diasporas in the world, in absolute as well as percentage terms. The largest single destination for permanent Filipino migrants in the 1990s continued to be the US. In a newer pattern since the 1990s, however, rapidly increasing numbers of OFWs on temporary contracts have gone to places requiring a combination of cheap, compliant, English-capable, and semi- or fully skilled labour. These new workplaces have included Saudi Arabia and the rest of the Gulf States, parts of Europe, Japan, Hong Kong, Taiwan and Singapore, and approximately 160 other countries and shipping lines around the world. The remittances sent back home shifted the consumption patterns, lifestyles and expectations of large sectors of the lower middle and lower classes of the population to higher levels.

Despite the government's celebration of the OFWs via officiously gushy airport reception and send-off rituals, and other displays of public gratitude for these 'New Heroes' (*ang mga Bagong Bayani*), the Philippines remained relatively powerless to intervene in the frequent instances of abuse and exploitation of these people abroad. Numerous cases emerged of OFWs in all types of occupation forced to pay extortionate recruitment fees. Others had their passports taken away from them as they were passed on from recruiting agency to labour contractor to third-party worksite, under conditions that locked them into unacceptable working environments abroad with little or no recourse. Tragic cases involving the abuse of female OFWs who took jobs as domestic helpers, or even their execution for alleged capital crimes committed abroad, particularly inflamed public opinion and drove the passage of legislation such as the Migrant Workers and Overseas Filipinos Act of 1995.

Among other things, this law set up a system for reviewing labour contracts with approved overseas employers and contractors, and arranging bilateral agreements with the governments of other countries where certain classes of Filipinos worked, to ensure their protection from abuse. Building on bureaucratic procedures from the Marcos era, the requirement to register as an OFW with the new Philippine Overseas Employment Authority (POEA) in order to be able to respond to labour contracts also imposed an additional level of screening to prevent underage or otherwise vulnerable people from exploitation by recruiters.

ABOVE
The personal data page of a sample (that is, not belonging to any real person) Philippine passport.

THE PERSISTENCE OF POVERTY

The growth in the OFW sector, no matter how the government wished to spin its remittances as a clear positive for the nation, was also a reflection of the Ramos government's inability to deal with stubbornly high levels of poverty in the population. The economy as a whole might have been a

LEFT
The OFW-heavy Filipino market in Kota Kinabalu, Sabah, Malaysia.

211

POEA EXIT CLEARANCE: A TWO-CLASS TRAVEL REGIME?

POEA registration arguably divided Filipinos looking to travel abroad into a two-class system. On the one hand, middle-class professionals and well-to-do tourists remain essentially free agents. They are able to come and go any time they wish (given the right entry visas to other countries). On the other hand, 'official' OFWs – relatively less well educated, many coming from the mass base of the population, generally with different optics at airport-departure checks – need POEA exit clearance. In theory this clearance is required only for travel to the countries that offer OFWs the employment they are seeking. However, once registered with the POEA (and therefore subject to its documentation requirements), or otherwise simply once a temporary working visa from another country is placed in their passport, many Filipinos have found out the hard way that exiting the country for any destination, even if no work contract is involved, has become increasingly complicated and difficult. Arbitrary exit delays, complete blocks at ports of departure because of missing 'exit clearance' paperwork, and other forms of clearly discriminatory treatment from their own government have become an increasing worry for POEA-registered people planning to travel for personal reasons or to cultivate professional possibilities abroad, in contrast to non-POEA-registered free agents. Developed to protect the human rights of all Filipinos abroad, the system seems to have begun endangering the human right of certain bureaucratically defined groups of Filipinos to travel without undue constraint out of their own country.

moderately successful success story, but the government neglected structural reform in fundamentals such as agriculture – the continuing source of livelihood for millions – or the creation of self-sufficient, vertically integrated systems of consumer demand and domestic manufacturing or entrepreneurship. It instead tied the country ever closer to pre-existing networks of export-oriented global trade and financing, and encouraged cheap labour flows whose ultimate logic remains an extension of exploitative neo-colonialism. Not coincidentally, this strategy also tended to concentrate more and more of the wealth from increased productivity in elite hands, and thereby prevented the emergence of a truly robust and self-confident native middle class.

In keeping with longer term post-war patterns, persistent poverty also existed in a more straightforward relationship with persistent corruption. With the return of the old trapo elite patronage machines to Congress, as much as 45 per cent of discretionary funding and 20 per cent of the entire government budget wound up in the pockets of politicians or their followers during Ramos's administration. Despite his interventions in selected sectors, much of the country's physical infrastructure thus remained neglected, and provision of basic sanitation, water, healthcare and housing remained inadequate.

INSURGENCY, AS ALWAYS

The discontent that poverty continued to generate spurred a revival of communist insurgent activity. A recruiting rebound doubled the number of active New People's Army combatants to 12,000 from the low of about 6,000 during the Aquino period. This uptick in the insurgency was occurring as the constabulary, Ramos's old internal security paramilitary force, was fused with the Marcos-era Integrated National Police to form the Philippine National Police (PNP). Though the police and army remained loyal to the government and politically quiet during Ramos's time in office, their record of extra-legal violence and killing or other human rights abuses continued to attract domestic and international concern.

THE BIRTH-CONTROL DEBATE

Some critics argued that the persistence of poverty was at least partly due to a deeply conservative Catholic society's failure to address the problem of overpopulation. They pointed out that the success of other newly industrialized countries had come with a demographic transition to a slower rate of population growth, allowing enough capital to accumulate within individual families for a general societal take-off into shared prosperity. Many such observers believed that use of artificial birth-control technologies was urgently needed in the Philippines. However, with more success than in Latin America or Ireland, pious Catholics and other opponents of birth control apart from the natural rhythm method questioned what was cause and what was effect in the demographic transition, or levelled essentially moralistic arguments against any expansion of reproductive rights or access to birth-control information via public means.

The Marcos regime's technocrats had put forward birth control as one of their priorities, setting up the Population Commission of the Philippines in the early 1980s. After some initial cooperation, subsequent Catholic resistance to any measures associated with the dictatorship meant that this issue had been dropped during the Aquino administration. When Ramos, a Protestant, appointed another Protestant, Juan Flavier, as Secretary of Health, the issue took on a confessional aspect that polarized public opinion further, even as Flavier's tenure saw the birth rate drop by a modest amount with the somewhat improved availability of birth-control methods or information in most communities.

BELOW: *The pairing of canal-side slum housing and prosperous high-rise structures beloved of foreign photojournalists persisted in the overcrowded cities of the Philippines into the 21st century.*

CRIMINAL ACTIVITIES

Despite police effectiveness in coordinating international anti-terrorism efforts, the inability of organizational reform to address underlying problems of corruption and a culture of predatory impunity in the security forces is evident in the spike in one variety of 'normal' crime during this period – kidnappings. Alongside the more generic and longer-established criminal gangs, the perpetrators often came from two other backgrounds – communist or Muslim guerrillas engaged in creative fund raising, or crooked police and former or active military personnel. A characteristically considerate, uniquely Filipino innovation introduced by some of these kidnappers was the occasional (and sometimes successful) demand for a pre-emptive payment of ransom to avoid a kidnapping in the first place. In urban areas, the targets were often children of wealthy Chinese or Chinese-Filipino families; many of these people started maintaining private security forces, or sending their children abroad.

Outside the cities, a pattern also emerged of kidnappers targeting beach resorts or other hard-to-defend locations where foreign tourists gathered. This became the specialty of a particular gang of kidnappers known as the Abu Sayyaf Group (ASG). Originating as one of the many splinter groups that supposedly broke off from larger organizations such as the MNLF after the latter's increasingly conciliatory position towards the Philippine government throughout the 1990s, the ASG was widely held to be a good example

THE BOJINKA PLOT

A form in which Islamist militancy began to make its mark on the Philippine scene became evident in the uncovering and neutralization of the Bojinka plot in 1995. This was an early version of the al-Qaida plan to crash international airliners into American high-rise buildings and landmarks, this time from flights originating on the East Asian seaboard heading to the US West Coast. Philippine police and intelligence authorities passed on vital information about Bojinka's planners (one of whom was also involved in early attacks on the World Trade Center in New York) to the Americans.

of a 'lost command' – the colloquial term in Philippine English for an armed illegal organization supposedly separated from its more legitimate parent, but in reality still cooperating with the latter on a basis of deniability. What is undeniable is that the ASG tied down significant numbers of government troops that would otherwise have been deployed against the MNLF or the MILF.

CONSTITUTIONAL CHANGE?

The last year of Ramos's time in office witnessed his efforts to gather support for constitutional changes to overturn the one-term limit on individual presidencies, a campaign quickly dubbed 'Charter Change', or Cha-Cha, by the press. Mobilizing arguments from the business community anxious to maintain the momentum of economic recovery under Ramos's proven leadership, Cha-Cha proponents nevertheless encountered powerful resistance and pushback from the Catholic Church and a broad spectrum of social and political interest groups. Even though she had endorsed Ramos's original run for the presidency, Cory Aquino herself weighed in on the issue in front of a crowd estimated at 200,000 people, remonstrating against Ramos and refreshing memories of the abuses of power during Marcos's extended time in office. Ramos quickly backed down, publicly pledging to ensure a smooth presidential transition in the coming 1998 elections and to avoid any constitutional changes to the one-term limit.

ACTION HERO

The presidential elections were won by Ramos's vice-president, Joseph Estrada, a former film actor and mayor of his hometown of San Juan in the Manila suburbs. An approachable and down-to-earth personality who could speak the earthy language of the masses – or at least the Tagalog-speaking ones – Estrada had an endearing tendency to mangle the English language, in the manner of many in his modestly educated electoral base. Supported by a trapo coalition that opposed Ramos, Estrada won by a landslide victory in 1998 over Ramos's own favoured presidential candidate. His victory had been aided by Imelda Marcos's commitment of her own electoral base to his campaign, after her own planned run for the presidency was disallowed by the election authorities. Conversely, Estrada got as his vice-president Gloria Macapagal-Arroyo, the standard bearer of another trapo coalition that

endorsed Ramos, and the daughter of a previous president, Diosdado Macapagal.

Although of solidly well-to-do, middle-class origins himself, Estrada had built a large fan base among the broad masses over the 30 years of his film career as a crime-fighting action-film hero. In the post-Reaganite world of populist, media-driven politics-as-entertainment, it was therefore inevitable that Vice-President Estrada would be appointed as an actual 'anti-crime czar' by the Ramos administration. Although exerting real efforts to address the kidnapping scourge, Estrada also received much international and domestic criticism for the rough frontier justice that his police minions, perhaps inspired by their boss's on-screen fictional exploits, casually meted out to suspects on the actual streets of a real country.

Estrada assumed office as the Asian financial crisis that had broken out in 1997 was deepening its effects on the country's economy. In the course of his tenure, the Philippines managed to recover from a low of -0.6 per cent growth in 1998 to a moderate positive trend of 3.4 per cent by 1999. Meanwhile, the political landscape was undergoing fundamental changes that challenged the old status quo, one based on the Nacionalista versus Liberal dichotomy of political musical chairs constantly rearranged by the traditional oligarchic families to suit the personal ambitions of their latest standard bearers. For the first time (as provided for in the 1987 Constitution), traditional politicians (trapos) were being joined in Congress and the halls of governmental power by 'party list' delegates. These were usually leftists of one kind or the other, delegates of social groups such as the urban poor, women, workers, farmers, environmentalists, youth, minority ethnic communities, homosexuals or various combinations thereof, all traditionally under-represented in electoral politics.

After Aquino and Ramos's rapprochement with the ageing and compromise-ready leadership of the Moro National Liberation Front, the breakaway Moro Islamic Liberation Front (MILF) continued to pursue a secessionist agenda in Mindanao with escalating levels of violence. In response, in April 2000 Estrada declared an 'all-out-war' against the MILF. The government eventually captured or cleared 46 MILF camps in Mindanao and Sulu, including the movement's headquarters, Camp Abubakar. Nevertheless, the fighting continued to drag on as MILF units and the original MILF splintered and disappeared into urban populations.

Estrada's presidency ended prematurely in January 2001, after mounting popular revulsion at revelations about the massive levels of corruption in his administration. Dissatisfaction over this issue had already started after Estrada began to reintroduce, on a more modest scale, the culture of cronyism that had been such a destructive part of the political culture under the Marcos regime. A group that the press labelled Estrada's Midnight Cabinet – favoured family members and hard-drinking friends (the kind described in most Filipino languages as one's *barkada*, or 'crew') – received favourable treatment in the disbursement of millions in regional pork-barrel funding and other kinds of government contract work.

Resentment at this creeping cronyism received a further boost when coupled with Estrada's increasingly obvious sympathy for the Marcos family, which had lent Estrada support during his election bid. In 1998, the Marcoses almost got approval from his government to have the dictator's body reinterred in the National Heroes' Cemetery (*Libingan ng mga Bayani*), before massive protests forced Estrada to call off the plan. However, the trigger for Estrada's fall from power came in October 2000, when he was accused of having accepted millions of pesos in pay-offs from illegal neighbourhood gambling franchises all over the country. He was impeached by the House of Representatives, but his impeachment trial in the Congress broke down when an Estrada-friendly majority in the Senate voted to block examination of the president's bank records.

This was the signal for what became known as 'EDSA II', a repeat of the precedent set in 1986, of People Power ousting Ferdinand Marcos ('EDSA' refers to Epifanio de los Santos Avenue). EDSA II definitively established this route as the preferred site to stage peaceful uprisings demanding the removal of a sitting Philippine president. Faced with massive protests, defections from his cabinet and a total loss of support from the armed forces and police, Estrada left office on 20 January 2001. His vice-president, Gloria Macapagal-Arroyo, was sworn in as president on the same day. Estrada was

BELOW
Senator Risa Hontiveros, a member of the relatively small Akbayan party whose three social democratic representatives in the House and Senate were elected by way of the party-list system.

217

The San Juan-class patrol vessel EDSA II of the Philippine Coast Guard, named for the second successful People Power uprising that ended Joseph Estrada's presidency in 2001.

arrested in April of that year on charges of plunder, and put in relatively comfortable house arrest for the next six years while his anti-corruption case wound its way through the courts. Although convicted, fined and sentenced to prison, he was pardoned in 2007 by Arroyo on condition that he stayed away from politics at the national level.

GLORIA MACAPAGAL-ARROYO

Unlike the original People Power revolution, which had met with overwhelming approval domestically and internationally (except of course for die-hard Marcos loyalists), the replacement of Estrada with Arroyo proved to be a divisive event. For the second time, mass demonstrations had intervened to change a Philippine government in ways that were not provided for in the written constitution. A parallel politics of the street was becoming institutionalized alongside the regular electoral process.

Arroyo had grown up amid the familiar touchstones of a 20th-century Philippine elite career – private exclusive schools followed by a stint at a prestigious US university (Georgetown), and a doctorate from the University of the Philippines. She was plucked from a post as professor of economics at Ateneo de Manila University to serve in the Cory Aquino administration as undersecretary for trade and commerce. A career in the Senate preceded her time as vice-president. In her first three years in office (serving out the rest of the presidential term Estrada vacated) she reversed herself on her initial promise not to seek re-election. In October 2003, still technically qualified to run because she had not been elected to her current job, she decided to seek her own mandate and six-year term in the coming presidential race. Victorious amid accusations of widespread voting irregularities against another action film star even more famous than Estrada named Fernando Poe, Jr, Arroyo was sworn in as elected president in her own right on 30 June 2004.

Right away, Arroyo began to have problems establishing her legitimacy. In 2005, a phone tap emerged of a conversation recorded immediately before the release of the 2004 voting results, featuring a woman with the voice of Arroyo and an election official discussing various creative ways to maintain her projected margin of victory. The recording sparked calls for a Congressional investigation and triggered mass protests demanding Arroyo's resignation. She admitted inappropriate conversations with an election official, but denied any wrongdoing and refused to step down. Impeachment attempts failed later that year. Eight members of her new cabinet resigned soon after the phone-tap revelations, and the rest of her presidency was marked by periodic calls from them and other critics for a definite reckoning with these electoral fraud allegations.

Given the cloud the phone-tap affair cast over the beginning of Arroyo's full, second term, perhaps only the Hebrew term *chutzpah* can describe her unsuccessful attempt to overhaul the constitution and transform the present presidential-bicameral republic into a federal parliamentary-unicameral form of government. Critics pointed out that such a move would have allowed Arroyo to stay in power as Prime Minister beyond her constitutionally stipulated single six-year term as president, in a similar way to the intended effects of Fidel Ramos's earlier, equally unsuccessful Cha-Cha efforts.

THE GLOBAL WAR ON TERROR

In the midst of all these challenges to the legitimacy of her administration, Arroyo was actively updating the Philippines' close relationship with the

LEFT

Then-President Dmitry Medvedev of Russia tries to shake Gloria Macapagal-Arroyo's hand, Saint Petersburg, 2009.

US for a new and ominous 21st century. Eight days after the collapse of the World Trade Center in September 2001, Arroyo became the first head of an Asian country to fully commit to supporting the Global War on Terror (GWOT) announced by US President George Bush. The immediate result of this stance was the commitment of 60 or so Filipino logistics, medical and security troops to support the 2003 invasion of Iraq (withdrawn the following year after hostage crises there involving kidnapped Filipino OFWs). In a sign of exactly how mimetic Philippine officialdom can still get when it comes to American models, Arroyo's government then went on to push through Congress the 2007 Human Security Act, a clone of the US Homeland Security Act that gave the government new powers to detain and surveil the population in the interests of anti-terrorism.

Arroyo's resumption of the familiar post-1945 Philippine role as loyal

THE MAGUINDANAO MASSACRE

Apart from undermining the hard-won legitimacy of a Philippine presidency still making its way through a long drawn-out post-Marcos political transition, an unfortunate continuity between the Arroyo years and the mainstream of post-war Philippine politics was endemic political violence of the good old trapo kind. This culminated in the Maguindanao massacre, one of the worst mass killings in peacetime Philippine political history. Fifty-eight people, many of them women and children, travelling to an election rally for a candidate in the 2010 gubernatorial elections of the province of Maguindanao, were taken from their vehicles to a newly dug mass grave on a nearby hilltop, where they were shot en masse and buried. Among those killed were 34 journalists, making the massacre one of the deadliest events for journalists in history, according to the international Committee to Protect Journalists. The main suspects in the massacre were members of the Ampatuan clan, a powerful political dynasty that had delivered the entire province to Arroyo during the 2004 election, often with no opposition votes tallied in rural voting precincts.

LEFT: *Monument to the 34 journalists killed in the Maguindanao (or Ampatuan) Massacre, 2010.*

A NEW AMERICAN PRESENCE

A yearly programme of joint US-Filipino military exercises resumed in 2002 under the code name *Balikatan* (Shoulder-to-Shoulder). The Arroyo government insisted that the constitutional ban on foreign military forces based in Philippine territory did not apply, because Balikatan was covered under a 'visiting forces agreement' signed in 1998 that permitted the temporary presence of foreign military personnel. Soon afterwards, American advisers began to accompany Filipino soldiers in operations in various parts of Mindanao, observing the polite fiction that they were mere advisers who would only shoot back if attacked. The more than $100 million yearly in additional US military and miscellaneous aid (after a decade of cut-off since 1992) provided the incentive for the Arroyo government to agree to these deployments, which included the 'pre-positioning' at various places in the archipelago of supplies and facilities for use on short notice by American forces.

RIGHT: *Philippine Navy special operations personnel during a security training exercise on board a visiting US Navy ship, 2005.*

ally and even sidekick in whatever geopolitical project currently preoccupied the US would also have broader consequences. It internationalized the ongoing communist and Muslim insurgencies that had been active since the late 1960s, allowing her government and the US to relabel selected local organizations involved as terrorist threats to the entire global system. Interestingly, only the communist New People's Army along with the Islamist Abu Sayyaf Group landed on the official lists of terrorist organizations maintained by the Americans and the EU. The MNLF and MILF were never put on such lists, because the Arroyo government was actively conducting negotiations with them. Nevertheless, going after Abu Sayyaf in particular became the justification for a gradual reversal of the Philippine policy of barring the permanent presence of foreign military forces in the archipelago, in force since the US vacated its military bases in 1992.

Towards the end of her time in office, Arroyo also managed the remarkable feat of uniting Cory Aquino and Joseph Estrada (whom she had fully pardoned) in joint demands for her to step down. These calls were made as part of a persistent popular campaign demanding a reckoning with the charges of fraud stemming from the 2004 elections. Providing another cause for popular discontent, the Arroyo years also generated their fair share of 'normal' corruption scandals. Perhaps the most high-profile of these were the alleged kickbacks from ZTE, a Chinese telecommunications company bidding for a national broadband network, supposedly paid to Arroyo's husband as well as an Arroyo ally in the Commission on Elections.

In their different ways, the Estrada and Arroyo eras damaged the hard-won legitimacy of the presidency, which Cory Aquino and (at least partly) Fidel Ramos had been struggling to stabilize through a long drawn-out post-Marcos political transition. Nevertheless, Arroyo ended her term as president in the legitimate, constitutionally prescribed manner in 2010, succeeded by Senator Benigno Aquino III. Although she ran for a seat in Congress the same year (becoming the second president after Jose P. Laurel to run for lower office following the presidency), Arroyo was arrested several times on the by-now familiar charges of electoral fraud and corruption, and kept until 2016 under detention in the various hospitals where she had gone for treatment for different ailments.

NOYNOY

Benigno Aquino III ('Noynoy') became the fifteenth President of the independent Philippines on the last day of June 2010. A bachelor and the son of former President Cory Aquino, he came into office on a fairly predictable, unremarkable platform. He promised a major effort at reforms that would build on the achievements of the last 20 years, to bring greater transparency, reduce poverty and corruption, and to pursue growth in an economy that was built on solid fundamentals.

Just as for his predecessor, the start of Aquino's administration began inauspiciously; foreign affairs in particular seemed to provide a regular supply of bad news. The 2010 Manila

BELOW

An effigy of Arroyo during demonstrations against her government in 2007. Note the person in the face mask with the pattern of the American flag gesticulating in front of it. The effigy would eventually be burnt in the course of the demonstration.

hostage crisis involving a bus-full of visitors from Hong Kong ended bloodily, with eight tourists killed before the security forces could neutralize the disgruntled former policeman who had taken them hostage. The incident massively strained relations between Manila and Hong Kong for some time, leading to cancellations of many scheduled events and visits, and incidents against Filipinos in the coastal Chinese city.

ABOVE
President-elect Benigno Aquino III in the Congress on the night of his electoral victory, 9 June 2009. The senator holding his hand on the viewer's left is Juan Ponce Enrile, Ferdinand Marcos's former defence chief and one of the two leaders of the military revolt that helped bring Aquino's mother to power during the 1986 People Power revolution.

Despite the friction between the Philippines and neighbouring countries, the foundations for economic recovery that were laid back in the Ramos era proved to be durable. In Aquino's first year, the economy was already performing well, with a growth rate of 7.2 per cent of GDP, the second fastest in Asia. By 2013, the growth rate was the fastest in Asia. In addition to the continued inflow of remittances from OFWs, another major contributor to this positive outcome was Business Process Outsourcing (BPO), a remote-location information-technology industry that encompasses customer-service call centres, back-office accounting, animation, software development, game development and medical transcription. In 2010, the first year of Aquino's term, the Philippines achieved the milestone of being declared BPO capital of the world in industry surveys, with about a million people employed in an industry that created 27 per cent of all new jobs in the country. In the call-centre subsector of BPO in particular, the Philippines could capitalize on a well-educated workforce proficient in international, relatively accent-free American English, yet paid at rates far below those doing comparable work in advanced industrial countries. The long-term investment in education begun with the Thomasites seemed to be paying off, a century later – if one ignored the criticisms of call centres as sources of a new kind of placeless anomie in sleep-deprived or reverse-body-clocked employees, confined in enclosed spaces while fielding calls using generic American-sounding aliases to serve clients in radically different time zones who have no idea they are talking to Filipinos.

In 2013, Typhoon Haiyan (or Yolanda, using its local Philippine name) struck the central parts of the country, with unparalleled devastation particularly in the province of Leyte and the regions around it. The massive international and domestic assistance effort was marred by some chaos, and the diversion, spoilage or misplacement of some relief funds and goods, often for purposes of political manoeuvring. In 2014, the government finally signed a comprehensive agreement on the Bangsamoro autonomous regional administration in Mindanao with the Moro Islamic Liberation Front. Although this meant that the bulk of mainstream MILF supporters had now joined the Moro National Liberation Front (from which it had split off in 1978 over the extent of autonomy demands) in coming to a negotiated agreement with the Philippine government, this did not solve the problem of splinter groups such as the Abu Sayyaf, the Bangsamoro Independence Freedom Fighters/BIFF (ex-MILF) and the forces under Nur Misuari (ex-MNLF) that continued hostilities against both the Philippine military and civilian communities.

THE SOUTH CHINA SEA

During the Aquino presidency, the Philippines (along with Vietnam) experienced intensifying political and diplomatic tension with the People's Republic of China over territorial disputes about outlying groups of islets, reefs and shoals in the South China Sea. The Philippines started calling the areas off the coasts of Palawan and Luzon the West Philippine Sea, while beefing up its civilian and military presence and generally avoiding direct confrontations between its relatively weak forces and those of the Chinese. As part of a larger Chinese push to assert a claim of historical sovereignty over most of the Sea's area (the so-called Nine-Dash Line), the PRC Navy began to build up massive permanent military installations on some of these maritime features, including airstrips, harbours and barracks.

While also intended for internal nationalistic consumption in China, the other, twin contexts of this activity were an effort to challenge the US as the dominant hegemonic power in the South China Sea basin, while reminding the countries lining its shores of China's historical suzerainty over their tribute-paying ancestors. Although this precipitated something of a mini-arms race among other countries in the region, the Philippines' limited fiscal resources and the historically close relationship with the US meant that much of the response within areas of Philippine maritime claims or nearby came from US naval forces, which in turn signalled a renewed readiness from the Philippine leadership to countenance the presence of the US military within the archipelago. On 12 January 2016,

LEFT
A typical call centre in Bacolod City, 2008.

the Philippine Supreme Court upheld the Enhanced Defense Cooperation Agreement signed by the Aquino administration, paving the way for the return of US Armed Forces bases into the country. In 2013, the Philippines had also filed a request for arbitration with the Permanent Court of Arbitration in the Hague on the basis of the United Nations Convention on the Law of the Sea.

RODRIGO DUTERTE

With personal roots in the Visayan migrations to Mindanao during the 20th century, Davao City mayor Rodrigo Duterte won the 2016 election to replace Aquino, becoming the first Mindanaoanon to occupy the presidency. The vice-president elect, Leni Robredo, was from an opposing political party and won with the second narrowest margin in history, against Bongbong Marcos, the son of the late dictator. Two weeks after Duterte's accession, on 12 July 2016, the Hague ruled in favour of the Philippines against China's claims in the South China Sea, but the Chinese government indicated that it would not accept the jurisdiction or validity of the court's decision. Meanwhile, Duterte was making good on his electoral promise to launch an intensified anti-drug campaign and wipe out criminality in six months by allowing police and security forces to extrajudicially execute suspects on the street, sidestepping due process.

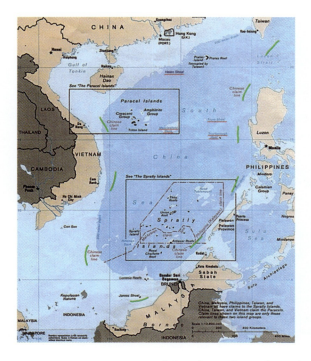

The Nine-Dash Line indicating Chinese maritime claims, marked in green.

This policy of dealing with symptoms first before addressing the root of a wider socio-economic syndrome proved to be quite popular among Filipinos suffering under a drug problem driven by unemployment and poverty. By March 2017, reliable estimates of the extrajudicial campaign's death toll had passed 8,000 people, with 2,679 killed in 'legitimate' police operations and the rest claimed by the government to be private homicide cases. Duterte responded to the opprobrium this campaign raised in observers from abroad by doubling down on an abrasive, earthy and sometimes shockingly vulgar kind of rhetoric that even scandalized some Filipinos unaware of the style's roots in Cebuano-Visayan satire and black humour. He also sought to demonstrate his independence from American hegemony by threatening to end mutual military cooperation and travelling to China to repair relations strained by the West Philippine/South China Sea dispute. In the end, though, Duterte did nothing that previous Filipino presidents had not already done in the delicate balancing act between too much submissiveness and too much defiance of the Americans.

Perhaps the most spectacular development of Duterte's time in office was the occupation of Marawi City, capital of Lanao del Sur province, by the radical Islamist Maute group in May 2017, and the recapture of the city by the Philippine military by November of that year. The worst urban fighting in the Philippines since the Second World War destroyed much of the city centre, and was the prelude to Duterte's declaration of martial law for the entire island of Mindanao. The Maute fighters were joined by the Abu Sayyaf Group and other breakaway Islamist factions, most of whom had pledged loyalty to the Islamic State in the Levant and Syria (ISIS). Even as their leadership was being killed during the Marawi fighting, unconfirmed reports were filtering in that survivors were recruiting and regrouping. What is clear is that the precarious peace agreements won at so much effort and patience between the government and the mainstream MILF and MNLF over previous years and decades did not spell the end of the long Muslim insurgency. If anything, reports of foreign fighters among the dead jihadists, the temporary infiltration of insurgents into parts of the Visayas like Bohol, and the scale of destruction left behind in Marawi suggested that the struggle between the two cultures and religions might be entering a new and even more dangerous phase. Meanwhile, Duterte's declaration of martial law for Mindanao was extended until the end of 2018, with the possibility of other areas being included.

The International Criminal Court formally began investigating the Philippines' drug war in 2018; in response, Duterte withdrew his country from the ICC. Aside from his controversial drugs policy, his administration addressed crime and corruption, taxation reform and infrastructure-building. He introduced laws enabling foreign ownership of property and businesses, intensified drives against terrorism and communist insurgency, and streamlined government processes. He also unsuccessfully proposed a shift to a federal system of government. The Philippines ratified the Paris Agreement on Climate Change after Duterte's initial misgivings about its impact on the country's industrialization. He later urged that rich industrial countries compensate smaller countries for damage caused by climate change.

Duterte's leadership style was described as 'populist' and 'nationalist' by many observers. Like Hungary's Viktor Orban, India's Narendra Modi, Brazil's Jair Bolsonaro, and Donald Trump in the United States, he seemed part of a shift in democracies around the world to quasi-authoritarian and anti-pluralist leadership amidst the decay of the neo-liberal, American-based world system. Despite such criticism, Duterte enjoyed high approval ratings, for example 87 per cent on a 2019 survey conducted by Pulse Asia. A 2019 Social Weather Station survey showing 82 per cent of 1,200 interviewed Filipinos 'overwhelmingly satisfied' with Duterte's extrajudicial war on drugs.

ABOVE
Rodrigo R. Duterte, 2016.

ABOVE

Protests against Duterte's drug war outside the Philippine Consulate General in New York City, 2016.

PANDEMIC

On 1 February 2020, the Philippines was the first country outside China to report a death from COVID-19. Despite difficulties with testing and vaccine procurement, the country's response has been comparatively effective; on May 15, 2022, the Philippines had around 3.5 million cases with 60,455 deaths — fifth place in Southeast Asia behind Vietnam, Indonesia, Malaysia and Thailand. Despite criticisms of long mass community quarantines (featuring the usual threats to shoot violators), Duterte also got high approval ratings from Filipinos for his handling of the pandemic.

2022 PRESIDENTIAL ELECTION AND THE RETURN OF THE MARCOS FAMILY

After a bewildering series of on-again, off-again decisions to run for vice president or senator, Duterte retired from politics in late 2021 after deciding not to face his daughter Sara in the vice-presidential race. After equally convoluted hesitations, Sara decided to run as vice presidential candidate for Ferdinand 'Bongbong' Marcos Jr, the late dictator's son, who announced his presidential candidacy in late 2021.

Bongbong Marcos won the presidency by a wide margin in the elections of 9 May 2022 amid claims of massive disinformation and trolling on social media. Nevertheless, most competing candidates (and the Catholic Church) quickly called for acceptance of election results as the country woke up the next day to the return to power of the country's most divisive political family.

ABOVE
The burning skyline of Marawi City during the Maute uprising, 2017.

THE MARCOS REBURIAL

On 8 November 2016, the Supreme Court of the Philippines ruled in favour of allowing the reburial of the late president Ferdinand Marcos in the National Heroes' Cemetery (*Libingan ng Mga Bayani*), setting off furious protests from thousands of young people, and Marcos-regime human rights victims and their relatives. Duterte, who needed support from voters in Ilocos Norte, the home province of Marcos, had made the reinterment a campaign promise. On 18 November 2016, Ferdinand Marcos was secretly buried in the cemetery by his family and friends, attended and protected by official police and military contingents. This was done despite stays put on the Supreme Court order pending review.

RIGHT: *Protests against the reburial of Ferdinand Marcos in the National Heroes' Cemetery, 2016.*

CONCLUSION: THE CHALLENGE TO IMAGINE

After centuries without control of their own destinies, the peoples of the Philippines are busy defining an authentic place for their fractious yet strangely resilient nation in a dangerously changing world. The burdens and dysfunctions inherited from the past are many and heavy. Oligarchy, corruption and extremes of poverty work in a demoralizing negative synergy. Inherited institutions and laws that did not emerge out of the decisions and collective experiences of ordinary people are not particularly good at representing their interests. The rule of the gun deepens the impact of sectarian and class conflict, while the armed coup and the mass popular uprising have recently joined constitutional procedures and the rule of law as all-too-convenient methods of forcing political change. A persistent sense of cultural shallowness and anomie emerges from the tenuousness of any links to authentic popular memories of the pre-Spanish and Spanish-colonial past. This drives a national tendency to creative fantasizing and wish-fulfilment in the search for the historical roots of national identity. The lure of emigration at any cost will continue to draw many, particularly among the best and the brightest (as well as the most industrious and long-suffering), whose absence has been crucial to undesirable political, economic and social outcomes from the 1970s until today. An unresolved tension lingers between the modest unifying effects of Tagalog-Filipino as the national language so far, and its equally real function as enforcer of an unreflected, semi-conscious Tagalog sense of entitlement to archipelago-wide cultural hegemony. This alienates many people in the other ethnolinguistic groups and holds them back from a fuller emotional investment in the many challenges of national life. A population of around 100 million is set to double sometime in the 2060s, as per capita income and provision of public services and infrastructure remain vulnerable to population growth rates that have barely begun a demographic transition to sustainable levels.

Yet the country's resilience is striking. It has a resource base, a skilled and cooperative workforce, and a beautiful natural environment that, if the ongoing wholesale exploitation by foreigners and their local elite partners can be kept to manageable levels, could nevertheless sustain and enrich both the still vigorously growing population and the more deserving among international partners. Plenty of social capital exists in the form of interlocking support systems of families, friends and other networks at almost all socio-economic levels. These are complemented by the broadening horizons for ordinary Filipinos made possible by information technology and a cultural commitment to education – if not yet by passports sufficiently respected internationally to allow easy physical entry into the global centres of power and culture. The time-tested national habits of compromise, mutually face-saving consideration, and dialogue have produced a robust social ethics, undergirded by powerful religious faiths that are practised emotionally, not intellectually. A broad cultural consensus in support of political democracy has been strengthened and tempered time and again by a difficult history.

This book appears around the time of perhaps the most important inflection point in Philippine history since the coming of American power to Manila Bay more than a century ago. Filipinos (along with Cubans and Puerto Ricans) were among the first and most uniquely situated people in the world to experience the full impact of an American century of global US power and influence. Now the Philippines (and the waters directly to the west of it) look set to be a key regional arena for the intensifying, if still early, stages of a possible – and epochal – historical transition to a post-American world. The growing tension between the US and China over hegemony and influence in Southeast Asia and the South China Sea in some ways echoes the growing tension between Japan and the Western colonial powers in the same region in the 1930s. The last two times the Philippines was caught in armed confrontations between the US and other major powers in Asia, it did not fare very well.

Yet the Nine-Dash Line conflict is only the politico-military and diplomatic face of a broader psychological and cultural challenge – the greatest since the Katipunan generation's repudiation of Spain – that Filipinos face, as the United States enters a period of change in its relations with the rest of the world. Whether in eager embrace, passive acceptance or active opposition, reacting to the US and all its works has been central to Filipino identities and ways of experiencing the world throughout the 20th century. Unlike other Southeast Asians occupied by the British, French and Dutch, Filipinos have not yet begun to imagine what national life might look like in a possible future where the hard – if not the soft – power of their most recent colonial ruler has been eclipsed. This challenge, and responsibility, to *imagine* is an increasingly urgent task.

TIMELINE

c.55,000 BC First *Homo sapiens* in the Philippines.

50–20,000 BC Australoid migrations. Stone tools in Tabon Caves, Palawan.

13,000–300 BC Break-up of Sundaland. Austronesian migrations.

c.4000 BC Earliest evidence of rice agriculture and chicken/pig domestication.

c.1000 BC Late Neolithic. Proliferation of pottery styles. Beginning of metalworking.

c.900 BC Emergence of Sa Huynh Culture based on Nusantao Maritime Trading and Communication Network.

AD 200–400 Trading networks and thalassocracies in Southeast Asia take on significant aspects of Hindu-Buddhist culture from India. Some elements of this, such as Baybayin script, ideas about rulership and vocabulary reach the Philippines.

AD 600–1000 Seaports in the Philippines such as Butuan, Ma-i and Namayan deepen their trade and diplomatic links with China.

AD 900 Laguna Copperplate Inscription gives written evidence of extensive trade and cultural contact between barangays in Manila Bay area and Majapahit and Bruneian cultural mandalas.

1174–75 Visayan pirates attack South Chinese Coast. Butuan recedes in importance while Sulu grows in wealth and power.

c.1240 Earliest Muslim missionaries arrive in Mindanao and Sulu.

1380 First mosque built in Jolo, Sulu.

1411 Embassy of Sulu seeks recognition at Chinese imperial court.

c.1450 Realm of Tondo becomes most important power in Manila Bay area.

1475 Sultanate of Sulu founded.

1500 Tondo incorporated into recently Islamized polity of Manila under rulers related to Bruneian royal house.

1521 Ferdinand Magellan lands successively on Homonhon, Limasawa and Cebu islands, claims territory for Spain, holds Christian Mass and baptizes Humabon, the ruler of Cebu and his wife. Magellan killed by Lapulapu from nearby Mactan. Remnant of his crew completes the first circumnavigation of the globe the following year.

1525–43 Spain sends three more expeditions to chart route to newly discovered islands and the Moluccas: Loaisa (direct from Seville), Saavedra and Villalobos (from Mexico). Villalobos names archipelago the Philippine Islands in honour of new Habsburg king of Spain, Philip II.

1565 Miguel Lopez de Legazpi leads a fifth expedition that marks beginning of permanent Spanish conquest and rule in the Philippines.

1568–70 Portuguese attacks on the new Spanish colony.

1571 Legaspi moves capital of new colony to Manila after defeating Rajah Soliman. Juan de Salcedo and Martin de Goiti begin planting new towns and settlements across lowland Luzon. Encomienda system initiated.

1574 Chinese pirate Limahong attacks Manila but is repulsed. Anti-Spanish revolt by Lakandula and other leaders in Manila/Tondo area crushed.

1576 Commercial treaty between Spain and China regulating trade and migration to the Philippines signed. Growing Chinese labourer and trader influx.

1579 Diocese of Manila established.

1580 Philip II of Spain also becomes King of Portugal, temporarily ending Portuguese threat to colony. Labour and service obligations (*polos y servicios*) are laid over entire lowland population.

1592 *Doctrina Christiana* appears in Chinese translation, first Western book published in the Philippines.

1595 College of San Idelfonso founded in Cebu.

1600 Pedro Bucaneg writes down the oral epic *Biag ni Lam-ang*. Start of galleon trade.

1602 Major Chinese revolt unsuccessful.

1611 College of Our Lady of the Holy Rosary (later University of Santo Tomas) established in Manila.

1621 Tamblot and Bangkaw Revolts.

1635–44 Governor-General Sebastian Hurtado de Corcuera confronts power of religious missionary orders and wages Mindanao campaign against Sultan Kudarat.

1646–47 Dutch naval attacks and blockades of the Philippines.

1662 Chinese revolt of 1662.

1663 Chinese warlord Koxinga threatens invasion of the Philippines. Spanish garrisons withdrawn from Mindanao to meet this threat, ending ongoing Spanish attempt to conquer southern Muslim sultanates there.

1686 Construction begins of Paoay church in Ilocos, prominent example of the 'earthquake baroque' style.

*c.***1660–1890s** Low-intensity war of Moro raids on coastal settlements and Spanish counter-campaign continues, without resolution of the essential conflict about survival of these southern Muslim states, increasingly coming under British influence.

1719 Governor-General Fernando Bustamante killed in anti-government rioting instigated by the Catholic Church leadership after disputes over the right of sanctuary in churches by suspects accused of major crimes. Manila archbishop Francisco de la Cuesta becomes acting governor-general.

1744–1829 Dagohoy Rebellion – longest in Philippine history.

1762–64 British invasion of the Philippines and occupation of Manila. Dawson Drake becomes British governor-general. Simon de Anda leads resistance movement and counter-government in Pampanga. Silang Revolt in Ilocos region. 1763 Treaty of Paris implicitly returns the Philippines to Spain. Last British troops and ships leave in following year.

1769 Jesuits expelled from the Philippines on royal orders.

1770s–90s Efforts to secularize parishes with diocesan priests by command of Charles III fail leaving missionary orders still in control of the majority.

1778 Governor-General Jose Basco y Vargas sponsors Real Sociedad Economica del Amigos de Pais as a vehicle for the Enlightenment-style modernization of the colony's economy and social relations, and the training of a future technocratic elite.

1783 College of San Carlos (now University of San Carlos) takes over premises of College of San Idelfonso in Cebu, closed with the Jesuit expulsion of 1769.

1808 Bourbon dynasty replaced by French puppet government in Madrid with Joseph Bonaparte as King of Spain.

1811 *Del Superior Gobierno*, the colony's first newspaper.

1812 Spanish Cortes promulgates the Cadiz Constitution, granting civil rights, citizenship and parliamentary representation to all non-black inhabitants of Spain's colonies. The Philippines sends two delegates from white European settler population to Cortes.

1813 Cadiz Constitution promulgated in Manila. Peninsular War in Iberia grows in intensity and violence until Napoleonic troops are driven out by an Anglo-Spanish alliance under the Duke of Wellington.

1814 Bourbon King Ferdinand VII regains Spanish throne. Royalist Conservatives gain control of Cortes.

1816 Cadiz Constitution rejected by conservative government and the Philippines loses representation in Cortes and guarantees of civil liberties.

1823 Novales Revolt breaks out among European criollo population of colony, leading to crystallization of a 'Filipino' identity, first only among Europeans born in archipelago.

1828 Massive earthquake damages much of Manila.

1830–37 Manila gradually opened to world market under terms of free trade.

1835 Chamber of Commerce formed.

1841 Execution of Apolinario de la Cruz (Hermano Pule), militant cult leader from Batangas.

1846 *La Esperanza* published as colony's first daily newspaper.

1859 Jesuits return to the Philippines, setting off reshuffling of parish and other clerical posts at expense of native secular priests, and in favour of European missionary clergy, strengthening existing 'frailocracy'. Jesuits set up the future Ateneo de Manila University.

1861 Birth of Jose Rizal, Philippine national hero.

1863 Another major earthquake destroys much of

Manila. Birth of Andres Bonifacio, future head of Katipunan.

1864 Birth of Apolinario Mabini, future 'Brains of the Revolution'.

1865 Jesuits set up Manila Observatory.

1869 Suez Canal opens, allowing easier travel and communication between the Philippines and Spain. Carlos Maria del la Torre becomes governor-general, introduces sweeping liberal reforms of law, government, and social policy to popular acclaim. Ilustrado reformers spread from criollo to native population, along with identity of 'Filipino'.

1871 Governor-General De la Torre replaced by conservative Rafael de Izquierdo, who cancels most of liberal reforms.

1872 Two hundred native soldiers stage unsuccessful mutiny at Cavite Arsenal. Activist Filipino priests Gomez, Burgos, and Zamora accused of complicity and executed, leading to wave of support for Filipino self-determination.

1880 Telegraph connects Manila with Europe. Another major earthquake in Luzon. The reformist Propaganda Movement begins effort to mobilize Spanish and European opinion in favour of Philippine liberalization.

1882 Rizal leaves for Spain to continue his medical studies. He is drawn into work of Propaganda Movement, along with Marcelo H. del Pilar and Graciano Lopez Jaena. Rizal begins writing *Noli Me Tangere*.

1884 *Polos y servicios* forced labour requirement reduced to 15 days from 46, the rest commuted to a tax payment.

1885 Cebu gets its own municipal government.

1887 *Noli Me Tangere* published. Rizal starts *El Filibusterismo*.

1889 *La Solidaridad* published in Spain as organ of Propaganda Movement.

1891 *El Filibusterismo* published in Ghent.

1892 Rizal returns to the Philippines and founds La Liga Filipina, causing his arrest and exile to Dapitan in Mindanao. Andres Bonifacio establishes Katipunan.

1896 Rizal receives permission from Governor-General Ramon Blanco to leave the Philippines for service as an army doctor in fighting against Cuban Revolution. Katipunan plans for an uprising discovered by Spanish, triggering Cry of Balintawak and premature start of Philippine Revolution. Rizal's journey to Cuba cut short with his arrest and return to Manila for trial as an instigator of the revolt. Rizal executed at the end of December.

1897
March–May Tejeros Convention elects Emilio Aguinaldo as President of Revolutionary government, bypassing Supreme Council headed by Bonifacio. Violent split in leadership leads to Bonifacio's arrest and execution on charges of sedition and treason. Aguinaldo establishes revolutionary government at Biak-na-Bato in Bulacan province.

August–December Aguinaldo begins negotiations with Spanish to end stalemate. Constitution of Biak-na-Bato promulgated. Aguinaldo agrees Pact of Biak-na-Bato with Governor-General Primo de Rivera. For a monetary indemnity and promise of no reprisals for Filipino rank and file, Aguinaldo and much of revolutionary leadership enter voluntary exile in Hong Kong.

1898
February–April Katipunan regional governments and fronts maintained as low-grade fighting continues. Aguinaldo in unofficial discussions with US representatives in Hong Kong and Singapore over possible support for Filipino independence. US declares war on Spain.

May–July Admiral George Dewey destroys Spanish fleet in Battle of Manila Bay. Aguinaldo and his followers return to the Philippines. Aguinaldo declares Philippine independence and forms a revolutionary government. Malolos Congress is convoked. US reinforcements arrive in the Philippines.

August–December Spanish forces surrender to Americans after mock Battle of Manila. Spain turns over sovereignty over the Philippines to US in Treaty of Paris. US President McKinley issues Benevolent Assimilation proclamation.

1899 Malolos Constitution promulgated. First

Philippine Republic inaugurated with Aguinaldo as President. Hostilities break out in Filipino-American War. The First Philippine Commission (Schurman Commission) arrives in Manila. Antonio Luna and Apolinario Mabini suppress attempts at compromise with Americans, Luna killed. Gregorio del Pilar and his troops killed delaying Aguinaldo's American pursuers at Battle of Tirad Pass.

1900 Schurman Commission returns to US. Taft Commission begins construction of permanent colonial administration. Federalista Party formed.

1901 Aguinaldo captured by American-led forces, takes oath of allegiance to US. William Howard Taft becomes first civilian governor-general. Philippine Constabulary organized. Balangiga Massacre.

1902 Thomasites assist in construction of school system. Miguel Malvar surrenders to US forces. Macario Sakay sets up second Tagalog Republic. Philippine Organic Act passed. Philippine Assembly established. Despite official declaration of end of Philippine Insurrection, fighting continues, with remaining insurgents classified by Americans as bandits. Iglesia Filipina Independiente separates from Roman Catholic Church.

1903 Taft declares policy of Philippines for Filipinos in government appointments, etc. Friar lands purchased, but distributed mostly to elites.

1907 Macario Sakay captured and hanged. University of the Philippines established. Nacionalista party formed.

1913 Francis Burton Harrison appointed governor-general.

1916 Jones Law creating all-Filipino legislature and formally promising eventual independence is de facto constitution until 1935. Nacionalistas dominate Philippine politics – Sergio Osmeña is Speaker of the House while Manuel Quezon is Senate President.

1921 Leonard Wood appointed governor-general.

1930 Communist Party of the Philippines established.

1931 Osmeña-Roxas Mission to US Congress secures Hare-Hawes-Cutting Act providing for timetable for independence after a period of Commonwealth status and detailed negotiations about immigration, trade and defence. Act is rejected by Quezon-influenced Philippine legislature.

1932 Communist Party declared illegal by Supreme Court.

1933 Frank Murphy, last American governor general, gives vote to women. The Sakdalista Party formed.

1934 Tydings-McDuffie Law, Quezon's near identical Commonwealth-Independence legislation, signed into law by President Roosevelt, ratified by Philippine Legislature.

1935 New constitution promulgated for new Philippine Commonwealth. Transitional period of 10 years until independence. Quezon elected President, Osmeña Vice-President. Failed Sakdalista uprising results in 30 dead and exile of Sakdalista leaders to Japan. Governor-generalship abolished; Frank Murphy becomes first US High Commissioner. Armed Forces of the Philippines created.

1939 First commercial radio station DZRH begins transmissions.

1941 Philippine Airlines starts operations. Quezon begins second presidential term. Japan attacks Pearl Harbor and US installations in the Philippines, starting Second World War in Asia. Manila declared open city. Quezon and his cabinet evacuated first to Corregidor, then to US via Australia. US and Filipino forces retreat to Bataan.

1942 Japanese troops enter Manila. Bataan and Corregidor fall, Death March to Tarlac for Allied prisoners. The People's Anti-Japanese Army (*Hukbalahap*) underground resistance organized by Communists. Other resistance forces emerge led by US and Filipino guerrillas. Japanese organize collaborators into *Kalibapi*.

1943 Japanese sponsor puppet Second Philippine Republic with Jose Laurel as President while mobilizing economy to support Japanese war effort. Economy veers toward collapse.

1944 Death of Quezon; Sergio Osmeña becomes Commonwealth President in exile. MacArthur lands in Leyte with Osmeña after Battle of Leyte Gulf. Major American air attacks on Philippine cities. *Makapili* pro-Japanese militia organized.

1945 Further American landings at Lingayen

Gulf en route to Manila. Battle of Manila destroys central city. General Tomoyuki Yamashita retreats to uplands in northern Luzon. Laurel's government evacuated to Japan. Japanese defeated in Cebu, Panay, and other parts of the Visayas. Osmeña reforms Commonwealth government. 1941 Congress meets for first time. Japanese surrender in Tokyo Bay. Laurel dissolves Second Philippine Republic. Yamashita's army surrenders in Ifugao Province. Manuel Roxas breaks away from Osmeña and Nacionalistas to form Liberal Party and contest coming presidential election.

1946 Generals Yamashita and Homma executed for war crimes. Manuel Roxas wins last Commonwealth presidential election. US recognizes independent Republic of the Philippines with Roxas as first President.

1947 Roxas declares amnesty for all collaborators with Japan. Hukbalahap declared illegal. Treaty of General Relations signed between US and Philippines. Peace Treaty signed with Japan.

1948 Manuel Roxas dies of heart attack at American military base. Vice President Elpidio Quirino becomes President.

1950 Philippines sends combat forces to Korean War. Ramon Magsaysay becomes Secretary of Defence.

1951 Mutual Defense Treaty signed between US and Philippines.

1953 Ramon Magsaysay becomes President.

1954 South East Asia Treaty Organization (SEATO) formed in Manila. Laurel-Langley Agreement signed.

1957 Magsaysay dies in plane crash in Cebu; Carlos P. Garcia becomes President.

1958 'Filipino First' policy promulgated.

1961 Diosdado Macapagal elected President.

1962 Macapagal changes date of Independence Day from July 4 (the 1946 anniversary) to June 12 (the 1898 anniversary).

1963 24 Philippine Boy Scout delegates to the 11th World Scout Jamboree in Greece killed in plane crash in Indian Ocean. Macapagal signs Agricultural Land Reform Code.

1964 Death of Emilio Aguinaldo.

1965 Ferdinand Marcos elected President.

1967 Association of Southeast Asian Nations (ASEAN) is formed with Philippines as a founding member.

1968 Jabidah massacre of Muslim Philippine Army recruits escalates radicalization of new Moro generation. New Maoist-style Communist Party of the Philippines (CPP) established by Jose Maria Sison after dissatisfaction with remnants of old-style PKP.

1969 CPP sets up its military arm, the New People's Army (NPA) and begins armed revolutionary struggle against Republic. Ferdinand Marcos re-elected president.

1970 Student protests reach peak in First Quarter Storm. Pope Paul VI survives assassination attempt on visit to the Philippines.

1971 Constitutional Convention begins work. Marcos suspends writ of *habeas corpus* after Plaza Miranda bombing.

1972 Moro National Liberation Front (MNLF) begins its armed struggle for independence of Muslim-majority regions of Mindanao. Wave of bombings with no clear claims of responsibility occur all over country.

September 21 Marcos signs Proclamation 1081 putting entire country under Martial Law. Not yet publicly announced. Alleged assassination attempt on Defence Minister Juan Ponce Enrile.

September 22 Martial Law proclamation officially announced. Media outlets shut down or placed under government control.

September 23 Opposition figures such as Ninoy Aquino and Jose Diokno and thousands of others arrested. Whole country is declared an Agricultural Land Reform area.

1973 Plebiscite/Referendum held among *ad hoc* 'citzens' assemblies' to ratify new constitution giving Marcos essentially dictatorial powers. Marcos's term extended by manipulated referendum. Chinese drug lord Lim Seng executed as part of anti-narcotics campaign. National Democratic Front (NDF) formed to coordinate efforts of leftist anti-government forces with CPP. Margie Moran crowned Miss Universe.

1974 Lieutenant Hiroo Onoda emerges from hiding in jungle of Lubang Island and formally surrenders as last Japanese straggler from Second World War, amidst media circus. He is pardoned for killing of Filipinos after 1945 by Marcos.

1976 Martial Law extended by new manipulated plebiscite. Tripoli Agreement leads to ceasefire between Army and MNLF.

1977 CPP leader Jose Maria Sison arrested. Ninoy Aquino and other detainees condemned to death by military courts, but sentences not carried out. Another referendum approves Marcos's stay in office and allows him to take additional title of Prime Minister.

1978 Interim *Batasang Pambansa* (IBP) is inaugurated as Marcos's rubber stamp parliament, filled with New Society Movement (KBL-*Kilusang Bagong Lipunan*) members.

1981 Pope John Paul II visits the Philippines for first time. Another manipulated general election-plus-referendum ratifies Marcos's rule for third term. Cesar Virata becomes Prime Minister. 169 workers killed during construction of Manila Film Center.

1983 Benigno Aquino Jr. assassinated on arrival at Manila International Airport.

1985 Special court acquits General Fabian Ver and co-accused of involvement in Aquino killing.

1986 Amid widespread accusations of regime cheating and manipulation, both Marcos and Cory Aquino claim victory in Philippine presidential elections. EDSA Revolution (People Power plus Enrile-Ramos military mutiny) deposes Marcos from power and Aquino becomes President. Marco goes into exile in Hawaii. Aquino sets up Revolutionary Government and Commission on Good Government, abolishes Interim Batasang Pambansa, and begins work to replace 1971 Constitution with new Freedom Constitution.

1987 Mendiola Massacre during agrarian protest rally. New constitution ratified in plebiscite. Bloodiest of several coup attempts launched by Gringo Honasan, leaving 53 dead and over 200 wounded. Lorenzo Ruiz canonized as first Filipino saint. MV *Doña Paz* and MT *Vector* collide and sink with 4,386 dead, deadliest peacetime maritime disaster in world history.

1988 Aquino signs Comprehensive Agrarian Reform program and (with the US) Interior Bases Agreement.

1989 Autonomous Region of Muslim Mindanao (ARRM) created. Death of Ferdinand Marcos. Gringo Honasan and other military officers launch most serious threat to Aquino's government so far, with 99 casualties and intervention by US aircraft needed to defeat uprising.

1990 Merger of Philippine Constabulary (PC) with Integrated National Police (INP) to form Philippine National Police (PNP). Mt Pinatubo erupts in second largest volcanic eruption of 20th century, covering much of central Luzon (including two major US military bases in ash). Clark Air Base rendered permanently inactive. Philippine Senate rejects renewal of bases treaty. US hands over Clark and prepares to leave Subic Naval Base.

1992 Fidel Ramos elected as President in first democratic presidential election since 1969. Last US forces leave country.

1994 First Philippine connection to the Internet. Bomb explodes on Philippine Airlines flight as test run for 'Bojinka' plot.

1995 Filipina housemaid Flor Contemplacion executed in Singapore for murder of fellow domestic and child of employer. President Ramos opens special Export Processing Zones in Subic and other locations. 'Ceboom' in second largest city of Cebu.

1996 'Permanent' peace agreement signed between government and MNLF.

1997 Asian Economic Crisis hits country.

1998 Joseph Estrada elected President. Centennial of Philippine independence.

2000 Estrada declares 'all-out war' against breakaway Moro Islamic Liberation Front (MILF). Abu Sayyaf terrorists hold 21 people hostage in Malaysian resort for four months. Estrada impeached in House of Representatives for corruption.

2001 Walkout at Estrada trial after senators vote to block release of possible evidence. Crowd gathers at EDSA II Revolution, Estrada deposed, Vice President Gloria-Macapagal Arroyo takes over as President. 20 hostages taken by Abuf Sayyaf at Palawan beach resort and held for 12 months.

2004 Abu Sayyaf bombs ferry near Manila Bay, killing 116 people. Macapagal-Arroyo elected to her own six-year term as President.

2005 'Hello Garci' scandal around recorded conversations allegedly between Macapagal-Arroyo and election commissioner over alleged manipulation of results.

2006 Death penalty law repealed.

2007 12th ASEAN Summit in Mandaue City. Exiled Communist Party head Jose Maria Sison arrested in the Netherlands, but extradition prevented by court order. Sandiganbayan convicts former President Estrada for plunder and sentences him to imprisonment, but case caught in appeal technicalities. Arroyo eventually pardons him. Manila Peninsula Hotel mutiny.

2008 Former First Lady Imelda Marcos, who had been allowed to return to the Philippines by Cory Aquino, acquitted by a Manila court of 32 counts of illegal money transfers. Other cases against her still pending. Hundreds of bomb components seized from house of Filipino with alleged links to Jemaah Islamiya pan-Southeast Asian terrorist network. Peace talks between government and MILF collapse.

2009 Death of Cory Aquino. Maguindanao massacre kills 58 in world's deadliest attack on journalists.

2010 Benigno Aquino III (Noynoy) wins the presidency in the first fully computerized national election in Philippine history. Hostage taking by disgruntled policeman of Hong Kong tourists results in deaths of nine people and tension between Philippines and Hong Kong.

2011 Former President Gloria Macapagal-Arroyo arrested on corruption, electoral sabotage and other charges while in hospital.

2012 Death of Philippine comedy king Dolphy. Agreement signed on Bangsamoro as new poltical entity to replace ARRM in southern Mindanao. Canonization of St Pedro Calungsod, first Visayan saint. Reproductive Health Bill signed.

2013 Bangsamoro forces declare independence from the Philippines but defeated in Zamboanga City crisis. Typhoon Haiyan (locally known as Yolanda, deadliest on record) and major earthquake in the Visayas devastate the east-central part of the country, particularly province of Leyte and its capital Tacloban, and also province of Bohol. The Philippines files a request for arbitration with China at United Nations regarding shoals and reefs in South China Sea. Philippine government begins using term 'West Philippine Sea' for this maritime area.

2014 Philippine officials sign agreements with their Indonesian counterparts regarding boundaries and economic zones in waters between them. Birth of baby girl in Manila hospital chosen as statistical milestone marking population growth to 100,000,000 Filipinos.

2015 Hostilities continue with Bangsamoro and other Muslim splinter groups. 51st International Eucharistic Congress held in Cebu City.

2016 Rodrigo Duterte elected president. As promised during his election campaign, wave of killings under dubious legality of people alleged to be involved in drug use or trafficking begins and sparks international criticism. The UN Permanent Court of Arbitration rules in favour of the Philippines against China over jurisdiction of areas in South China Sea. China does not recognize decision and continues island- and base-building activities in close proximity to Philippine and US military vessels. Former president Gloria Macapagal-Arroyo acquitted of corruption and plunder charges. Former president Ferdinand Marcos re-buried in the National Heroes' Cemetery (Libingan ng mga Bayani), sparking intense protest.

2017 Duterte mandates universal access to modern family-planning methods. The Philippines signs Paris Agreement on Climate Change. Clashes between army, police and Abu Sayyaf in Inabanga, Bohol province. Major military campaign to re-take Marawi City after it falls to Maute group and other jihadist forces. Results in worst urban fighting in the Philippines since Second World War that destroys most of Marawi City centre.

2018 A state of Martial Law in Mindanao extended until 31 December 2018.

2022 Ferdinand 'Bongbong' Marcos Jr wins the Presidency of the Republic of the Philippines.

BIBLIOGRAPHY

Abinales, Patricio & Amoroso, Donna J. (2005) *State and Society in the Philippines* New York: Rowman and Littlefield.

Abu-Lughod, Janet (1989) *Before European Hegemony: The World System A.D. 1250–1350.* New York: Oxford University Press.

Agoncillo, Teodoro A. (1990) *History of the Filipino People* (8th edn) Quezon City: University of the Philippines.

Arcilla, Jose S. (1994) *An Introduction to Philippine History* (4th edn) Quezon City: Ateneo de Manila University Press.

Bellwood, Peter (2017) *First Islanders: Prehistory and Human Migration in Island Southeast Asia* Oxford: Wiley-Blackwell.

Celoza, Albert F. (1997) *Ferdinand Marcos and the Philippines: The Political Economy of Authoritarianism* Westport, CT: Greenwood Publishing.

Coedes, George (1968) *The Indianized States of Southeast Asia* Honolulu: The University Press of Hawaii.

Constantino, Renato (1978) *The Philippines* (2 vols) Quezon City: Foundation for Nationalist Studies.

Coronel, Sheila S., Chua, Yvonne T., Rimban, Luz & Cruz, Bomma B. (2004) *The Rulemakers: How the Wealthy and Well-born Dominate Congress* Quezon City: Philippine Center for Investigative Journalism.

Feleo, Anita (ed.) (2001) *KASAYSAY: The Story of the Filipino People* (rev. edn) Manila: University of Santo Tomas Press.

Fish, Shirley (2003) *When Britain Ruled the Philippines, 1762–1764: The Story of the 18th Century British Invasion of the Philippines during the Seven Years' War* 1st Books Library.

Francia, Luis H. (2014) *A History of the Philippines: From Indios Bravos to Filipinos* New York: The Overlook Press.

Go, Julian 2008) *American Empire and the Politics of Meaning: Elite Political Cultures in the Philippines and Puerto Rico during U.S. Colonialism* Durham, N.C.: Duke University Press.

Ileto, Reynaldo (1979) *Pasyon and Revolution: Popular Movements in the Philippines, 1840–1910* Quezon City: Ateneo de Manila University Press.

Joaquin, Nick (2005) *A Question of Heroes: Essays in Criticism on Ten Key Figures in Philippine History* Pasig City: Anvil Publishing.

Jocano, F. Landa (2001) *Filipino Prehistory: Rediscovering Precolonial Heritage* Quezon City: Punlad Research House.

Junker, Laura Lee (1999) *Raiding, Trading, and Feasting: The Political Economy of Philippine Chiefdoms* Honolulu: University of Hawaii Press.

Karnow, Stanley (1990) *In Our Image: America's Empire in the Philippines* New York: Ballantine Books.

McCoy, Alfred W. (1994) *An Anarchy of Families: State and Family in the Philippines* Quezon City: Ateneo de Manila University Press.

McCoy, Alfred W. (2009) *Policing Americas Empire: The United States, the Philippines, and the Rise of the Surveillance State* Madison: University of Wisconsin Press.

Mijares, Primitivo (1986) *The Conjugal Dictatorship of Ferdinand and Imelda Marcos* New York: Union Square Publications.

Miller, Stuart Creighton (1984) *Benevolent Assimilation: The American Conquest of the Philippines, 1899–1903* (4th edn) New Haven: Yale University Press.

Newson, Linda (2009) *Conquest and Pestilence in the Early Spanish Philippines* Honolulu: University of Hawaii Press.

Oppenheimer, Steven (1999) *Eden in the East: The Drowned Continent of Southeast Asia* London: Orion Publishing.

Quibuyen, Floro C. (2008) *A Nation Aborted: Rizal, American Hegemony, and Philippine Nationalism* (rev. edn) Quezon City: Ateneo de Manila University Press.

Ramírez, Dámaso de Lario (ed.) (2009) *Re-shaping the World: Philip II of Spain and His Time* Quezon City: Ateneo de Manila University Press.

Rizal, Jose (trans. Augenbraum, Harold) (2006) *Noli Me Tangere* London: Penguin Classics.

Schumacher, John N. (1973) *The Propaganda Movement: 1880–1895* Manila: Solidaridad Publishing House.

Scott, William Henry (1994) *Barangay: Sixteenth-Century Philippine Culture and Society* Quezon City: Ateneo de Manila University Press.

Silbey, David (2008) *A War of Frontier and Empire: The Philippine–American War, 1899–1902* New York: Farrar, Straus and Giroux.

Solheim, Wilhelm G. II. (2006) *Archeology and Culture in Southeast Asia: Unravelling the Nusantao* Quezon City: University of the Philippines Press.

Warren, James Francis (2007) *The Sulu Zone: 1768–1898* (2nd edn) Singapore: National University of Singapore Press,.

Wolff, Leon (1991) *Little Brown Brother: How the United States Purchased and Pacified the Philippines* Oxford: Oxford University Press.

Yu-Jose, Lydia N. (1999) *Japan Views the Philippines, 1900–1944* Quezon City: Ateneo de Manila University Press.

INDEX

A

Abu Sayyaf Group (ASG) 214–215, 221, 224, 226
Aetas (Negritos) 28, 29, 30, 51, 103
Aglipay, Father Gregorio 136
agriculture 45–46, 86–87, 96, 191, 212
Aguinaldo, Emilio 15, 16, 114, 116, 117, 118, 119, 122–125, 126, 127, 128, 132–134, 149, 172
Americanization 17, 19–20, 145–146, 168
Anda, Simon de 84, 85
animism 13, 45, 49, 50–51, 55, 76, 102
anitos 50
anti-drug campaign 225
Aquino, Benigno, Jr 21, 22, 175, 179, 193–194, 199–203
Aquino, Benigno, Snr 149
Aquino, Benigno, III 222–223
Aquino, Corazon 22, 184, 194, 195–196, 198–202, 203, 205, 206, 215, 221–222
architectural projects 185, 186
Armed Forces of the Philippines (AFP) 180
Asian economic crisis (1997) 209, 216
Association of Southeast Asian Nations (ASEAN) 173–174
Ati-Atihan festival 29
Augustinians 75, 77, 79, 101
Australoids 28, 30, 32
Austronesians 25, 29, 30, 31, 32, 33, 34, 45, 55, 71

B

Balangiga Massacre (1901) 134
Balboa, Vasco Nuñez de 58
Balikbayan Boxes 210
Balikatan 221
Bangsamoro Independence Freedom Fighters (BIFF) 224
barangays 11, 14, 47, 62, 84
Basco, Jose 86, 87, 96
Bataan Death March 149
Bataan Nuclear Power Plant 191
baybayin syllabary 51–52
Benedicto, Roberto 191
Benevolent Assimilation proclamation (1898) 126
Bilibid Prison, Manila 135
Biñan 9, 23
birth-control debate 213
Blanco, Ramon 110, 111–112, 113
Blood Compact 62, 63, 111
boat designs 37, 46–47
Bohol 26, 62, 72, 73, 227
Bojinka plot (1995) 214
Bonifacio, Andres 110, 111, 112, 113–114, 115, 116–118, 172
Borneo 12, 27, 34, 42
Boxer Codex 36, 45
Bracken, Josephine 110
British occupation (1762-1764) 83–85
Brunei 43, 54, 63
Bud Dajo Massacre (1906) 137, 141
Buddhism 10, 40, 47
Burgos, Father José 105, 106
burial practices, early 49–50
Bush, George H.W. 183
Bush, George W. 220
Business Process Outsourcing (BPO) 223–224
Bustamante, Fernando 79

C

Cadiz Constitution (1812) 90, 91, 92
call centres 223, 225
Carlist Wars (1833–1876) 92
Catholic Church 12, 13–14, 15, 17–18, 51, 62, 69, 72–80, 81, 87, 91, 96, 98, 100, 101–103, 104–106, 135, 136, 196, 197, 199, 213, 215, 229
see also missionary orders
Cavite 114, 116
Cavite Mutiny (1872) 106
Cebu 38, 43, 58, 61, 64, 66, 96, 100, 150, 153, 208
Champa 35, 36, 40
Charter Change campaign (Cha-Cha) 215, 219
China 25, 36–37, 38, 39, 40, 65, 68, 147, 224–225, 226, 231
Chinese community 20, 66–67, 81–83, 84, 91, 94, 97, 99–100, 168, 214
CIA 19, 165, 167, 171, 182
Civilian Home Defence Forces (CHDFs) 187
civilizing mission 122
Clark Air Base 162, 164, 197, 202, 203
Cofradía Revolt (1840–1842) 101–102, 103
coinage, early 49
Cojuangco, Eduardo 191
Cold War 19, 155, 156, 157, 160, 163, 206
Colegio de San Jose 76
colonial uprisings 15, 71–72, 73, 82, 85, 93, 106
Columbus, Christopher 57
Commonwealth of the Philippines 18, 20, 144–145, 148, 156, 160
communist insurgency 174, 192, 213
Communist Party of the Philippines (PKP) 167, 192
constitution 125, 126, 135–136, 140, 145, 161, 174, 181, 199, 201–202, 215
corruption 18, 20, 79, 163, 168, 169, 178, 190, 196, 199, 212, 214, 217, 222
coup attempts 200, 201, 202
criollos 89, 90, 91, 93, 94, 96, 100, 105, 106
crony capitalism 18, 21, 190–191, 196, 200, 217
Cry of Balintawak 112, 113
Cuban Revolution (1895–1898) 121–122

D

Dagohoy Revolt (1744–1829) 73, 85
Dasmariñas, Luis Perez 36
Datu Lapulapu 11
Datu Summangol 37
datuship 11, 42, 47, 53, 84
Dewey, Commodore George 122, 123, 124
diaspora 21, 23, 107, 108, 190, 207, 209–211
dictatorship *see* Marcos, Ferdinand
Diokno, Jose 179
Disini, Herminio 191
Dominicans 75, 76, 77, 101, 105, 108, 109

drug war 227
Dutch East India Company 67–68
Duterte, Rodrigo 184–185, 225–227

E

early man 26, 27–33
early Philippine history 25–55
earthquakes 26
economic development 17, 80–83, 86–87, 95–96, 169, 207, 209, 223
Economic Development Corps (EDCOR) 167
economic imperialism 121
EDSA Revolution *see* People Power
EDSA II 217–218
education 75–76, 87, 94, 96, 97, 98–100, 104, 130, 131, 145–146
encomienda system 68–69
English-language education policy 17, 130, 131, 143, 168
Enrile, Juan Ponce 177, 196, 197, 201, 205, 223
epic literature 52–53
Estrada, Joseph 215, 216, 217–218, 221–222
export market 96, 97, 145, 154, 193
export-processing zones (EPZs) 208
extrajudicial killings 21, 185, 213, 226

F

Federalista Party 129, 137
Ferdinand VII of Spain 91, 92
festivals 13, 29, 67
Filipino self-identification 15, 89, 94, 95, 107, 141
Filipino-American War (1899–1902) 16, 126–134, 137

Filipino First Policy 167–168, 169
First Philippine Republic *see* Malolos Republic
flag, national 123
Flavier, Juan 213
forced labour (*polo*) 71, 72
foreign debt 21, 200
Francis, Pope 14
Franciscans 75, 77, 78, 101
free trade 95–96, 100
Freemasonry 111
friarocracy (*frailocracia*) 101, 106
Funston, General Frederick 132, 133

G

galleon trade 79–81, 82, 95
Garcia, Carlos P. 167, 168
GDP 169, 223
General Agreement on Tariffs and Trade (GATT) 193
geothermal energy 188, 207
Global War on Terror (GWOT) 220
GNP 196
Gomburza Affair (1872) 106–107, 113
guerilla warfare 128, 130, 132, 150, 153

H

haciendas 69, 97
Hare-Hawes-Cutting Independence Bill (1933) 143
Harrison, Francis Burton 139, 140
Hidalgo, Felix Resurreccion 79
holy mountains 103
homesteading projects 167
Homma, General Masaharu 151
Honasan, Gregorio 201
Hontiveros, Risa 217
Huks 150, 163–165, 166

I

illustrados 10, 15, 18, 94–95, 104, 106, 107, 114, 115, 117, 128, 129, 133, 136, 143
Ilocos 85, 180, 181
Iloilo 62, 66, 95, 96, 150, 153
Indianization 10, 13, 25, 40–44, 49, 50, 52, 53, 54, 55
Indios 14, 15, 66, 70, 71–72, 73, 76, 78, 81, 91, 93, 94, 100, 101, 102, 104, 105, 107
Indonesia 10, 13, 21, 27, 41, 54, 68, 142
insulares 91, 94, 101
International Criminal Court 227
Isabella II of Spain 92, 105
Islam 10, 12, 13, 25, 43, 47, 137
Islamist militancy *see* Abu Sayyaf Group (ASG); Maute group; Moro Islamic Liberation Front (MILF); Moro National Liberation Front (MNLF)
Islamization 10, 13, 53–55, 63
Izquierdo, Rafael de 106

J

Japan 148, 153, 156, 160, 193
Japanese occupation 19, 20, 147–151, 158–159, 164
Jaudenes, Fermin 124
jeepneys 154, 155
Jesuits 75–76, 77, 100, 104, 110
John Paul II, Pope 196
Johnson, Lyndon 172, 173
Jones Law (Philippine Autonomy Act, 1916) 140
Jopson, Edgar 187

Juan Tamad (Lazy Juan) 72

K

Kalanay 34, 35
kidnappings 214–215
Kissinger, Henry 182
KKK (Katipunan) 15, 16, 18, 23, 104, 110–118, 122, 124, 125, 129, 136, 172
Koxinga 82

L

La Liga Filipina 109, 110, 111, 124
La Naval de Manila 67
Laguna Copperplate Inscription 43, 44
Laguna de Bay 25, 54–55
land ownership 69, 78–79, 97, 136, 138
land reform 170–171, 173, 188, 200
languages and linguistic tensions 28–29, 36, 98, 141–142, 143
see also English-language education policy; Tagalog
Lansdale, Colonel Edward 165, 166
Lapulapu 58, 59
Laurel, José P. 149, 158, 222
Laurel, Salvador 195–196, 201
Laurel-Langley Agreement 193
Legazpi, Miguel Lopez de 61, 62–63, 64, 66, 72
Leyte 72, 150, 172, 187, 223
Liberal Party 159–160, 161, 165, 169, 175, 216
liberation theology 196
Limahong 65, 66
Lingayen Gulf 38, 150
literature, early 52–53
Loney, Nicholas 95
Lopez, Eugenio 179

Lopez Jaena, Graciano 107–108, 110
Luna, General Antonio 126, 128
Luzon 26, 27, 36, 47, 49, 53, 63, 64, 84, 85, 114, 117, 119, 124, 150, 164, 167, 171

M

Ma-i 36, 37
Mabini, Apolinario 124, 125, 126, 128
Macabebe Scouts 132, 133
Macapagal, Diosdado 169–170, 171, 172, 216
Macapagal-Arroyo, Gloria 205, 215–216, 218–222
MacArthur, General Douglas 148, 149, 150, 155, 156, 157, 158, 159, 160
McKinley, William 122, 126, 128
Mactan 58–59
Magellan, Ferdinand 58–59, 62
Magsaysay, Ramon 165–167
Maguindanao Massacre (2010) 220
Maine, USS, sinking of 122, 123
Majapahit 41, 43
Malacca 54, 57
Malaysia 10, 13, 34, 54, 171, 173–174
Malolos Republic 125, 126, 127–128, 129, 133, 143, 198
mandalas 41–42, 43, 53, 54
Manila 22, 38, 54, 63, 64, 65–66, 68, 77, 81, 82, 83–84, 96, 100, 106, 111, 114, 123, 124, 127, 144, 148, 153, 209
Manila Bay, Battle of (1898) 16, 122

Manila hostage crisis (2010) 222–223
Manila Massacre (1945) 151
Manunggul Jar 35
Marawi City 226–227
Marcos, Bongbong 225, 229
Marcos, Ferdinand 20–21, 22, 171–183, 194, 195, 197–198, 205, 217, 229
Marcos, Imelda 21, 172, 181, 184–185, 186, 194, 198, 215
martial law period (Duterte presidency) 226, 227
martial law period (Marcos presidency) 20, 171, 175, 177–178, 183, 185, 187, 188, 193
Maute group 226–227
Mendiola, Battle of (1970) 174–175
Mendiola Massacre (1987) 200
mestizos 91, 96, 97, 99–100, 105, 107
Metal Age 35, 45
Mexico 15, 59, 68, 80, 91, 95
Mijares, Primitivo 184
Military Bases Agreement (MBA) 162, 193
millenarianism 101–103, 104, 146
Mindanao 13, 26, 47, 53, 54, 63, 68, 93, 137, 148, 150, 165, 167, 217, 221, 224, 226
Mindoro 26, 36, 37, 150
missionary orders 18, 66, 75, 77, 78, 79, 98, 101, 104–105, 106, 136
Misuari, Nur 224
Mitra, Ramon 203
Moluccas (Spice Islands) 12, 57, 59, 68
Moro Islamic Liberation Front (MILF) 217,

221, 224, 226
Moro National Liberation Front (MNLF) 174, 214, 215, 216, 221, 224, 226
Moro Wars (1899-1913) 137
musical instruments 33

N

Nacionalista Party 137–139, 140, 143, 144, 145, 159, 166, 171, 216
National Progressive Party 137
nationalism 18, 19, 91, 95, 102, 103, 104, 105, 136, 137, 138, 141, 142, 143, 150
Negros 26, 143, 191
Nehru, Jawarharlal 10
New People's Army (NPA) 174, 192, 213, 221
New Society Movement 20–21, 179, 180–181
Nine-Dash Line 226, 231
Novales Mutiny (1823) 93
Nusantao Maritime Trading and Communication Network (NMTCN) 33–35

O

Organic Act of the Philippine Islands (1902) 135–136, 140
Osmeña, Sergio 138, 140, 143, 144, 145, 149, 150, 156–157, 158, 159, 167
overseas Filipino workers (OFWs) 209–211, 212

P

Pacquiao, Manny 184
Paduka Pahala 39
Palaris, Juan de la Cruz 85
Palawan 26, 27, 37, 113

Palermo Conspiracy (1828) 93
Panay 26, 44, 62, 64, 167
pandemic 228
Pangasinan 72, 85
Pardo de Tavera, Trinidad 128, 129
Paris Agreement on Climate Change 227
parity rights plebiscite 161
party-list system 216, 217
Patiño, Pedro 112
Patronato Real 74, 78
peninsulares 15, 91, 93, 94, 105, 106
People Power 22, 194–195, 197, 205, 218
People's Liberation Army 164
Philip II of Spain 61
Philippine Army 161, 165
Philippine Congress 160, 161, 167, 178
Philippine Constabulary 137, 164, 197, 205, 213
Philippine Independence Day 172
Philippine Independent Church 136
Philippine National Police (PNP) 213
Philippine Rehabilitation Act (1946) 161
Philippine Revolution (1896-1898) 15, 112–119, 143
Pigafetta, Antonio 45
Pilar, General Gregorio del 128
Pilar, Marcelo H. del 107, 108, 110
Pinatubo eruption 202–203
piracy 37, 65, 67
Poe, Fernando 218
Polavieja, Camilo 113, 116, 119
Portuguese colonialism 57, 59, 60
prehistory 26–31

Presidential Commission on Good Government (PCGG) 199
press censorship 100, 105, 106, 178
principalia 14, 15, 70–71, 95, 100, 117, 129, 136, 139, 158
private militias 20, 153, 178, 187
Propaganda Movement 107–110
Pule, Hermano (Apolinario de la Cruz) 101, 102, 103

Q

Quezon, Manuel L. 17, 138, 140, 141, 143–144, 145, 146, 148, 149, 150, 158, 198
Quirino, Elpidio 18, 159, 165, 166

R

Rajah Humabon 43, 58, 62
Rajah Soliman 63, 66
Ramos, Benigno 146, 147, 149
Ramos, General Fidel 197, 203, 205–207, 209, 212, 213, 215, 219, 222
Reagan, Ronald 182–183, 197
reconcentrados 134
reduccion (resettlement) system 74–75
Reform the Armed Forces Movement (RAM) 196, 201, 205
reformism 91, 94–95, 105, 107–111
remittances 23, 207, 209–210, 223
Ricarte, Artemio 149
Rizal, Jose 107, 108–112, 113, 172
Robredo, Leni 225
Romualdez, Benjamin 191

Roosevelt, Eleanor 166
Roxas, Manuel 18, 143, 158–159, 160, 162, 164–165
Royal Company of the Philippines 91
Royal Economic Society of Friends of the Country 86–87, 96

S

Sa Huynh-Kalanay network 35, 36
Sabah 171, 173–174
Sakdalistas 146–147
Salazar, Domingo de 73, 74
Salcedo, Juan de 63, 66
Samar 72, 134, 187
San Isidro 127
San Juanico Bridge 187, 188
Santo Tomas, University of 76, 99, 100, 105, 108
Schurman Commission 127, 129
sea people 34
Second Indochina War 173
Second Philippine Republic 149, 158
see also Japanese occupation
Second World War 19, 147–151, 153–154
secularization 77–78, 98–99, 104, 106
Seven Years' War (1756–1763) 83
shamans 49, 72
sharecropping 170, 191
Silang, Diego 85
Silang, Gabriela 85
Sin, Cardinal 195, 196, 197
slaves 47, 48, 49, 84
social structure, early 47–49
socio-economic inequality 146, 189, 211–213
South China Sea 23, 27, 54, 224, 226, 231
Spanish colonialism 12, 13–15, 16, 17, 45, 55,

56–87, 89, 90–91, 92, 95, 96
Spanish language 143
Spanish literacy 98, 99
Srivijaya 41, 43, 44
Subic Bay Naval Base 162, 202, 203, 208
Suharto 21
Sukarno 10
Sulu 13, 38, 39, 48, 63, 171, 217
Sulu Sultanate 53, 54
Sundaland 26, 27, 29, 32

T

Taft, William Howard 129, 134
Taft Commission 129, 130, 145
Tagalog speakers 15, 43–44, 47, 49, 50, 95, 101, 103, 110, 111, 114, 134, 141–142, 230
Tao (Yami) 31
Taruc, Luis 150, 163–164, 165, 166, 194
Tejeros Revolutionary Government 116–117
Third Philippine Republic 160–175
Thomasites 130, 131, 223
timawa 48–49
Tirad Pass, Battle of (1899) 128
Tondo 43, 54, 63, 71, 111
Torre, Carlos María de la 105, 106
trade 34–35, 36, 38, 41, 42, 46, 49, 79–80, 95–96, 193
see also export market
Treaty of Biak-na-Bato (1897) 119
Treaty of Paris (1898) 125–126
Treaty of Tordesillas (1494) 57, 58, 60
Treaty of Zaragoza (1529) 59–60

Truman, Harry S. 156, 157
Tydings-McDuffie Act (1934) 144
Typhoon Haiyan/Yolanda (2013) 223

U

Underwood Tariff Act (1913) 145
United States–Philippine relationship 12, 16, 18, 19, 119, 121–163, 167, 168, 182, 192–193, 195, 203, 220, 221, 224–225, 227, 231
United States imperialism 125–160
United States military presence and bases 162, 167, 182, 193, 201, 203, 221
universities 76, 99, 100, 105, 108
Urdaneta, Andres de 61, 62

V

Varela, Luis Rodriguez 94
Ver, Fabian 180, 194
Vietnam 35, 39
Vigan 65
Villalobos, Ruy Lopez de 60–61
Virata, Cesar 188
Visayas 26, 27, 37, 44, 47, 49, 50, 53, 54, 55, 62, 63, 141, 165

W

Wainwright, General Jonathan 148
wartime collaborators 149, 150, 156–158, 162
women's suffrage 139
Wood, General Leonard 140–141
writing systems 51–52

Y

Yamashita, General Tomoyuki 150, 151

ACKNOWLEDGEMENTS

Thanks to John, Rosemary and the editorial team for seeing the promise of this book; to Luis H. Francia, who showed the way; to Talk of the Town, the Gilleras, the Borromeos, and their bands; to Albert, Steven, Oscar, Jake, Elmer, Eugene, the Gaunas, and Jack Hammer and the Weirdos; to the Bolardes and the rest from Talavera; to the Lees, the Gimarinos and Lala, and the visible and invisible at La Vista Village in those final summers; to the Guadalupe-Mandaue-Banawa axis, Fr. Bilbao, Wally and Snow Rabbit at SHS; to Jess, Flor, Mads, Sofie, Fred, Rosette, Felisa, Fe, Daniel, Sgt. Flores and the rest from UP Cebu; to that one year at USC; to the Scouts, CAT and ROTC; to Ben and his magazine; to Rhine Marketing, Sandra, Bradley Hrutfjord and the Plaza architectural office; to R.J. Mitchell at Vickers Supermarine, Yamamoto Isoroku and the Dai Nippon Teikoku Kaigun, and the crewmen from the USS *New Orleans* and the USS *Grayback*; to Tura, Anun, Walding, Flor (and Tito), Jun and their families; to Nena, Jose and Ludy, Beth, Charles, Sonia, Jingjing, Helena, Jesus, Dulce, Inday and the victims of the Kamagayan district fire; and to my parents, Susing and Letty – for, among other things, surviving the Second World War.

All of the above made the book come alive.

Special thanks to Sasai, Len, Chu, Denz, Bong, Pong, Don, Dondon, Maning, Judith, Agnes and Lynley, for making our own phase of this history so uniquely... ours. A very special thank you to Mario and Abet, and to all the other ones who couldn't get away.

PICTURE CREDITS

The following institutions and persons have made available images in this book that are in the public domain, and are acknowledged by the author without individual images being enumerated: Malacañang Palace Presidential Museum and Library at www.malacanang.gov.ph; Armed Forces of the Philippines; The Lilly Library, Indiana University; U.S. Department of State; U.S. Information Agency; U.S. National Archives; U.S. Department of State; U.S. Army; U.S. Navy; U.S. Air Force; U.S. Geological Survey; Florentino Floro (Judgefloro); Dr. W.G.N. van den Sleen, Tropenmuseum Amsterdam; Goya Museum

The following copyright holders are acknowledged by the author for images used in this book. Every effort has been made to ascertain full names/identities with information from Wikimedia Commons, Flickr and other sources before publication. However, some remain known only by usernames. Corrections or full names are most welcome and appreciated. Ramon FVelasquez pp.11, 24, 40, 67, 161, 170, 186; Bernardo Arellano III pp.29, 95; Sarahli777 pp. 66, 158; Dennison Uy p. 2-3; Jsinglador p. 6; Burningbatsu p.9; www.nehrumemorial.nic.in p.10; Squalluto 11; CEphoto/Uwe Aranas p.12; Adolfo A. G. Galache p.13; Benhur Arcayan p.14; Francinehihao p.15; Hans Olav Lien p.22; Thomas Mercado p.23; Robert Breivik p.25; Ken Ilio p.28; Sasaki Chunichi p.31; Thomas Quine/Hiart p.33; Dr. A. Hugentobler/Vassil p.34; Philip Maise p.35; Ajchacon p.37; Adam Daley p.43; Muffin Wizard p.44; Kashmut p.46; Reuel Mark Delez p.50; Jason Audrey Licerio p.52; Joaquim Alves Gaspar p.56; Lencer p.58; The Ogre p.60; Alexey Mukhranov/Victor D. Kintanar p.62; ControlFreakMe p.63; Joelaldor p.65; The Wellcome Trust p. 67; Qaalvin p.73; Irene Dolphin p.76; Francisofmconv p.78; Gisling p.82; Elmer B. Domingo p.88; istolethetv p.102; Alternativity p.103; Tsambaproductions p.109; Mello47 p.112; MIKELAAGAN p.113, Andy Mitchell p.114, Eugene Alvin Villar p.117; The Wiccan/Jan's Cat Philadelphia p.123; Ranieljose p.125; Felipamestiza p.128; Palafox Associates p.130; JoRitchCht/Flashbang p.131; University of Texas Libraries p.138; Kleomarlo p.140; Gaetano Faillace p.151; Victor Jorgensen p.152; Joost J. Bakker p.154; Magalhães p.155; Val Gempis p.162; caladcarens p.175; Angus Townley p.181; Rodsan18/danny@bambooman.com /Marcelo Chan p.182; The Sun King p. 185; Jopson Family Collection/Altheooo p.187; Oscar W. Rasson/Chajedidian p188; Exec8 p.189; Jiru27 p.191; Christian Razukas p.192; MakiR p.195; International Rice Research Institute (IRRI) p.200; Richel King p.203; Brian Biller p.204; Michael Gonzales p.207; Rio Hondo p.208; drcw p.210; Eric in SF p.211; Helene C. Stikkel p.216; Cesar Tomambo p.217; Lieutenantpdg p.218; www.kremlin.ru p.219; David J. Ham p.221; Matikas Santos p.222; Titan One p.225; VOCAL-NY p.228; Bro. Jeffrey Pioquinto, S.J./Mark Jhomel p.229.